THE GREAT LAWRENCE TEXTILE STRIKE OF 1912
New Scholarship on the Bread & Roses Strike

Edited by

Robert Forrant
University of Massachusetts Lowell

Jurg Siegenthaler
American University

Work, Health, and Environment Series
Series Editors: Charles Levenstein, Robert Forrant, and John Wooding

Baywood Publishing Company, Inc.
AMITYVILLE, NEW YORK

Copyright © 2014 by Baywood Publishing Company, Inc., Amityville, New York

All rights reserved. No part of this book may be reproduced or utilized in any form or by any means, electronic or mechanical, including photo-copying, recording, or by any information storage or retrieval system, without permission in writing from the publisher. Printed in the United States of America on acid-free recycled paper.

Baywood Publishing Company, Inc.
26 Austin Avenue
PO Box 337
Amityville, NY 11701
(800) 638-7819
E-mail: baywood@baywood.com
Web site: baywood.com

Library of Congress Catalog Number: 2014005721
ISBN 978-0-89503-861-6 (cloth)
ISBN 978-0-89503-862-3 (alk. paper)
ISBN 978-0-89503-863-0 (e-pub)
ISBN 978-0-89503-864-7 (e-pdf)
http://dx.doi.org/10.2190/BRS

Library of Congress Cataloging-in-Publication Data
The great Lawrence Textile Strike of 1912 : new scholarship on the Bread & Roses Strike / edited by Robert Forrant, University of Massachusetts, Lowell, Jurg Siegenthaler, American University.
    pages cm. -- (Work, health, and environment series)
  Includes bibliographical references and index.
   ISBN 978-0-89503-861-6 (cloth : alk. paper) -- ISBN 978-0-89503-862-3 (pbk. : alk. paper) -- ISBN 978-0-89503-863-0 (e-pub) -- ISBN 978-0-89503-864-7 (e-pdf) 1. Textile Workers' Strike, Lawrence, Mass., 1912. 2. Strikes and lockouts--Textile industry--Massachusetts--Lawrence--History. 3. Textile workers--Massachusetts--Lawrence--History. 4. Textile workers--Labor unions--Massachusetts--Lawrence--History. I. Forrant, Robert, 1947- editor of compilation. II. Siegenthaler, Jurg, 1939- editor of compilation.
  HD8039.T42U556 2014
  331.892'86770097445--dc23

2014005721

Table of Contents

Preface v

CHAPTER 1
Introduction 1
   Robert Forrant and Jurg Siegenthaler

CHAPTER 2
"'Believe Comrades . . . the Day is Coming When Those at the End of Their Rope Will Require Struggle. It Will Be, Perhaps, Tomorrow.' Franco-Belgian Immigrants and the 1912 Strike" 15
   Janelle Bourgeois

CHAPTER 3
The Committee of Ten: The Local Heroes Who Faced Lawrence's Mill Men and Won in 1912 37
   Clarisse A. Poirier

CHAPTER 4
In Harm's Way: The Lawrence Textile Strike Children's Affair 59
   Lawrence Cappello

CHAPTER 5
Why Labor Won: Tactical Innovation, Failed Repression, and Turning Points in the Bread and Roses Strike 79
   Robert Biggert

CHAPTER 6
The Parades: Evolving Views of God and Country and the IWW in Lawrence 91
   Ken Estey

Strike Images 113

CHAPTER 7
The "American Dream" and the 1912 Lawrence Textile Strike 121
   Frank Fletcher

CHAPTER 8
Voices of Labor Militancy in Lawrence, 1912–1931 135
  Ethan Snow

CHAPTER 9
Striking Women: Massachusetts Mill Workers in the Wake of
Bread and Roses, 1912–1913 153
  Anne F. Mattina and Domenique Ciavattone

CHAPTER 10
The Triangle Fire Centennial Commemoration 171
  Adrienne Sosin and Joel Sosinsky

CHAPTER 11
The Cloth From Which We Are Cut: Using Music, Narration, and
Images to Tell the Story of the 1911 Triangle Shirtwaist Fire 187
  Vicki Gabriner and Linda Stern

CHAPTER 12
Lessons Learned: A Comparison of the Textile and Apparel Industry
of Early 19th-Century Lawrence and Lowell with China Today 205
  Virginia M. Noon

CHAPTER 13
Bread and Roses: Why the Legend Lives On 219
  Robert Ross

Editors' Biographies 231

Author Biographies 233

Index 235

Preface

In the Baywood series *Work, Health, and Environment,* the conjunction of topics is deliberate and critical. We begin at the point of production—even in the volumes that address environmental issues—because that is where things get made, workers labor, and raw materials are fashioned into products. It is also where things get stored or moved, analyzed or processed, computerized or tracked. In addition, it is where the folks who do the work are exposed to a growing litany of harmful things or are placed in harm's way. The focus on the point of production provides a framework for understanding the contradictions of the modern political economy.

Despite claims to a post-industrial society, work remains essential to all our lives. While work brings income and meaning, it also brings danger and threats to health. The point of production, where goods and services are produced, is also the source of environmental contamination and pollution. Thus, work, health, and environment are intimately linked.

Work organizations, systems of management, indeed the idea of the "market" itself, have a profound impact on the handling of hazardous materials and processes. The existence or absence of decent and safe work is a key determinant of the health of the individual and the community: what we make goes into the world, sometimes improving it, but too often threatening the environment and the lives of people across the globe.

We began this series to bring together some of the best thinking and research from academics, activities, and professionals, all of whom understand the intersection between work and health and environmental degradation, and all of whom think something should be done to improve the situation.

The works in this series stress the political and social struggles surrounding the fight for safer work and protection of the environment, and the local and global struggle for a sustainable world. The books document the horrors of cotton dust, the appalling and dangerous conditions in the oil industry, the unsafe ways in which toys and sneakers are produced, the struggles to link unions and communities to fight corporate pollution, and the dangers posed by the petrochemical industry, both here and abroad. The books speak directly about the contradictory effects of the point of production for the health of workers, community, and the environment. In all these works, the authors keep the politics front and foremost. What has emerged, as this series has grown, is a body of scholarship uniquely focused and highly integrated around themes and problems absolutely critical to our and our children's future.

CHAPTER 1

Introduction

Robert Forrant and Jurg Siegenthaler

> *What we choose to emphasize in this complex history will determine our lives. If we see only the worst, it destroys our capacity to do something. If we remember those times and places—and there are so many—where people have behaved magnificently, this gives us the energy to act, and at least the possibility of sending this spinning top of a world in a different direction. – Howard Zinn*

"In Lawrence, Massachusetts, fully one-half of the population 14 years of age or over is employed in the woolen and worsted mills and cotton mills, and approximately 60,000 of the 85,982 people living in Lawrence are directly dependent upon earnings in these textile mills." Thus began the federal government's *Report on Strike of Textile Workers in Lawrence, Massachusetts in 1912*. Completed at the end of June 1912 under the direction of Commissioner of Labor Charles Neill, the report offered readers an extraordinary look at the strike that unfolded between January 11 and March 14, 1912. Neill noted: "Although dissatisfaction over the possibility of a reduction in earnings on account of the shortened hours had really begun before the 1st of January, it is evident that the mill officials did not appreciate the extent of their (workers) dissatisfaction or the possibilities latent in it."[1] According to Neill, the city's mill agents believed that the worst reaction "would probably be confined to a strike in a single mill." Mill overseers went to their beds on the evening of January 10, 1912, oblivious to the commitment workers had made to each other to stand firm and fight for a better life for themselves and their children.

---

[1] Charles P. Neill, *Report on Strike of Textile Workers in Lawrence, Massachusetts in 1912*, 62 Cong., 2 sess., (Washington, D.C.: Government Printing Office, 1912) 11.

LAWRENCE BORN

During the 1830s Daniel Saunders, called the "Founder of Lawrence," purchased strips of land on either side of the Merrimack River to gain control of waterpower rights. On behalf of the Essex Company, he also acquired land in Andover, which eventually became part of the new city of Lawrence. The so-called Boston Associates had already developed the nearby city of Lowell as one of the first planned industrial cities. They sought to replicate their success twenty miles downriver from Lowell's cotton mills. Lawrence and its woolen and cotton mills were soon located at the convergence of the Merrimack, Shawsheen, and Spicket rivers. The Essex Company was chartered in 1845 explicitly to build a dam and canals on the Merrimack River for the purpose of providing waterpower for textile mills. Its directors included the wealthy, interlocked families—Lawrences, Lowells, Appletons, Jacksons and others—who controlled much of the New England textile industry. On March 22, 1845, Abbott Lawrence pledged $100,000 to purchase stock in the Essex Company; 82 others put up $900,000 and construction began on the infrastructure for a new mill city.

At the time it was completed in 1848, the dam over the Merrimack River was possibly the largest in the world. The Essex Company also constructed the Mechanics Block, "an architecturally unified set of fifty single-family brick row houses" for workers because its directors were "concerned with getting and keeping a skilled staff of machinists." Through a company jointly owned by the Essex Company and Lowell's Proprietors of Locks and Canals, all necessary land and water rights for the Merrimack River up to and including Lake Winnipesaukee and the other large lakes of New Hampshire were purchased. Finally, the Essex Company commenced the task of building the rest of the city, turning the land into one gigantic workshop.[2]

The Great Stone Dam created the foundation for the city's growth. From the stone dam, a canal was constructed to the north of the Merrimack River to carry water to the mills. It eventually empties back out to the river. The mile-long North Canal provided greater space for manufacturers to position their mills parallel to the river on what appears to be an "island" of red brick. "And all along the river's banks, merchants, peddlers, blacksmiths, and machinists set up shop. . . ."[3] Incorporated as a city in 1853, the name Lawrence was chosen as a token of respect for Abbott Lawrence, a director of the Essex Company. Three years after incorporation, the city contained 8,358 people. It more than doubled by 1860, with 17,639 residents, 42 percent foreign born, most the result of Irish

---

[2] Duncan Erroll Hay, "Building 'The New City on the Merrimack': The Essex Company and its Role in the Creation of Lawrence Massachusetts," (PhD diss., University of Delaware, 1986) 127.

[3] Bruce Watson, *Bread and Roses: Mills, Migrants, and the Struggle for the American Dream.* (New York: Penguin Books, 2005) 34.

immigration. Between 1845 and 1860, some one-third of Ireland's population emigrated due to famine, high employment, and mass evictions off small holdings. The Irish accounted for more than 65 percent of Lawrence's foreign-born population.

In 1870 some 29,000 people lived in the growing city; the number grew to just over 39,000 by 1880. At that time, Irish, Scots, and French Canadians accounted for 77 percent of the city's foreign-born population. Testifying to the growth of woolen mills and numerous supporting industries and commercial establishments, the population approached 45,000 in 1890. Forty-five percent of them were foreign born, attracted by the possibilities of mill employment. The last decade of the 19th century saw a massive influx of southeastern European and Middle Eastern immigrants and the population in 1900 reached nearly 63,000. In 1910, 85,892 people lived in Lawrence; 48 percent of the total was foreign born. Seventy-four percent of the city's total work force of 42,526 people engaged in manufacturing, compared to 54 percent for all of Massachusetts.

The Essex Company laid out the city with blocks for worker housing, vast expanses of industrial space, long commercial boulevards such as Essex Street, and a meticulously planned park. Roadways out of the neighborhoods led workers over several North Canal bridges, highly contested spaces during the strike, and into the mills.

Twenty-three miles from the mouth of the Merrimack River grew what *The Lawrence Survey* (1912) called "a great workshop."[4] In his four-volume history of Massachusetts industries, Orra Stone has this to say about the city. "The influx of Boston capital created a mill city almost overnight and for nearly a mile on both banks of the stately Merrimack there tower the red brick walls of manufacturing establishments . . . ."[5] Fewer than 40 years after the Essex Company's incorporation, 338,100 spindles, 9,057 looms, and 10,200 employees wove two million yards of worsted a week. The Lawrence Machine Shop, built between 1846 and 1848, constructed most of the machinery used in the mills and also for a time built railroad locomotives. Somewhat diversified, Lawrence was also one of the most important centers in the United States for the production of paper-making machinery. Stone noted,

> The city manufactures a wider variety of paper-making machinery than any other one center; a larger total volume than any other city in the United States, while a buyer can purchase in Lawrence a larger percentage of the complete machinery required for making paper than in any other place in this country.[6]

---

[4]Robert E. Todd and Frank Sanborn, *The Report of the Lawrence Survey.* (Lawrence: Andover Press, 1912).

[5]Orra Stone, *History of Massachusetts Industries: Their Inception, Growth, and Success,* Vol. 1. (Boston: S.J. Clarke Publishing Company, 1930) 327.

[6]Stone, 338-339.

With the construction of the Everett Mills, the Pacific Mills, the Washington Mills, and numerous other factories, the city grew exponentially. After 75 years, Lawrence led the world in the production of worsted wool cloth. In 1900 its mills churned out nearly 25 percent of all the woolen cloth in the United States. The Pacific Mills had the mechanical equipment capable of producing 800 miles of finished textile fabrics every working day of the year (see Figure 1, p. 113). Sixty-five percent of manufacturing output, 67 percent of all the capital invested in the city, and 52 percent its wages came from the woolen mills. Lawrence, in other words, had grown into a gigantic workshop complete with thousands of restive workers.

THE STRIKE

In 1912 Lawrence, Massachusetts, erupted in a dramatic struggle between mill owners and workers from several countries, including Belgium, France, Ireland, Italy, Lithuania, Poland, Russia, Syria, and Turkey. When it commenced, a call went to workers across Lawrence and beyond, from the citywide strike committee. It read in part:

> . . . now that the combination of capitalists have shown the unity of all our adversaries, we call on you as brothers and sisters to join hands with us in this great movement. Our cause is just. . . . Workers quit your hammers, throw down your files, let the dynamos stop, the power cease to turn the wheels and the looms, leave the machinery, bank the fires, tie up the plants, tie up the town.[7]

Sparked by a wage cut when the legal work week in Massachusetts went from 56 to 54 hours for women and children, simmering resentments over nearly every aspect of mill workers' lives came to a boil as 1912 opened.

In 1910 Lawrence had the eighth highest death rate per 1,000 in the country and the seventh highest death rate for infants. The Massachusetts Labor Commission found that "the lowest total wages for human living conditions for an individual . . . was $8.28 a week." A third of families in Lawrence earned less than $7.00. The U.S. Bureau of Labor's *Report on the Strike* (1912) noted that weekly rents varied from $1 to $6, but the amount commonly paid in Lawrence was $2 to $3 for a 4-room apartment and $3 to $3.50 for five rooms (see Figure 5, p. 116). Thus, wages couldn't cover food and family necessities. Life was desperately short for mill workers. Lawyers and clergy had the longest life expectancy at 65.4 years; manufacturers were next at 58.5; for mill operatives it was 39.6 years.[8]

As the strike spread, it defied the popular assumption that immigrant, largely female, and linguistically and ethnically distinct workers could not or would not

---

[7]"A Call For Action," Appendix to Neill, *Report on Strike of Textile Workers*, 499.

[8]Neill, *Report on Strike*, Chapter 3, "Housing Conditions and Family Earnings," 143-162.

organize. First to shut off their machines when they realized that their wages had been cut approximately 30 cents to reflect the shorter work week were Polish women weavers at the Everett Cotton Mills. The next day 25,000 more workers joined the fray. Amherst, Massachusetts-born journalist Mary Heaton Vorse, who covered the strike for *Harper's Weekly*, described what she witnessed:

> New England was appalled by Lawrence. It was a new kind of strike. There had never been mass picketing in any New England textile town. Ten thousand workers paraded. They stoned mills and broke windows and, almost storming a factory to bring the workers out, were kept back only by a stream of icy water from a fire hose. It was the spirit of workers that seemed dangerous . . . They were always marching and singing. The gray tired crowds ebbing and flowing perpetually into the mills had waked and opened their mouths to sing, the different nationalities all speaking one language when they sang together. "Revolution," screamed the conservative press.[9]

Blocked by the militia from standing in front of mills and canal bridges, strikers perfected the loud, moving picket line. Upwards of 5,000 singing, chanting strikers regularly marched across the city's commercial district, challenging the militia and police to stop them (see Figure 6, p. 116). They maintained soup kitchens and nurseries for children. Meetings were simultaneously translated into nearly 30 languages. And, to keep workers unified, representatives from every nationality formed a 50-person strike leadership group. A reporter for *The Outlook* wrote on February 10:

> The impression of Lawrence, which I gained during my first evening, was that of a besieged city. The militia armed with guns and bayonets, guarded the streets and bridges in the mill district and challenged all comers. The hulking factories, with their massive gates and iron doors, appeared in the semi-darkness like fortresses, and along the face of these mills there played a strange, trembling light from the search lanterns opposite.[10]

Mill owners wrongly predicted a quick end to the strike. They were shocked when they learned that enraged Italian women who had happened upon a lone police officer on an icy bridge stripped him of his gun, club and badge, sliced the officer's suspenders, took off his pants, and dangled the officer over the freezing river. "One policeman can handle 10 men," Lawrence's district attorney lamented, "while it takes 10 policemen to handle one woman." A horrified boss, described women activists as full of "lots of cunning and also lots of bad temper. They're everywhere, and it's getting worse all the time."

---

[9] Mary Heaton Vorse, *A Footnote to Folly: Reminiscences of Mary Heaton Vorse*, (New York: Farrar and Rinehart, 1935) 6.

[10] Walter Weyl, "The Strikers at Lawrence," *The Outlook*, Vol. 101, February 10, 1912, 310.

TURMOIL

The city's mayor wasted little time calling in the militia. To discredit the strikers, William Wood, the powerful head of the American Woolen Company, hired a local undertaker and school board member to plant dynamite in several known locations where strike leaders met. The move backfired when it was determined that undertaker John Breen planted dynamite around the city at the behest of Wood. On January 29, the militia cornered a large group of marchers at the corner of Union and Garden Streets. After some pushing and shoving, a shot rang out; Annie LoPizzo, a 34-year-old striker, lay dead in the street. Witnesses charged that the bullet was fired by police officer Oscar Benoit, but he and others insisted someone specifically targeting LoPizzo fired the shot from behind the police. Two important strike leaders—Arturo Giovannitti and Joseph Ettor—were arrested for murder conspiracy in her death. Striker Joseph Caruso was arrested in April and charged with murder. The three remained in jail without bail until the end of November 1912.

Though the initial arrests were made, in part, to break the strike, it didn't happen. The week following the arrests witnessed the largest turnout during the whole strike. Other dramatic events marked the strike, including the death of striker John Ramey, a 'children's exodus' from the city, a train station riot that featured the arrests of several mothers with children in hand, and stunning Congressional testimony by several young workers. In October, a third striker, Jonas Smolskas, lost his life as some city residents turned against the Industrial Workers of the World (IWW) and the memory of the walkout.

TURNING POINT AND SPRINGTIME

As the strike dragged on, scores of children were sent from Lawrence to live with supporters in several cities. When police and the militia tried blocking children from boarding a train to Philadelphia, the ensuing melee led to injuries and arrests and the sort of negative publicity the mill owners didn't need. The United States Congress held hearings on the strike where child workers and others described the horrors of life and work in Lawrence. The publicity forced mill owners to the settlement table where an agreement was reached and then voted on by strikers in an open-air meeting on the Common on March 14th. The workers had won.

By spring, attention turned to the fates of Caruso, Ettor, and Giovannitti. *The Outlook's* reporters returned to Lawrence, and a June 1st article on the pending trial explained why the three were arrested and remained in jail. "The strike was then at its height and the situation was so dangerously tense that the authorities took advantage of the homicide to arrest Ettor and Giovannitti, two leaders of the working men. No one claims that they were anywhere in the vicinity of the killing. No one supposes that they desired the death of the victim, who, indeed, was one of the strikers. They are to be put on trial for life, however, charged, as leaders of the strike, with using language which incited riot, the incidental result of which was the homicide."[11] In their fall 1912 trial, a jury largely composed of skilled workers found them not guilty.

ABOUT THIS BOOK: NEW UNDERSTANDINGS OF THE BREAD AND ROSES STRIKE

Historians of many stripes encounter early on in their career the claims of 19th-century Historicism that it is possible to tell "history as it really was" and learned that it was not possible. Many have also come across the saying, "The past is a foreign country: they do things differently there."[12] This is one of the challenges writers and readers of history always face. How well have the contributors to this book done in telling us what happened in that fateful year of the Lawrence Textile Workers' Strike and in the years beyond? Do they help us understand such a complex and monumental event better, even through the filter of time and given observers' different perspectives? And do we come away with lessons learned from that distant "country" for our own today?

It is a pleasure to recall that all participants in the April 2012 Centennial Symposium did remarkably well in focusing precisely on the task of understanding the Bread and Roses Strike more thoroughly. And the authors in this book, perhaps even better, have unfolded the story to the point where we appreciate much better what happened at different levels and in different domains. The contributors' accounts also complement each other very well.

Three factors loom large in helping us understand past events—just as they assist us in understanding our own present: organization, communication, and the time dimension (both shorter and longer). Organization is perhaps a first crucial factor that helps answer the apparent contradiction in the events of 1912: a city's population and a work force made up of numerous different ethnic segments managed to mount a strike of strong solidarity across those segments. Janelle Bourgeois' study of Franco-Belgian immigrants and the 1912 Strike (chapter 2) reveals how that particular community competed and debated with other groups, among them the fellow-French-speaking Quebecois workers, about the right way to defend one's interests. Cooperatives were its preferred organizational device. As Bourgeois found, the Franco-Belgians had established themselves for a decade at the "forefront of radical labor organizing in Lawrence, just as they were in France and Belgium. They preached for revolution and the demise of capitalism but regularly lent their hall to any labor effort, conservative and radical alike." Once the strike was underway, Franco-Belgians supported

---

[11] "The Aftermath of a Strike," *The Outlook,* June 1, 1912, 238.
[12] L. P. Hartley, *The Go-Between* (London: H. Hamilton, 1953).

everyone, unselfishly and efficiently, by means of their cooperative store, soup kitchens, and a meeting hall open to all.

The power of organization is demonstrated in several other chapters as well. Here is clear evidence how groupings with organizational sophistication made the January walkout anything but a spontaneous action. We are amazed to witness in Clarisse Poirier's lively discussion of the strike's Committee of Ten (chapter 3), how workers actions were deeply rooted in organization in the city's ethnic neighborhoods and then strengthened through city-wide structures. Thus, a cohesive and powerful group of workers operated flexibly and with purpose in numerous encounters with state and business adversaries. In many instances, we are reminded of what today is being discussed as a remedy for declining union membership: whole-worker organizing and representative collective bargaining. Lawrence 1912 is a testimonial to how well that approach works.

Secondly, communications made the strike run effectively. Already the early contribution by Ardis Cameron told us how women were crucial in spreading everyday information, then the news on strike events, from household to household in the city's densely packed neighborhoods. In absorbing the story of the strike, we often notice how sophisticated communication was in an industrial city even before electronic media: a multitude of newspapers in different languages, regular public meetings, and the constant contact in the streets, shops, co-ops, union meetings, or places of worship kept workers in touch. Frequent travel of leaders and others, by train and streetcar, was swift and inexpensive even before the automobile. The extraordinary mobility of IWW leaders and the extensive world-wide publicity around the imprisonment and trial of Joseph Ettor, Arturo Giovannitti, and Joe Caruso are illustrations of the advanced levels of communication that prevailed at the time.[13]

Thirdly, this book sheds a great deal of light on the time dynamic of the strike at the various, interconnected levels of action, best illustrated by the example of the Children's Exodus. The original suggestions at the level of the leadership, discussed and planned at meetings, eventually came down to an early morning confrontation on a train platform, all in interaction with newspaper reporting and public opinion at the regional and national range. It is extremely useful to have this "movement within a movement" explained and placed in the whole time-line of strike events.

As Lawrence Cappello notes in chapter 4, the Children's Exodus was among other things "a public relations gambit aimed at re-energizing an amenable socialist base and, in the process, possibly capturing broader sympathy from outsiders by calling attention to the abysmal conditions inside the textile city. The tactic was used decades before in labor struggles throughout Europe, but

---

[13] Ardis Cameron, *Radicals of the Worst Sort: Laboring Women in Lawrence, Massachusetts. 1860-1912* (Urbana: University of Illinois, 1995).

never to such avail in America." Robert Biggert adds to our understanding of the Children's Exodus by analyzing why the 1912 strike succeeded. He succeeds in situating the children's campaign within a larger theoretical framework to better understand the entire strike in chapter 5.

Additional chapters, in the second half of the book, serve to lengthen that time perspective carefully and in longer sweeps. Many individuals are accustomed to celebrating the Bread and Roses Strike looking back from today, but we often zero in too narrowly. Though let us credit the most thorough, major investigation of the Merrimack Valley strikes by Dexter Arnold for having provided an important longer view.[14] The present volume makes us acknowledge that there were not only the winter and spring events, but also what happened in the autumn of 1912, the following year, then 1919, then 1931. Several chapters help us remember that the very passing of time changed the structure, the networking, and the dynamic of what occurred in Lawrence and how it was remembered. As Ethan Snow reminds us, only seven years after the 1912 strike another walkout of similar scale and duration rocked Lawrence, though it barely makes it into the history books. In 1919 in Massachusetts, "there was a massive Boston police strike, a successful telephone workers' strike, a strike involving more than 5,000 New England fishermen looking for improved job security and wages, and a Boston trolley car operators' strike" (chapter 8). The Bread and Roses Strike is a part of this time-line of action.

Here, we should acknowledge the continuing hardship that Lawrence's workers encountered in the wake of the strike. The rapid decline of the New England textile industry, the first Red Scare, the Great Depression, World War II, the Korean War, and McCarthyism, all shaped the history of the city and the lives of the Great Lawrence Textile Strike generation. In fact, just a few short months after the 1912 strike concluded, Lawrence business and religious leaders sought to erase the event from the community's collective memory through a God-and-Country Parade. As Kenneth Estey points out in chapter six, the assertion of working people's "agency as workers became deeply contested territory; the forces of religion and state in this city served as a formidable weapon against the workers who resisted injustice." At the height of the Cold War, on the 50th anniversary of the 1912 strike, it was this parade that took center stage, not the memory and lessons of the strike. Living links to the strike were not sought out nor were those workers' lives post-1912 investigated. As Esty summarizes, "The God-and-Country parade of 1912 cemented mounting opposition to the IWW in many quarters and contributed, through the parade of 1962, to continued marginalization within Lawrence of the strike and the mill workers' resistance."

---

[14] Dexter Arnold, "A Row of Bricks: Worker Activism in the Merrimack Valley Textile Industry, 1912–1922." (PhD diss., University of Wisconsin Madison, 1985).

The reader who is led through a complex set of stories and interpretations, may well ask in the end what the message is that we can take away from the 1912 strike. Frances Fox Piven, an authority on social movements, has summarized the forces that make for protest and social action: "new hardships, broken compacts, and the uprooting of peoples from familiar places and accustomed ways of life."[15] There is good evidence here that the factors of the strike that we reviewed—organization, communication, and the dynamic of time—were answers to the uprootedness, immiseration, and feeling of broken promises (see Fletcher, chapter 9), with respect to the "American Dream" that made up the reality of Lawrence workers and their families in 1912. These conditions, had to change, and the strike delivered. Historically, the wave of sit-down strikes in the 1930s can be seen in a similar vein. The question of whether and why, in other places and other times, unions' job actions did not prompt such powerful protests and results goes, however, beyond the scope of this brief overview.

Our book concludes with studies of remembrance and a comparison of labor conditions in Lawrence in 1912 and China in 2012, leading us to the present day. The commemoration of the 1911 Triangle Shirtwaist Factory Fire involved a multitude of participating groups and, utilizing the power of the arts, heightened our intellectual and emotional ability to get closer to past events. The historical links and connections between the Triangle Factory Fire in March 1911 and the Lawrence textile strike cry out for full exploration.

One wonders, for example: How much did Lawrence workers know about the horrors that took place on March 25, 1911? Walking to and from work, did they talk about the fire and wonder out loud whether their own workplaces were equally dangerous? Further, how many women around the country were outraged by the fire and became activists who supported the Lawrence strike ten months later? We know that many women with knowledge of the Triangle Fire, including Helen Keller, Frances Perkins, and Margaret Sanger, became outspoken supporters of the strike, as did members of the Women's Trade Union League. Did they and others engage with Lawrence strikers because they were responding along a path to labor activism from their anger regarding the fire?

Women and children suffered from industrial violence in both cities and events in both places challenged progressive-era notions that social improvement was possible. Early in the strike, Arturo Giovannitti, Joseph Caruso, and Joseph Ettor were jailed and charged with complicity in the death of striker Anna LoPizzo, shot by a militia rifle. The three were nowhere near the scene of her death. The trial, which opened in late September 1912, drew international attention and a committee raised funds for the men's defense. Prominent among those speaking out for the three was Keller, who wrote: "The crime with which he (Giovannitti) was charged was, of course, a legal fiction devised by the mill

---

[15] Frances Fox Piven, "Movements Making Noise," *The Nation*, February 18, 2013, 11-14.

owners and their agents. Giovannitti's real crime was helping the strikers in their assault on the pocketbooks of the owners." Dolly Sloan, wife of artist John Sloan, participated in numerous labor and suffrage events in New York City, was well aware of the Triangle Fire, and became a leader in the movement of strikers' children for safe keeping. She and her husband took in two children.

Margaret Sanger played a critical role in the Lawrence Textile Strike, traveling from New York City to Lawrence to bring the children of striking textile workers to New York City, where sympathetic families cared for them for the duration of the strike. In her brief *New York Call* article, "The Fangs of the Monster at Lawrence," Sanger described what she found in Lawrence:

> As soon as you board the train for Lawrence at Boston, you are aware that war is going on about you somewhere not far off. Dozens of soldiers in uniform, relieved for a few hours of such laborious work as waiting for trouble, are seen strutting in and out of the railway trains, pompous and important as defenders of the bosses and private property.
>
> When you get to Lawrence, on every corner are soldiers with guns bayoneted, ready at a moment's notice to plunge this deadly instrument into the living flesh of the working men or women who have rebelled against these degrading conditions of wage slavery which has reduced them and their families to human machines used only to pile up enormous profits for the bosses of the mills.

Many women in both events—whether those dead and injured in the Triangle Fire and engaged in acts of protest and organization in its aftermath or the thousands of young women in the cold winter-time streets of Lawrence—were immigrant teenagers, working hard and struggling for better lives at the height of the progressive era. Taken together, these events thrust the inequities of early 20th century industrial capitalism onto the front pages of newspapers around the world. And, they challenged individuals like Keller, Sloan, and Sanger to action. Linked events in 1911 and 1912, they were powerfully commemorated in 2011 and 2012. How they were memorialized and, indeed, this volume are parts of the remembering.

Little can be added to Clark University Professor Robert Ross' expert review of how Bread and Roses as a "legend" lives on (chapter 13). For Ross, the Lawrence textile strike of 1912 "has come to represent working class struggles for dignity and respect and a more expansive ambition for a full life—the 'roses' part of the iconic duality." That the legend of the Bread and Roses Strike continues "to grip the imagination of workers and feminists and intellectuals is indicative of a deeper reality—that aspirations for dignity and respect loom large in a working class life."

The centennial celebration of which this book is a part has offered an excellent vantage point from which to evaluate the "longue durée" of even such a twisted debate as the one on why the strike was forgotten or why its remembrance was revived with a historically incorrect name just before 1980. As social and economic historians, we may emphasize that the 1970s constituted a real turning point of the nation's well-being, which helped revive old memories. As already pointed out above, hardship after hardship had met the generation of 1912 strikers.

The 1960s, in turn, offered some good times. If earlier decades had pushed memories of 1912 to the back burner because other worries loomed larger (the Great Depression, World War II), or because of political repression (Red Scare, McCarthyism), the 1960s tempted people to forget because bad times seemed finally gone. That all changed with the oil crisis of 1973, and don't we remember how—and how long—its impact lasted, especially for the working class! The 1976 Bicentennial was a spark to reexamine our history, by the way, and lots of constituencies did. Under this constellation, the strike was rediscovered and given a more permanent name that seemed to encapsulate hope along with material reward.

According to Kirk Savage, collective memory such as that of the 1912 Lawrence Textile Workers' Strike, like for so many events in history, is "'constructed,' amidst a perpetual political battleground." We owe this now widely shared awareness to Maurice Halbwachs, who argued that all memory is a social process, shaped by various groups. But it does not emerge in one piece. John Bodnar, a social historian of ethnic and immigrant communities, makes a distinction between "official" and "vernacular" memory, the first constructed by the authorities and (in our case, business or religious) organizations, the second by ordinary people. We have posited that these two kinds of collective memories were more apt to merge since the 1970s.[16]

Another theme has influenced the recent literature on remembrance: the distinction between sculptural and living memory. The first is represented by monuments, the second, for example, by ". . . performance and consumption that may leave no lasting trace on the landscape."[17] The Bread and Roses Centennial included both, as have other commemorations discussed in the accounts by Sosin and Sosinsky (chapter 10) and Gabriner and Stern (chapter 11) of the 1911 Triangle Shirtwaist Factory Fire centennial. The Bread and Roses anniversary year of 2012 saw concerts, conferences, exhibits, and theater performances and the creation and unveiling of a powerful Strikers' Monument on the Lawrence Common. Just how the monumental and living realms of collective memory

---

[16] Kirk Savage, "History, Memory, and Monuments: An Overview of the Scholarly Literature on Commemoration," online essay commissioned by the Organization of American Historians and the National Park Service, 2006. http://www.nps.gov/history/history/resedu/savage.htm; Maurice Halbwachs, *On Collective Memory* (1925) (Chicago, IL: The University of Chicago Press, 1992); John Bodnar, *Remaking America: Public Memory, Commemoration, and Patriotism in the Twentieth Century* (Princeton, NJ: Princeton University Press, 1992).

[17] Savage, 7.

interpenetrate one another—and they do—is still an open research question among scholars. But we know from our experience in celebrating the centennial, and now also through the writings in this book, that everyone benefited immensely from coming together in efforts to understand better and memorize more vividly what happened in Lawrence in 1912, and beyond.

Finally, after 1912 local memory of the strike was dominated by the "God-and-Country" version of history. Since then, people in Lawrence and around the world have debated, suppressed, celebrated, and reexamined the strike's legacies. A new, more favorable interpretation of the strike finally emerged in Lawrence in the late 1970s. Instrumental figures included three New Yorkers: folk artist Ralph Fasanella, *Village Voice* journalist Paul Cowan, and labor leader/historian Moe Foner; some local Lawrence historians: Attorney Ignatius Piscitello, Lawrence History Center founder Eartha Dengler, and Mayor Lawrence Lefebre; and some academic practitioners of the "new social history," including James Green and Ardis Cameron. Most of these people were present for "Bread and Roses Day" on the Common on April 27, 1980, the first officially sanctioned pro-strike public commemoration in Lawrence. Fasanella was famous for his colorful images of the American working class. His interest in the history of the U.S. labor movement attracted him to Lawrence where the Great Textile Strike of 1912 had taken place. There, he painted people, places, and events.

The Bread and Roses Labor Day Festival—held in celebration of the ethnic diversity and labor history of Lawrence every year since 1985—includes music and dance, poetry and drama, ethnic food, historical demonstrations, and walking and trolley tours. The Festival also makes explicit links to contemporary struggles for social justice. The Festival's September 2012 welcome to attendees read in part: "Today we gather on the very Common that witnessed and fostered solidarity among Lawrence's workers. In this spirit, we have created a program that honors Lawrence's many cultures, both past and present. In addition to performances, we extend our support to unions and other community organizations for social justice in their fight to secure and improve the lives of all."

Shortly after the walkout began, strikers circulated an "open letter" explaining what they hoped to gain from their effort.

> In our fight we have suffered and borne patiently the abuse and calumnies of the mill owners, the city government, police, militia, state government, legislature, and the local police court judge. We feel that in justice to our fellow workers we should at this time make known the causes which compelled us to strike against the mill owners of Lawrence. We hold that as useful members of society and as wealth producers we have the right to lead decent and honorable lives; that we ought to have homes and not shacks; that we ought to have clean food and not adulterated food at high prices; that we ought to have clothes suited to the weather and not

shoddy garments. That to secure sufficient food, clothing and shelter in a society made up of a robber class on the one hand and a working class on the other hand, it is absolutely necessary for the toilers to band themselves together and form a union, organizing its powers in such form as to them seem most likely to affect their safety and happiness.

These words offer a fitting entry point to new scholarship on the Bread and Roses strike. We hope our collective efforts have done justice to the heroism of thousands of Lawrence mill workers during that desperately cold winter of 1912.

CHAPTER 2

"'Believe Comrades . . . the Day is Coming When Those at the End of Their Rope Will Require Struggle. It Will Be, Perhaps, Tomorrow.' Franco-Belgian Immigrants and the 1912 Strike"*

Janelle Bourgeois

> *It is absolutely foolish to say 'it happened without any apparent cause;' 'that it was lightning out of a clear sky,' etc. As a matter of fact, it was a harvest, it was a result of seeds sown before. . . . In Lawrence it was a determined band of Franco-Belgian workers who kept up the agitation . . . held aloft the banner of industrial unionism until the great strikes and victories of this year came to reward their efforts and prove their propaganda had not been in vain.*[1]
> *– James P. Thompson, IWW Organizer, October 1912*

On a cold Thursday afternoon in January 1912, the opening curtain was drawn on the 1912 Lawrence textile strike, one of the most studied strikes in American labor history. On that day, 200 Polish women walked out of the Everett Mill to protest a pay cut proportional to a legislatively mandated reduction in the hours of the work week. They shouted, "Short pay! Short pay!" and thousands of their fellow workers followed them out of the mills.[2] In the words

---

*This chapter uses extensive French-language primary and secondary sources. The author did all translations. This chapter builds on the painstaking research of French scholars who compiled a biographical dictionary of French speaking radicals in the U.S. See: Michel Cordillot, ed., *La Sociale en Amérique: Dictionnaire Biographique du Mouvement Social Francophone aux États-Unis, 1848-1922* (Paris: Les Editions de L'Atelier, 2002).

[1] James P. Thompson, "Report as General Organizer: the Seventh Annual IWW Convention." *Solidarity*, October 2, 1912.

[2] Bruce Watson, *Bread and Roses: Mills, Migrants and the Struggle for the American Dream* (New York: Penguin Books, 2006), 9.

of one overseer, "like a spark of electricity,"[3] the strike began. The curtain closed a little more than two months later on an unequivocal victory. On that day, an agreement ended the strike on the strikers' terms. Twenty thousand strikers stood in rainy weather on the Lawrence Common for hours as the agreement was read and approved in all of the city's languages.[4]

These scenes are well known. They mark a dramatic beginning and a triumphant end. Telling the story of the strike in this way gives it an air of spontaneity, as if the strike was a random eruption; passive workers bore the burdens of starvation wages silently until the moment they could take no more. If, however, one follows those mill operatives down into the streets, one of their destinations opens the curtain on a different strike story. The day after the walk-out, those strikers marched to the Franco-Belgian Hall at 9 Mason Street (see Figure 2, p. 114). There the strikers formed what would become the strike committee and telegraphed for the Industrial Workers of the World (IWW).[5] Two months later workers filled the hall, which served as strike headquarters and housed the largest soup kitchen, beyond capacity when Bill Haywood announced the settlement that ended the strike.[6]

The destination of the strikers begs several questions: Who were the Franco-Belgians? Why did the strikers think their hall would be of use to them? What was their relationship to the radical organization they helped call into the city? The answers lie not in the scenes described above but in the immigrant journey of the Franco-Belgians to Lawrence. Those strikers marched to that hall because during the previous ten years the Franco-Belgians had established themselves at the forefront of radical labor organizing in Lawrence, just as they were in France and Belgium. They preached for revolution and the demise of capitalism but regularly lent their hall to any labor effort, conservative and radical alike.

Telling the strike story through the Franco-Belgians shifts the historical lens in important ways. Through one lens, it restores history to the grassroots level. Workers were not passive until the minute they could take no more but instead pushed back against the injustices they faced. They did not just strike; they also developed alternative social institutions like the hall. This telling is important, essential even, because through it we must acknowledge that social change is not something spontaneous but something built on years and decades of the thankless, dogged efforts of people whose names history has long since forgotten. In this telling, the strike becomes not a random, "spark of electricity," but, to borrow the words of James P. Thompson, a harvest. This chapter aims to tell the story of the Franco-Belgians; a group who helped sow the strike's seeds.

---

[3] Ray Stannard Baker, "The Revolutionary Strike," *The American Magazine,* May 1912, 20.
[4] Watson, 206.
[5] *Lawrence Evening Tribune,* January 12, 1912; Sidney Lens, *Radicalism in America* (Cambridge, MA: Schenkman Publishing, 1982), 236.
[6] Watson, 206.

PUSH AND PULL

France on strike was above all the France of textiles, its capital Roubaix, its leading actors the weavers, who alone monopolized 23 percent of the conflicts.[7]

On November 19, 1901, 31-year-old August Detollenaere, a French-speaking Belgian, boarded the *S.S. Saxonia* in Liverpool, England bound for Boston, Massachusetts.[8] Detollenaere, a skilled worsted weaver from the French textile center Roubaix, left France to try his luck in an American textile center—Lawrence, Massachusetts.[9] His decision to sail for America was intertwined with two trends that conspired to bring him and other French and Belgian immigrants to American textile centers. The first trend occurred in France over the course of 1870-1890 when an economic recession hit the French textile cities of Roubaix and Tourcoing. The crisis deepened when the U.S.'s 1890 McKinley and 1897 Dingley tariff halved woolen imports to the U.S.[10] French workers were warned of impending, "unprecedented unemployment in the textile industry."[11] Mills closed, and by 1898 mass lay-offs occurred.

The second trend, linked to the first, occurred in the United States. In response to the protectionist tariffs French and Belgian mill owners invested in the U.S. woolen industry. Before this investment American mills, including those in Lawrence, utilized English style manufacturing. The French method was, arguably, superior and "revolutionized the woolen and worsted industry in the United States."[12] Gradually all American mills adopted the method including those in Lawrence around 1900.[13] The adoption of French methods created a demand for skilled French operatives. Franco-Belgian migration to Lawrence began as early as 1868, but peaked in 1900-1910 after the adoption of the French method. American mill owners recruited loyal French foremen who in turn

---

[7] Perrot, *Workers on Strike: France, 1871-1890* (New Haven, CT: Yale University Press: 1987).

[8] National Archives and Records Administration (NARA); Washington, D.C.; Crew Lists of Vessels Arriving at Boston, Massachusetts, 1917-1943; Microfilm Serial: T938; Microfilm Roll: 43. Ancestry.com. Boston Passenger and Crew Lists, 1820-1943 [database on-line]. Provo, UT, USA: Ancestry.com Operations, Inc., 2006.

[9] Roubaix, Ibid; Occupation: 1910 US Census, Essex County, Massachusetts, Lawrence, Ancestry.com, retrieved 02 Dec. 2011.

[10] Mary Blewett, "The Transatlantic Worsted Trade 1830-1930," in *Connectng Seas and Connected Ocean Rims: Indian, Atlantic, and Pacific Oceans and China Seas Migration from the 1830s to the 1930s,* ed. Donna Gabaccia and Dirk Hoerder (IDC: Leiden, 2011).

[11] Jean-Claude Gilbert, *Textile Workers, Trade Unions and Politics: Comparative Caste Studies, France and the United States 1885-1914*. Thesis, Tufts University, 1980.

[12] Mira Wilkins, *The History of Foreign Investment in the United States to 1914* (Cambridge, MA: Harvard Univ Press, 1989), 358.

[13] Ibid., Gary Gerstle, *Working Class Americanism: The Politics of Labor in a Textile City 1914-1960* (Princeton, NJ: Princeton University Press, 2002), 74.

recruited loyal French operatives. Recruits were promised good employment in the United States and that there were other immigrants from the same place who spoke the same language.[14]

Mill owners hoped to avoid the labor unrest that characterized mills in France. From 1895-1900, textile workers in Roubaix staged more than 100 strikes.[15] An 1893 strike wave is worthy of particular mention for the resonance it occasioned 19 years later. That strike wave began in November 1892 when legislation limited the work hours of women and children which translated to a de facto pay cut for all workers. Across various industries workers conducted 55 strikes in protest.[16] As they recruited from the ranks of these workers American mill owners quickly found, that like many of the best-laid plans, things went awry. Black-listed operatives in France heard of recruiters and it was not long before the radicals appeared throughout American textile cities.[17]

As Detollenaere, who would later be described as "no man's fool," carried his luggage to his cabin, it was likely a spot earned on such a black list that spurred his departure.[18] His experiences in Roubaix's textile mills convinced him of the irreconcilability of the interests of workers and their employers. Within ten years, that conviction transformed itself in Lawrence and found expression in the Franco-Belgian Co-operative, the formation of the French Textile Federation within the Industrial Workers of the World (IWW) and, finally, the publication of the monthly labor paper *L'Emancipation*. It was this experience that made Detollenaere and the broader Franco-Belgian community the integral and militant group it was during the 1912 strike.

SETTLING IN

> *These people are for the most part French-speaking textile workers . . . who have been coming to . . . American wool and worsted towns where they find employment as skilled operatives. The larger part are weavers . . . an annual immigration is expected . . . true to the traditions of their homeland, they are quick to espouse the cause of trade unionism in their new home.*[19]

---

[14] Mary Blewett, *"A Lifetime of Gentle Strength,"* Women in American History, Manuscript, Franco-Belgian Box, Lawrence History Center, Lawrence, MA.

[15] U.S. Department of Labor, *Bulletin of the Department of Labor* 12-15, 1897, 792.

[16] Edward Shorter and Charles Tilly, *Strikes in France 1830-1968* (New York: Cambridge University Press, 1974), 385 n. 16.

[17] Gerstle, *Working Class Americanism,* 74.

[18] Justus Ebert, *The Trial of a New Society* (Cleveland: IWW Publishing Bureau, 1913), Chapter 2.

[19] United States Immigration Commission, *Reports of the Immigration Commission: Immigrants in Industries*, Edited by William Dillingham. Vol. 4. Washington DC: Washington Government Printing Office, 1911.

Detollenaere disembarked the *S.S. Saxonia* in Boston and boarded a train north to Lawrence with $60 in his pocket. After an hour's journey, he arrived in Lawrence where a community of about 225 Franco-Belgians had taken root. Whatever fears he had about the black list following him to America were alleviated when he found work as a worsted weaver. After less than six months, his wife and son sailed from Belgium to make their new home in Lawrence. The family settled in at 4 Nightingale Court.[20]

It is difficult to say how many Franco-Belgian radicals like Detollenaere came to Lawrence. A 1902 strike, however, provides a clue. The strike started in Olneyville, Rhode Island. William Wood's decision as head of American Woolen to institute the two-loom system in his fancy mills, which produced more complex patterned cloth, precipitated the strike.[21] Weavers correctly perceived two looms as a way for American Woolen to halve the number of workers and still maintain production levels. Two looms also staved off union organizing because they created unemployment.[22] The situation for weavers worsened with introduction of the premium system which rewarded workers when they produced beyond their ever-increasing quotas.

In response to the introduction of two looms, the Socialist Trade and Labor Alliance (STLA) in Olneyville launched a strike.[23] As the unrest spread, 2,800 looms ceased, shutting down 30 percent of American Woolen's production capacity.[24] According to the *American Wool and Cotton Reporter* "discontent and discord were immediately communicated to other mills . . . an endemic of . . . 'sympathetic' strikes followed."[25] As the strike wave spread American Woolen weavers in Lawrence attempted to join. A total of 60 weavers walked out in sympathy with the Olneyville strikers. While only a small number of weavers walked out over the two loom system in Lawrence other workers, led by German immigrants, demanded a 20 percent pay increase and the abolition of the premium system.[26]

Franco-Belgians were essential to the strike led by the Germans and among the first to walk out. While neither the Olneyville nor the Lawrence strike met with success, the strikes had a radical tone in the press and leaders were called

---

[20] Thirteenth Census of the United States.
[21] Philip Scranton, *Figured Tapestry: Production, Markets and Power in Philadelphia Textiles, 1855-1941* (New York: Cambridge University Press 1989), 208.
[22] "Report as General Organizer," *Solidarity,* October 12, 1912.
[23] "American Woolen Strike," *American Wool and Cotton Reporter* 16 (1902), 23.
[24] *Figured Tapestry,* 208.
[25] "American Woolen Strike," *American Wool and Cotton Reporter* 16 (1902), 23.
[26] Rhode Island. Office of Commissioner of Labor, *Report of the Commissioner of Labor Made to the General Assembly, Volume 16* (Providence: EL Freeman & Sons, State Printer, 1903), 144; Donald Cole, *Immigrant City: Lawrence Massachusetts 1845-1921* (University of North Carolina Press: 1963), 94.

"red button socialists" and "extremists."[27] It was, perhaps, the new arrivals like Detollenaere who drove this radicalism. On strike within the first year of his arrival in Lawrence, Detollenaere may have begun to feel at home.

It is unclear whether the Lawrence strike was conducted under the auspices of the STLA local in Lawrence. The STLA, a militant split from the Knights of Labor and the American Federation of Labor, advocated the "smashing" of conservative American labor organizations.[28] Franco-Belgians comprised the majority of the members of the Lawrence STLA local.[29] The local had failed to grow in Lawrence, however, due to high rents and maintenance costs for meeting spaces. These costs absorbed half or more of the revenue of the local and prevented members from engaging in organizing propaganda.[30]

L'UNION FRANCO-BELGE

The Union is the place of combat. For us, the cooperative should be a financial and moral support. Its value in this role is incontestable and the worker's party of the old world owes to it a great part of its power.[31]

As the Lawrence STLA local floundered under financial pressure, Detollenaere and many Franco-Belgians paused to consider the cooperative tradition they carried across the Atlantic. They remembered that in Roubaix Belgian-inspired cooperatives had strengthened the unions. When Detollenaere sailed in 1901, *La Paix*, the premier working-class cooperative in Roubaix had a membership of 5,000 families and provided spaces for the local textile union and section of the Socialist Party.[32] Linked to cooperatives that owned their own physical spaces, trade unions took money otherwise wasted by rent payments and redirected it to propaganda. Further, as alternatives to capitalist enterprises, consumer cooperatives sold food, fuel, and other goods to members at cost. In this

---

[27] Ibid., 94.

[28] "Preceding the ST&LA." *The Daily People* (New York), July 3, 1910.

[29] "Etre Chez Soi," *L'Union des Travailleurs,* December 22, 1910. Reprinted from *L'Emancipation.* Only 2 complete copies of *L'Emancipation* exist. Many articles were reprinted by Louis Goaziou in *L'Union des Travailleurs.*

[30] Ibid.

[31] "Syndicat et Coopérative," *L'Union des Travailleurs,* December 22, 1910. Reprinted from *L'Emancipation.* French scholar Michel Cordillot has assumed that *L'Emancipation* articles signed with the initials A.D. were authored by August Detollenaere. This chapter also operates under that assumption. See Michel Cordillot, ed., *La Sociale en Amérique: Dictionnaire Biographique du Mouvement Social Francophone aux États-Unis 1848-1922* (Paris: Les Editions de L'Atelier, 2002), 161.

[32] Carl Strikwerda, "France and the Belgian Immigration," in *The Politics of Immigrant Workers,* ed. Camille Guerin-Gonzales and Carl Strikwerda (New York: Holmes & Meier, 1993), 113.

way, members withdrew from the economic system they so resented. In these *Maisons du Peuple,* consumption itself became an act of protest.[33]

With this in mind, the Franco-Belgians embarked on a cooperative venture modeled after institutions in France and Belgium. Detollenaere and seven other Franco-Belgian immigrants formally chartered L'Union Franco-Belge on June 19, 1905.[34] The cooperative operated its own bakery as well as its own grocery store. At the club, Franco-Belgians spoke their own language and, according to one Franco-Belgian, members found a place where "good friends meet to discuss the tough social issues" and "families can relax after the hard work of the week."[35]

Membership was open to all families, with subscription consisting of one $10 share called an individual's *part sociale*.[36] Ten percent of profits earned went to a reserve fund to be used during strikes or to aid needy members, 10 percent more went to a socialist propaganda fund. The cooperative distributed the balance of any profits back to members proportional to the amount they purchased throughout the year.[37] Socialist principles also applied to those working at the cooperative store, managers received a salary no greater than other employees, $15 per week.[38]

Detollenaere intended the cooperative to be tied to labor activity in Lawrence. For him, "The union is the place of combat; the cooperative must be . . . a financial and moral support." He acknowledged that the "workers' party of the old world owes much" to cooperatives. On a more pragmatic level, Detollenaere argued that since workers spent their days being exploited in the factories, they ought to seek institutions such as the cooperative that would not do so when they were off the clock.[39]

The cooperative enjoyed tremendous success by 1910. In that year, it operated with a budget surplus of $800.[40] Also in 1910, the club purchased its headquarters at 9 Mason Street. The building had a 500-seat auditorium, committee rooms, a library, a gymnasium, and a pool and billiards room. Members installed a new steam heat system in the building and paid with cash.[41] By 1913, it conducted

---

[33] "Etre Chez Soi."

[34] Charter of L'Union Franco-Belge. June 19, 1905. Franco-Belgian Box, Lawrence History Center, Lawrence, MA.

[35] Where their own language could be spoken: Autobiography of Henry Claus, Manuscript, Franco-Belgian Box, Lawrence History Center, Lawrence MA; Detollenaere quote: "Etre Chez Soi."

[36] James Ford, *Cooperatives in New England, Urban and Rural* (New York: Survey Associates, 1913), 38.

[37] Charter of *L'Union Franco-Belge.*

[38] James Ford, 38.

[39] "Syndicat Et Cooperative."

[40] Ibid.

[41] "Notes From New England: Progress of the IWW in Textile and Other Industries," *Solidarity,* March 26, 1910.

$100,000 in yearly business.[42] As the cooperative enjoyed its success, members increasingly acted in solidarity with the efforts of American and French workers. In July 1910, a strike was declared in Halluin, France. Workers struck over pay differentials, which according to Franco-Belgians in Lawrence amounted to huge profits for the mill owners.[43] The cooperative sent nearly $100 to support the strike.[44] Similarly, during another 1910 strike in New Bedford, Franco-Belgians donated $34.25.[45]

While the propaganda fund financially aided the strikers, the hall provided necessary, but otherwise hard-to-obtain physical spaces, that strikers needed. In 1911, a group of 87 women walked out of the Ayer Mill to obtain a pay increase. Mill agents responded that they should be grateful they had jobs. Unorganized, the women affiliated with the Textile Workers Protective Association, not the IWW. Despite this choice, the Franco-Belgians offered their hall as a meeting place and the strikers accepted.[46] In 1910, the hall also became the meeting place for a newly organized weavers union.[47]

THE INDUSTRIAL WORKERS OF THE WORLD

The Franco-Belgian Federation of the IWW has the following goals:
To group workers of the French and Flemish languages for the defense of their interests, moral and material, economic and professional; To group workers of both sexes, belonging to any political school with the principle of class struggle. . . . It places itself purely and simply in economic action.[48]

In 1907, with the increasing strength of the cooperative behind him, Detollenaere turned his attention back to labor agitation. This time, he turned to the IWW, which was founded in Chicago in 1905. The IWW espoused revolutionary syndicalism and was arguably the most radical union ever to make headway in the United States. While revolutionary syndicalism developed along its own trajectory in the United States, similar philosophies in France influenced it. The core of revolutionary syndicalism held that the state and the capitalist economy must be destroyed and that the general strike and trade

---

[42] James Ford, *Cooperatives in New England, Urban and Rural* (New York: Survey Associates, 1913), 38.
[43] "Nouvelles de France," *L'Union des Travailleurs,* December 22, 1910.
[44] "En France," *L'Union des Travailleurs,"* January 19, 1911.
[45] "Contributions to Textile Strikers," *Solidarity,* June 18, 1910.
[46] Annual Report of the Adjunct General of the Commonwealth of Massachusetts, Vol. 10, 1912.
[47] *Reports of the Immigration Commission: Immigrants in Industries*, Edited by William Dillingham.
[48] "Fédération Franco-Belge IWW, Réglement, But et Consitution," *L'Emancipation,* September 1911. From one of two complete surviving editions of *L'Emancipation*, held by the Wisconsin Historical Society.

unionism were the best means to that end. Workers would then take over industry and run it for the benefit of the masses.[49]

The American Federation of Labor (AFL), which organized white, skilled, male workers, did not appeal to the Franco-Belgians. They viewed the AFL as, "divert[ing] the working class from the true path."[50] They equated the AFL with conservative unions in France and Belgium that never addressed the social ills at the foundation of the capitalist system nor called for an end to wage slavery. With these philosophies, it was a foregone conclusion that Franco-Belgians would seek out the most radical labor organizations in the United States.[51]

Further, the AFL, unlike the IWW, excluded African-American and women workers. Franco-Belgians saw both groups as important to labor organization. Detollenaere derided men who claimed to represent civilization on one hand but sought to deny full rights to African-Americans on the other. According to him, the duty of workers' organizations was to want justice for African-American workers. Unions must make "clear to the descendants of the slaves, that the organized working-class condemns [the principle of racial separation] . . . that all men whether black or white, yellow or red are equal . . . having the right to life and freedom."[52]

The French Textile Federation within the IWW also organized female workers. Franco-Belgian radicals, however, viewed the radicalism of women in highly gendered terms. In 1908, the Franco-Belgian branch of Local 20 invited David Mikol, a French socialist living in Boston, to speak to a group of workers including many women. Mikol explained to the women that their radicalism found best expression in their children's education. By educating their children in radical principles they created "a resolute and strong generation of men who will be able to break the horrible chains of capitalism."[53] That women may have engaged in radical labor organizing in accordance with their own principles like the men did was apparently not considered.

The practical work of organizing with the IWW began in December 1907 when IWW Organizer James P. Thompson visited Lawrence. He arranged a meeting with August Detollenaere and Gilbert Smith, two of the few remaining members of the STLA local. At the meeting, the Franco-Belgian branch of Local 20 IWW was formed with 31 members.[54] Thompson reported, "There is splendid material in this new French branch, and great things are expected from the new

---

[49] Philip Foner, *History of the Labor Movement in the United States: 1905-1917. The Industrial Workers of the World* (International Publications: 1965), 20-21.

[50] "Notre Ideal," *L'Union des Travailleurs,* September 18, 1910. Reprinted from *L'Emancipation.*

[51] Ibid.

[52] "Conflit de Races," *L'Union des Travailleurs,* January 19, 1911. Reproduced from *L'Emancipation.*

[53] "Travailleurs Industriels du Monde," *L'Union des Travailleurs,* October 22, 1908.

[54] "Report as General Organizer," *Solidarity*, October 19, 1912.

recruits, some of them having received their training in the French Confederation of Labor."[55]

The new French branch of Local 20 capitalized on the experience its members brought from France. A small population of Franco-Belgian weavers also lived in Lowell, nine miles from Lawrence. In March 1908, weavers in Lowell went on strike. During the strike, two Belgians scabbed on strikers. When the Franco-Belgians in Lowell realized this they organized to get the scabs to leave work. Initially, the AFL affiliated United Textile Workers (UTW) planned to organize the workers. Before the UTW moved, however, Detollenaere, on behalf of the IWW, stepped in with an organizational meeting and the Belgians signed up for a charter with the IWW.[56] Thompson was so pleased by the collaboration between workers in Lawrence and Lowell that he hoped the UTW would find out so the IWW could have a laugh at their expense.[57] Two years later, the Belgian branch in Lowell traveled to Lawrence, this time to help Detollenaere and IWW organizer Fred Isler organize a Flemish branch in Lawrence.[58]

A few months later, in May 1908, the National Industrial Union of Textile Workers (NIUTW) became the first chartered industrial branch within the IWW in Paterson, New Jersey.[59] Representatives from the French branches of both Lawrence and Lowell were present. August Detollenaere of Lawrence and J. Youngsjohn of Lowell were elected members of the National Executive Board. Within the NIUTW, the French textile workers formed the French Textile Federation. Some members of the NIUTW were concerned that language branches would tend to fragment immigrant workers in the American labor movement.[60] Despite these misgivings, however, the language branches represented a pragmatic way of creating unity from an immense ethnic and linguistic diversity.

As the NIUTW got underway, the Franco-Belgians branched out their efforts to organize the French-language populations across the textile centers in New England. The French textile locals held their first congress in Woonsocket, Rhode Island in 1907. At the first congress, three branches from Providence, Lawrence, and Woonsocket were present. The branches planned a second congress for 1908.[61] In the year between the first and second congress, the organizing efforts of the French workers paid off. A total of 16 French-speaking delegates attended

---

[55] Yates, William. The Work in New England. *Industrial Union Bulletin*, January 11, 1908.
[56] Notes From the Front." *Industrial Union Bulletin*, March 21, 1908.
[57] Ibid.
[58] "L'Organisateur Isler à Lawrence," *L'Union des Travailleurs,* July 7, 1910.
[59] IWW chronology (1904-1911). Available from http://www.iww.org/en/about/chronology/1 (accessed 05/11/2012); "Minutes of the Convention of Textile Workers," *Industrial Union Bulletin*, May 16, 1908.
[60] "Language Federations in the National Unions," *Solidarity,* September 7, 1910.
[61] "French paper needed. *Industrial Union Bulletin*, April 18, 1908.

the 1908 congress with additional delegates from Philadelphia, New Bedford, Olneyville, and Lowell seated.[62] Subsequent annual congresses were held until at least 1915.[63]

L'EMANCIPATION

> *By the voice of our humble bulletin our adherents will be kept current on the general situation . . . but the primordial duty that we pursue will be, without respite, the battle against capitalism, against the exploitation of one class for the benefit of another, against the minority of the idle for the productive majority.*[64]

By 1910, the Franco-Belgian Co-operative and Local 20 I.W.W were well established in the Franco-Belgian community. August Detollenaere had passed eight years in Lawrence. In 1910, the French Textile Federation started to issue *L'Emancipation,* its own French-language IWW newspaper.[65] As early as 1908, Franco-Belgians in Lawrence linked with radical French printer Louis Goaziou from Charleroi, Pennsylvania.[66] Goaziou was born in 1864 in Brittany, France. He arrived in Pennsylvania when he was 16 years old and found work in the anthracite mines. Within two years, he had gone on strike for the first time and joined the Knights of Labor and the United Mine Workers of America.[67] An avowed anarchist, Goaziou published a succession of radical papers that often went out of print for want of an audience.[68]

Goaziou, however, was determined to publish a successful French-language paper and finally got it right in 1901 when he issued *L'Unions des Travailleurs*. Goaziou shifted away from anarchism towards socialism and aimed this paper at socialists of all stripes.[69] The paper gained popularity and Goaziou embarked on speaking tours to areas with large French-speaking populations. In March and April 1908, he left on a Socialist speaking tour beginning in Montreal, Canada, with stops in Claremont, Manchester, and Nashua, New Hampshire; Lawrence, Worcester, and New Bedford, Massachusetts; Providence, Rhode

---

[62] "Compte Rendu: Deuxieme Convention Annuelle des Travailleurs Francais du Textile," *L'Union des Travailleurs*, September 17, 1908.

[63] "French Branches Meet," *Solidarity,* June 27, 1914.

[64] "Noveau Journal," *L'Union des Travailleurs,* July 7, 1910.

[65] Ibid.

[66] "Réunions socialistes: Tournée de Propagande du Louis Goaziou," *L'Union des Travailleurs*, March 26, 1908.

[67] *La Sociale en Amérique,* 210.

[68] Ibid., 212.

[69] Ronald Creagh, "Socialism in America: The French-Speaking Coal Miners in the Late Nineteenth Century," in *In the shadow of the statue of liberty: Immigrants, workers, and citizens in the American republic, 1880-1920,* ed. Marianne Debouzy (Chicago: University of Illinois, 1992).

Island; and Danbury, Connecticut. Goaziou met August Detollenaere and other members of the Franco-Belgian community while in Lawrence.[70] In 1910, the cooperative announced that *L'Union des Travailleurs* would print its advertisements and notifications.[71] Shortly after, the French branches issued the first edition of *L'Emancipation* printed by Louis Goaziou. The paper claimed its first duty was to pursue the battle against capitalism and exploitation without respite.[72]

FORGING CONNECTIONS

We are under no illusions and know perfectly well that we will have much work to bring our ideas to the organized masses which in Lawrence have never experienced the principles of emancipation; there is the desire in some of them; industrial unionism first and then the complete suppression of the exploitation of man by man.[73]

While Detollenaere and other similar-minded Franco-Belgian radicals formed the French Textile Federation within the IWW, they found a receptive audience among their fellow radicals. They also organized outside of their own radical circles. They began with non-unionized French and Belgian workers in the United States. While the adoption of French technology in America spurred the emigration of black-listed radicals, it also attracted less dedicated unionists. In 1910, Detollenaere expressed frustration with this group saying they were "incomprehensible . . . the French and Belgians who have suffered the arrogance of exploitative employers at home, were part of workers' unions, have completely lost the notions of the social question in America."[74]

In France, they struck at every opportunity but here, another Franco-Belgian claimed, "The salary they receive has given rise to a ferocious pride and egoism." He further exclaimed, "What good is it to tell them that in . . . Lawrence the great woolen trust built immense mills without asking for a penny from its shareholders while workers are earning $5 to $8 per week. These people have eyes but do not want to see." While these French and Belgians were motivated by their own personal profit, they also were concerned with their reputation in their new country. Sometimes, "they read a newspaper and even then it is a 'right thinking' newspaper to avoid being noticed." At the mills, they were

---

[70] "Réunions socialistes: Tournée de Propagande du Louis Goaziou," *L'Union des Travailleurs*, March 26, 1908.

[71] "Merci, camarades . . ." *L'Union des Travailleurs*, December 10, 1910.

[72] "Nouveau Journal," *L'Union des Travailleurs,* July 7, 1910.

[73] "Alliance Textile," *L'Union des Travailleurs,* March 7, 1911. Reprinted from *L'Emancipation.*

[74] "Woonsocket," *L'Union des Travailleurs,* October 20, 1910.

the employees who could be abused without a hint of revolt.[75] Articles in *L'Emancipation* frequently exhorted these workers to join the IWW.

Radical French and Belgians also encountered another group that confounded them—the French-Canadians. The French-Canadians spoke the same language but existed at the opposite end of the ideological spectrum: conservative, loyal to their churches, and resistant to labor organizing, Franco-Belgian radicals focused much organizing attention on them.[76] According to Louis Picavet, a French-Canadian member of the IWW and the cooperative, his fellows were "dull and kept in ignorance by priests and politicians."[77] The French-Canadians lived

> Day to day to work ... to kill themselves. ... It is they who, in weave rooms of the Pacific Mills, operate up to 16 looms. They withstand the poverty and the hunger, accept the sickness and the accidents as an inevitability because they have always instilled in themselves the idea of resignation to their miserable fate ....[78]

In 1908, radical Franco-Belgians launched a campaign to educate the French-Canadians, their "brothers and sisters in chains." The campaign ended in frustration.[79]

While the French-Canadians seemed deaf to the appeals of the Franco-Belgians, the community was hardly homogenous. It had its own group of radicals, among them Louis Picavet, mentioned above. Another was Joseph Bedard, financial secretary of the 1912 strike, and a representative on the Committee of Ten that settled the strike. Bedard likely occupied a unique position between the two communities: respected for his radicalism by the Franco-Belgians but at home among the French-Canadians. In 1903, Franco-Belgians forged their connections with Bedard at a party he presided over to celebrate the 1st of May, international workers' day.[80]

As they organized among their countrymen and those who shared the same language, Lawrence's Franco-Belgians also looked to the many other immigrant groups who called Lawrence home, in particular, the city's Italian population. Years later, Angelo Rocco, a prominent Italian immigrant who was active in the 1912 strike, recalled, "You know why it started? Franco-Belgians from the province of Lille became textile workers. They formed a club of the IWW. ...

---

[75] "Egoistes," *L'Emancipation*, September 1912. This is one of two known, complete, copies of *L'Emancipation*. It is held by the University of Michigan.

[76] *Reports of the Immigration Commission: Immigrants in Industries.*

[77] "Travailleurs Industriels du Monde," *L'Union des Travailleurs*, October 22, 1908.

[78] "Aux Canadiens-Français," *L'Emancipation*, September 1912. From one of two surviving complete editions of *L'Emancipation* held at the Univ. of Michigan.

[79] "Compte Rendu de la Deuxième Convention Annelle des Travailleurs Français du Textile," *L'Union des Travailleurs*, September 17, 1908.

[80] Michel Cordillot, *La Sociale en Amérique*, 43.

They began to sow socialism."[81] To organize among the Italian workers, Detollenaere requested an Italian speaker at a meeting of the executive board of the NIUTW.[82]

In 1910, the Franco-Belgians invited Joseph Ettor to organize but "the times were hard. His warm, eloquent, and catchy speech was not heard because the workers cared little for the organization."[83] Instead, Ettor spent his time among the Franco-Belgians on the Merrimack where he charmed them and learned the refrain of *L'Internationale*.[84] Ettor returned to agitate among Italians during a convention of French branches in 1911. Ettor "was not sailing any more but in meetings and in the streets he accompanied his strong voice with the fiery song of revolt by Eugene Pottier."[85] He presided over packed meetings of Italian textile workers and organized an Italian branch.

Detollenaere and the Franco-Belgians also approached other trade unions in the city. The French branches had no problem with the idea of "boring from within" that challenged the broader IWW. "Boring from within" was an embraced labor policy in France and England. The tactic called for radical workers to infiltrate conservative unions to radicalize them. Franco-Belgians in Lawrence did not advocate the infiltration of conservative unions; they did try to radicalize them. In 1910, IWW member Louis Picavet said, "The idea of meeting with the unions, even the conservative ones, can only result in good because ... we can lead them first of all in a more progressive direction, and finally to a revolutionary conception."[86] Picavet referred to Local 20 joining Lawrence's Alliance of Textile Workers' Unions. The alliance coordinated propaganda efforts of member unions for increased strength when conflicts broke out between unions and employers.[87]

When they joined this alliance, Franco-Belgian IWW members were clear about their motives and goals. Detollenaere and Picavet said the alliance was a way to bring publicity to the IWW since the press remained conspicuously silent toward the organization. Due to this silence, workers in Lawrence knew nothing of the principles of the IWW. This laid the foundation for the introduction of more revolutionary ideas.[88] Detollenaere wanted discussions between IWW Local 20 and other unions to be open and frank. He felt conservative unions in the United States, like their counterparts in France and Belgium, consistently avoided of open discussion, especially with radicals.[89]

---

[81] Studs Terkel, *American Dreams Lost and Found* (New York: Pantheon Books, 1980), 97.
[82] "National Textile Union," *Industrial Union Bulletin,* December 12, 1908.
[83] "Petit Souvenir," *L'Emancipation,* September 1912.
[84] Ibid.
[85] Ibid.
[86] Melvyn Dubovsky, *We Shall Be All: A History of the Industrial Workers of the World.* (Chicago: Quadrangle Books, 1969).
[87] "Alliance Textile," *L'Union des Travailleurs,* March 2, 1911. Reprinted from *L'Emancipation.*
[88] Ibid.
[89] "Toujours Pas des Reponses," *"L'Union des Travailleurs,"* October 13, 1910.

Despite the success of the Franco-Belgian Cooperative, the French Textile Federation and the organizing efforts of Detollenaere and others, by 1911 the IWW in the Eastern United States was, at best, an embryonic organization. Few inroads were made organizing the French-Canadian population. Franco-Belgians in Lawrence assisted in the formation of Polish and Italian branches of the IWW, but these locals, like their own, remained small. The frustrations of efforts to organize the masses of textile workers were reflected in a spring 1911 *Solidarity* article. The article demanded to know whether the IWW in the East was alive or dead. Detollenaere responded saying economic conditions unfavorable to organizing were turning around.[90] The French locals hoped to breathe new enthusiasm with a campaign for the eight-hour work day.[91] Anyone looking for activity in the East did not have long to wait for things to pick up as Detollenaere expected.

THE HARVEST BEGINS

The worm has turned at last. He [the textile worker] has been stepped on in such a way that there is nothing left for him to do. . . . The IWW is to the front in Lawrence.[92]

For the Franco-Belgians, local agitators for more than ten years, the last months of 1911 and the first of 1912 must have felt, to use James P. Thompson's words, like a harvest. It began in August 1911, when 100 weavers walked out of the Atlantic Mill. Management tried to increase output requirements while cutting compensation. Detollenaere and Bedard were members of the strike committee.[93] The Franco-Belgian Cooperative provided organizational and financial support to the strike.[94] In October, 500 members of an independent textile workers union surrendered their charter and joined the IWW. One hundred English weavers took similar action. These changes are important to note given how essential it was to the 1912 strike that skilled workers concentrated in more established immigrant groups also struck. Thompson was called once again to the city. The situation in Lawrence was described as "rotten, ripe for reaping the harvest . . . so diligently sown. . . ."[95]

---

[90] "Les IWW dans l'Est," *L'Union des Travailleurs,* March 30, 1911.
[91] "Huit Heures de Travaile," *L'Union des Travailleurs,* March 2, 1911.
[92] "James P. Thompson's Report as General Organizer."
[93] "Fight Against Oppression," *Solidarity,* October 21, 1911.
[94] Ardis Cameron, *Radicals of the Worst Sort: Laboring Women in Lawrence, Massachusetts. 1860-1912* (Urbana and Chicago, IL: University of Illinois Press: 1995).
[95] "James P. Thompson's Report as General Organizer."

The strike was headquartered at the Franco-Belgian Hall where workers drew up plans for agitation. They distributed ten thousand flyers; thousands of stickers and posters alerted workers about the strike and derided scabs. The IWW hosted open-air meetings every day outside the mills and enormous crowds attended and cheered for speeches made by the IWW. In the midst of the Atlantic Mill strike, in October 1911, the Massachusetts legislature passed its law that reduced the working hours of women and children from 56 to 54. The IWW did not use the legislation as a call to strike but workers across the city saw it as a rallying point.[96]

Approaching 1912 it is clear that Franco-Belgians had the militancy and necessary social institutions to support strikers. Franco-Belgians weavers, among the highest paid operatives, also bore witness to the city's grinding poverty. Although they did not face such poverty, they possessed a keen sense of moral outrage toward the city's mill powers who they blamed for the suffering. In a 1911 *L'Emancipation* article, Detollenaere responded to a statement made by a railroad magnate Jim Hill that "decadence" was destroying the American people. Detollenaere likely thought of his own friends and family from Lawrence when he said capitalists thought, workers ought to "eat less expensive foods, wear inexpensive clothes, accept rent from the children, pass over parties, theatre and other distractions," nor should workers expect to be attended to by doctors when they got sick; in this way they could save themselves the pharmacy bills.[97]

Detollenaere added, "Luxurious and warm clothes are for Jim . . . the parties, the banquets and other orgies are for the financiers and other entertainments are for the sons of . . . millionaires. . . ." Speaking to workers, he said, "When you have a cold or any other illness, work yourself to death." Detollenaere attacked the press saying it praised the honor and virtue of exploitative capitalists and never considered the human cost of accumulated wealth. While the Franco-Belgians had the institutions to aid strikes, it was this moral outrage that propelled the IWW and arguably, all the workers in Lawrence forward.[98] This moral outrage, combined with the experienced core leadership of Detollenaere, Bedard, and their Polish and Italian counterparts, provided a link between their respective ethnic communities and labor organizations. When the strike began, unorganized workers knew where to turn. As events snowballed, resistance seemed more and more possible and it was the IWW leading the way.[99]

---

[96] "La Loi de 54 Heures," *L'Union des Travailleurs,* October 12, 1911.
[97] "Conseil de Jim Hill Magnat des Chemins de Fer," *L'Union des Travailleurs,* 1910.
[98] Ibid.
[99] Ibid.

THE GREAT 1912 STRIKE

The Franco-Belgians who were, after an expression of Giovannitti, "lost sentinels in the great battle of January-March," demonstrated courage, cohesion and admirable initiatives which contributed largely to the success of the strike.[100]

On January 12, 1912, August Detollenaere opened the doors of the cooperative to thousands of mill workers who felt the moment was right to fight back. On that day, they formed a strike committee and Angelo Rocco telegraphed Joseph Ettor to board a train for Lawrence. The strikers set up a mass meeting for the next day at City Hall.[101] At the meeting, Detollenaere spoke for the French workers.[102] As the strike got underway, the community connections, like the labor connections that the Franco-Belgians had forged in the prior decade, all came into play.

Among their non-union and conservative fellow French and Belgian immigrants, Detollenaere and the radicals framed the strike as a purely economic issue with neither mention of politics nor the radical goals of the IWW. They said the strike, "rests purely upon an economic basis. . . . We have enough differences as it is. We have among us Catholics, Protestants, freethinkers; Republicans, Democrats, Socialists, opportunists."[103] While nearly all of the Franco-Belgians struck, some—perhaps those who read only 'right-thinking newspapers'—struck with an eye to their reputation and not to principle. A young French weaver named Celeste decided to strike because she did not want to lose her reputation by being a scab.[104]

The local press picked up on the divide between radical and conservative French and Belgians. In the Lawrence papers, an article ran that described the return of a French family who had visited France and returned with $1,200. The article proclaimed, perhaps taking aim at the city's radical Franco-Belgians, that not all weavers were unhappy in Lawrence.[105] In the national press, the diversity of the community was either not recognized or ignored. In an article for *The Outlook*, a reporter said the French and Belgians were not concerned with the "proletarian will to revolt." He observed a "temperate objective attitude" among them.[106] His article emphasized the, "generous, though often cautious impulses of the Gallic workman." The author perhaps intended his article as a counterpoint to racially charged articles that presented the strikers as radical foreigners. It is ironic that the author attempted to distance

---

[100]"De L'Action," *L'Emancipation,* September 1913.
[101]*Lawrence Evening Tribune,* January 13, 1912.
[102]*Lawrence Evening Tribune,* January 14, 1912.
[103]"The Strikers at Lawrence," *The Outlook,* February 10, 1912.
[104]Ibid.
[105]*Lawrence Evening Tribune,* February 7, 1912.
[106]"The Strikers at Lawrence."

the strike from the radicalism of the IWW by highlighting the temperate nature of one of the radical immigrant groups most dedicated to it. Indeed, it was the Franco-Belgians who sarcastically suggested that all scabs be thrown into the river.[107]

The strike also reflected the complicated and conflicted relationship the radical Franco-Belgians had with the city's French-Canadians. In the third week of the strike, the French-Canadians wanted to organize a mass meeting and requested the assistance of the Franco-Belgians.[108] By February, these efforts came to fruition and large meetings of French-Canadians took place at the hall.[109] According to one French-Canadian writing in *L'Emancipation* during the strike, the eyes of the French-Canadians were "opening to reality . . . because they are beginning to understand this terrible class struggle which still continues across the world."[110] Others, however, resented the Franco-Belgians for the radical image they cultivated and refused to use the hall.[111]

During the strike, the Franco-Belgian Hall fulfilled its role as a support system for the IWW. Workers used the hall as general strike headquarters and it provided meeting places for Finnish, Lithuanian, and Russian workers.[112] The soup kitchen run by the cooperative opened on January 22 and fed 1,300 workers twice a day without regard for nationality.[113] There, "the workers met to discuss their problems and to obtain renewed courage." Strike observers recognized that "there is something substantial about the primitive custom of meeting in the presence of food to thresh out social questions."[114]

Franco-Belgians weavers served generous portions in a morning meal of bread, pressed ham, and tea and an afternoon meal of bread, beef, potatoes, peas, and tea. Women strikers prepared the food and men helped serve it to the hall's long tables. Food was procured through donations or purchased from the same suppliers that the Cooperative Franco-Belgian grocery store (and other grocers in Lawrence) already utilized. Early in the strike, Franco-Belgian delegates on the strike committee offered to assist other nationalities in setting up their own soup kitchens.[115]

The hall served as a hub for the Children's Exodus, another famous European tradition the radical Franco-Belgians brought to Lawrence. According to the

---

[107]Ibid., Patrick Renshaw, *The Wobblies: The Story of the IWW and Syndicalism in the United States* (New York: Rowan & Littlefield, 1999), 102.
[108]*Lawrence Evening Tribune*, January 24, 1912.
[109]*Lawrence Evening Tribune*, February 8, 1912.
[110]"Aux Canadiens-Français."
[111]*Lawrence Sun American*, January 26, 1912.
[112]*Lawrence Evening Tribune*, January 20, 1912.
[113]*Lawrence Evening Tribune*, January 29, 1912.
[114]"Labor's Commissary," *Consumers' Cooperation (5)*, May 1919.
[115]Charles Neil, *Report on Strike of Textile Workers in Lawrence, Mass in 1912*, United States Bureau of Labor, Government Printing Office, 1912.

IWW newspaper *Solidarity*, a Franco-Belgian delegate suggested the idea to the strike committee and told stories of how it had been done in Belgium. French, Italian, and English delegates told similar stories.[116] In the Belgian tradition, children in the Flemish provinces were regularly sent to live at homes of Walloon, or French-speaking Belgians. In this way, the children spoke both languages fluently and in times of labor unrest had a place to go.[117] Given the high number of French-speaking Belgians in Lawrence, it is not improbable that someone like Detollenaere could have experienced such an exchange as a child.

On February 10, the first group of children left the city from the Franco-Belgian Hall; 70 were Belgian or French-Canadian.[118] One such child was a French girl named Marthe. She was sent in the first group of children to New York. In a letter printed in *L'Emancipation,* she recalled, "The great strike . . . prompted my exodus," and that her parents greatly benefited from the strike. She became close friends with the daughter of the family that took her in. On March 9, another group of 12 children, ten of whom were Belgian, departed Lawrence for Manchester, New Hampshire where they were taken in by Franco-Belgian cigar makers.[119]

The Children's Exodus also revealed the limitations Franco-Belgian radicalism towards women. According to an article in *L'Emancipation,* Franco-Belgian mothers and their babies took a place at the front of the ranks at the train station during the second exodus. There they were "hit by the policemen's batons while their husbands face[d] the bayonets."[120] The author claimed the women's families motivated their activism. He said, "Is it not the mothers of the family who have the most to rejoice from the wage increases . . . ?" In labor struggles, women could "present in a gesture of vengeful defiance that which is dearest in [the] world, their babies." While the article said Franco-Belgian women defied the old world adage that women should stay in the home, it also narrowly defined the activism of women in relation to their children.

On March 14, 1912, the Franco-Belgian hall filled beyond capacity, with strikers on the stage and flowing out the back doors, to hear Haywood's announcement of the strike settlement.[121] Two weeks later, when the children returned, Marthe among them, described the scene, "On the station platform of Lawrence thousands and thousands of people were pressing against each other. I managed to embrace my father. . . . I was joyful, very happy to see these

---

[116]"The Labor Contract and the IWW," *Solidarity,* April 6, 1912.

[117]"Consumers' Cooperation-The New Mass Movement," *The American Review of Reviews,* Jan-June 1913, 461.

[118]"The Labor Contract and the IWW," *Solidarity,* April 6, 1912; *Lawrence Evening Tribune,* February 10, 1912.

[119]"Lawrence, March 9," *Boston Evening Transcript,* March 9, 1912.

[120]"Aux Mères," *L'Emancipation,* September 1912.

[121]Watson, 206.

people celebrate our return."[122] On the day of Marthe's return, Detollenaere, the Franco-Belgian community, and all of Lawrence's workers were, for a moment, equally joyous to welcome their children home to parents who felt "We are a new people. We have hope. We will never stand again what we stood before."[123] (See Figure 12, Final strike meeting on Lawrence Common, p. 120.)

Et s'il n'en reste qu'un je serai celui-là
(And If Only One Remains, I Shall Be That One)

By their . . . noble attitude [during the 1912 strike the Franco-Belgians] heaped on themselves and their work the employer's hatred. . . . They have become the scapegoat on which all the blows must fall. Discharge without reason, blacklisting, the invasion by the police of their Club . . . having taken for themselves the famous phrase, "et s'il n'en reste qu'un je serai celui-là.[124]

On Monday March 18, 1912, as 20,000 textile operatives woke up and returned to the mills, August Detollenaere walked to 9 Mason Street and opened the Franco-Belgian Club. It was the emptiest and quietest the club had been for more than two months. Soon, members of the Defense Committee for Ettor and Giovannitti would arrive. The club offered its spaces as headquarters for that effort and Detollenaere was on the committee. As Detollenaere walked through the quiet building he, perhaps, paused to reflect on the path his life had taken. A mere two years prior, he had joined Lawrence's protective textile alliance to break the media silence toward the IWW. Now the IWW in Lawrence was on the tip of tongues the world around. Eight years before, he had left France with only $60 and his radical convictions. Now he operated a successful cooperative that did $100,000 in business and that aligned itself at every opportunity with agitation for social change. He had entered a city, unorganized, chaotic, exploited, and, with thousands of like-minded others, helped those within it to organize and empower themselves.

Well versed in labor agitation, remembering his spot on French black lists, Detollenaere likely realized that this quiet morning could not last and that a new storm was gathering strength just over the horizon. It would come in the following months as his fellow Franco-Belgians found themselves on American black lists. Adding insult to injury, mill owners recruited "10,000 Canadian workers for Lawrence to replace the Europeans" who they wanted "to send back to the

---

[122]"Lettre à Liline," *L'Emancipation,* September 1912.
[123]"Bread and Roses," 216.
[124]"De L'Action," *L'Emancipation,* September 1912.

old country."[125] Franco-Belgians were the particular targets of these recruiting efforts.[126] Progress, however, was evident in the outrage expressed by French-Canadians who called the recruitment "an appeal dishonoring our race and insulting our honor." Further, French-Canadians expressed shame for not continuing the strike and contended that when those who did not strike picked up their pay envelope, their "fingers burn and the face reddens with shame."[127]

On another morning, Detollenaere would unlock the club for the Lawrence police, the radical reputation of its operators considered a menace to the city. On that morning, Detollenaere may have reflected that, for all their radicalism, the Franco-Belgians had, in reality, fed the city's workers when they were hungry and accepted the strike agreement when it came. Despite these challenges and likely because of their radicalism, the Franco-Belgians persevered. For these workers, while the 1912 strike was certainly momentous, it did not end wage slavery; the fight continued. In the words of Victor Hugo they resolved, "if only one remains, I shall be that one."[128]

For his part, Detollenaere remained a life-long resident and labor activist in Lawrence until his death in 1929.[129] It is this longevity, this persistence in pursuit of their radical vision, which should resonate most with the modern reader, the modern worker, and the modern labor agitator. While context renders the Franco-Belgians fundamentally a product of their time and place, it does not render them irrelevant. Examining that context, in particular the immigrant journey, provides a more nuanced view of how radical ideas are formed and how immigrant communities adapt in their new countries.

Viewed from the grassroots level, too much of history presents social change as the product of great leaders, of great moments, and of spontaneous action. By this view, social change becomes something that just happens rather than something that is made to happen, that is the product of dedication, sacrifice, and persistence in the face of failure. The Franco-Belgians in Lawrence provide another example to those who would argue that social change, far from being spontaneous, is something that coalesces from years, sometimes decades, of unnoticed but dedicated effort.

---

[125]"Aux Canadiens-Français."
[126]"No Peace in Lawrence," *Solidarity,* July 6, 1912.
[127]Ibid.
[128]"De L'Action."
[129]Lawrence City Directory, 1930.

http://dx.doi.org/10.2190/BRSC3

CHAPTER 3

The Committee of Ten: The Local Heroes Who Faced Lawrence's Mill Men and Won in 1912

Clarisse A. Poirier

The story of the Lawrence Strike of 1912 is well known to historians: 25,000 to 30,000 striking textile workers led by such legendary figures of the American labor movement as "Big" Bill Haywood (1869–1928), Joseph J. Ettor (1886–1948), and Elizabeth Gurley Flynn (1890–1964) stared down the powerful corporations of one of the most important textile cities in the world. When local police used force on February 24 to prevent strikers from sending their children out of the city, Lawrence became the focus of national attention. The Congressional investigation that followed exposed the plight of the strikers, and pressured the city's textile interests into acceding to the strikers' demands. The now familiar story has, however, tended to ignore the role of the local strike leadership. Inspired by a photograph labeled, "The Committee of Ten Which Met the Mill Bosses—and Won," this author was prompted to find out just who these eight men and one woman were and what role they played in the Lawrence strike.[1]

The "Committee of Ten" included nine Lawrence textile workers and Joseph Ettor, a New York-based organizer for the Industrial Workers of the World (IWW). As memorialized in the photograph, the nine local leaders included Ettore

---

[1] The photograph on p. 117 (Figure 7) first appeared in Justus Ebert, *The Trial of a New Society: Being a Review of the Celebrated Ettor-Giovannitti-Caruso Case, Beginning with the Lawrence Textile Strike That Grew Out of It* (Cleveland, Ohio, 1913), between 50-51; it was later reproduced in William Cahn, *Lawrence 1912: The Bread and Roses Strike,* (1954; New York, 1980), 127.

Giannini, Thomas Holliday, William Born, John Bienkowski, Joseph Bedard, Gilbert Smith, Annie Welzenback, Archie Adamson, and Edward Riley. Striking workers authorized this committee, a subcommittee of the larger strike committee, to settle the strike that broke out in Lawrence on January 11, 1912. The strike spread throughout the city's factories as textile workers realized that a Massachusetts law that went into effect on January 1, 1912, reducing the number of hours women and children could work each week from 56 hours to 54 hours, not only shortened the work week by two hours, but also resulted in a proportionate loss of wages. Beginning on January 25, when the Committee of Ten was formed, this subcommittee worked to advance wages beyond the two hours of lost pay, and to force changes in how the corporations compensated overtime and calculated production premiums. When Joseph Ettor was arrested on January 30, 1912, charged as an accomplice to the murder of Annie LoPizzo, the Committee of Ten assumed more responsibility in maintaining the momentum of the strike, the solidarity of the strikers, and the negotiations with the corporations. The leadership of these nine members of the committee, just as much as the public pressure that the "exile" of the children elicited, was pivotal to the final victory of Lawrence's striking workers in 1912.

This chapter first examines the process by which the strike was finally resolved and the role of the nine local members of the Committee of Ten in those negotiations. It then describes the many other ways these local leaders contributed to the work of the strike committee, as well as their fate in the aftermath of the labor battle.

The strategy of negotiating a resolution to the strike through direct meetings between the Committee of Ten and the corporations evolved during January, though productive negotiations did not materialize until early March when three fundamental questions were answered: first, would the corporations and the strikers submit their differences to mediation; secondly, if mediation failed, how then would direct negotiations be conducted, between representatives of all the corporations meeting with representatives of all the strikers, or on a company-by-company basis; and finally, who legitimately spoke for the striking workers? Did the strike committee, publicly identified with the IWW, have the authority to speak for the thousands of Lawrence strikers, or did the trade unions allied to Lawrence's Central Labor Union (CLU) and the American Federation of Labor (AFL)?[2]

The possibility of mediating a quick end to the strike dominated press coverage throughout its first two weeks, though neither striking workers nor the corporations supported this approach. In fact, the only thing both sides in the labor battle appeared to agree on was that neither would deal with the other through

---

[2] "Strikers Hold to Old Demands," *Boston Daily Globe*, March 2, 1912, 5, http://search.proquest.com/docview/501868662 (accessed April 22, 2011).

a third party. Nevertheless, Lawrence's Mayor Scanlon announced on January 13 that the city council had established a committee to negotiate with mill managers and strikers. The council's efforts went nowhere, and city leaders quickly joined with Dudley M. Holman, secretary to Massachusetts' Governor Eugene Foss (1858–1939), to encourage strikers to submit their grievances to arbitration by the State Board of Conciliation and Arbitration. Holman spoke to the strike committee in Lawrence on January 16 and asked them to submit to arbitration through the Board. Ettor encouraged the strike committee to talk with the State Board, on the condition that it came to Lawrence. Ettor also advised the committee to meet with the manufacturers, in the presence of representatives of the board, though he doubted that anything would result from such efforts.[3]

While some local and state officials continued to push for a mediated end to the strike after January 18, other community leaders worked to arrange a face-to-face meeting between the strike committee and representatives of the textile corporations. The Citizens' Committee that had been formed by business leaders in Lawrence in the hope of ending the strike, went to Boston on January 20 to meet with representatives of the corporations and encourage them to engage in direct talks with the strikers. The strike committee insisted all along that only direct talks between strikers and the corporations could end the strike, but such discussions were impossible until the strike committee and the corporations resolved their inherently conflicted positions as to how to conduct direct talks. The committee sought direct negotiations between a committee representing all the strikers and a committee representing all of the mills. The corporations, on the other hand, insisted that if they were to meet at all with strikers they would only speak with representatives of the striking workers from their own company. Certainly, none of the corporations publicly recognized the legitimacy of the *de facto* strike apparatus, the strike committee, organized under the leadership of IWW Local 20 (Local 20).[4]

---

[3] Charles P. Neill, *Report on Strike of Textile Workers in Lawrence, Massachusetts in 1912*, 62 Cong., 2 sess., 1912, 35, 38; Ebert, *Trial of a New Society*, 55; U.S. Congress, House, *The Strike at Lawrence, Mass.: Hearings before the Committee on Rules of the House of Representatives*, 62 Cong., 2 sess., March 2-7, 1912, 345-55; Unpublished Transcript of Trial Testimony in *Commonwealth v. Joseph Caruso, Joseph J. Ettor, Arturo Giovannitte, alias*, Salem, Massachusetts, Sept. 30-Nov. 8, 1912, Volume 4:2496, 2727-29. Accession Number 2012.022 (Lawrence History Center, Lawrence, Massachusetts). (Hereafter "Trial Testimony," with the specific volume and page numbers following).

[4] The Citizens' Committee was chaired by Justin E. Varney, and included L. E. Bennink, C. E. Bradley, F. N. Chandler, C. J. Corcoran, Walter Coulson, Fred H. Eaton and A. B. Sutherland, "Executive Committee Favor Meeting Owners," *Lawrence Evening Tribune*, Jan. 22, 1912, 3; Neill, *Report on Strike*, 42; "Operatives Told To Appoint Committee," *Lawrence Evening Tribune*, Jan. 23, 1912, 3; the strike committee was made up of representatives of each of the ethnic and skill groups that joined the strike. Its size fluctuated throughout the nine weeks of the strike, but, for most of the strike, it included fifty-six members, "Trial Testimony," 4:2184.

Despite its public insistence on direct negotiations through committees representing all workers and all corporations, the strike committee began private discussions with the American Woolen Company on January 23, 1912. Apparently, in response to the entreaties of the Citizens' Committee, William M. Wood, president of the American Woolen Company, agreed to reach out to the strike committee through a third party, Max Mitchell. Mitchell, the former manager of the Federated Jewish Charities in Boston, telephoned Joseph Ettor, inviting the strike committee to send a small delegation to Boston for preliminary discussions with "two officials of a third party and the controller of the American Woolen Company."[5] On January 21, when the strike committee first took up the issue of the proposed Boston meeting, delegates were divided on the issue of discussing any propositions on a company-by-company basis. Harriet Hanson, a strike committee delegate, was particularly vocal, though not alone, in her opposition to a separate meeting with the American Woolen Company. Nevertheless, encouraged by Ettor, the strike committee agreed to explore the possibility of such talks.[6]

On Monday afternoon, January 22, about 3,000 strikers gathered on the Common and authorized a delegation to travel to Boston to establish the ground work for a future conference with representatives of the textile corporations. Strike leaders publicly maintained the position that they would not engage in company-by-company negotiations, but the strike committee understood that the purpose of the proposed meeting was to explore the possibility of substantive negotiations with the American Woolen Company. Such an approach was certainly practical since nearly half of Lawrence's textile workers were employed by the American Woolen Company, and the other corporations could be expected to follow the lead of the textile giant.[7]

On Tuesday, January 23, Ettor and a five-member delegation from the strike committee, travelled to Boston and met with Max Mitchell and two other men at the restaurant of Young's Hotel on Congress Street. Edward Riley, Archie

---

[5]Mitchell resigned that position in 1911 to head the Cosmopolitan Trust Company, a bank organized expressly for immigrants, "Personals," *Survey*, Nov. 18, 1911, 1237; "Trial Testimony," 4:2351; "Was Without Result," *Lawrence Evening Tribune*, Jan. 27, 1912, 1.

[6]U.S. Congress, *Strike at Lawrence,* 121; "Trial Testimony," 4:2217, 2184, 2351, 2725; "Executive Committee Favor Meeting Owners," 3; "Agree to Confer With Mill Men," *Boston Daily Globe*, Jan. 22, 1912, 1, http://search/[proquest.com/docview/501865798 (accessed April 21, 2011).

[7]"Agree to Confer With Mill Men," 1; "Operatives Told to Appoint Committee," 3; "Trial Testimony," 4:2181; "Lawrence Strikers Indorse Plan to Meet Their Employers," *Boston Daily Globe*, Jan. 23, 1912, 1, http://search.proquest.com/docview/501901584 (accessed April 22, 2011); "President Wood Meets Strikers Committee," *Evening Tribune,* Jan. 27, 1912, 3; Maurice B. Dorgan, *History of Lawrence Massachusetts with War Records* (Cambridge, Mass., 1924), 112.

Adamson, Thomas Holliday, Samuel Lipson and Annie Welzenback represented the strike committee. Max Mitchell, Frederick E. Atteaux, and Parry C. Wiggin spoke on behalf of the American Woolen Company.[8]

The meeting on January 23 in Boston appears to have been an effort to resolve the differences between the mill owners and the strikers as to how to conduct negotiations, between committees representing all the workers and all the corporations (committees of all), or on a company-by-company basis. Both strategies were explored at the meeting, though it appears likely that the American Woolen representatives were setting up conditions that would assure the failure of negotiating through committees of all, and force strikers to negotiate on a company-by-company basis. First, Mitchell, Atteaux, and Wiggin encouraged the strike committee to participate in a meeting with representatives of all the textile corporations. This meeting was scheduled for Wednesday evening at Lawrence City Hall. Ettor and the five strike committee delegates were assured that the corporations would be represented at the meeting, and that members of the State Board of Conciliation and Arbitration would be present, but not conduct the meeting. Consequently, this meeting, if successful, would comply with the strikers' demand for direct negotiations between committees representing all the strikers and all the corporations. Simultaneously, Mitchell and his colleagues guaranteed that if the January 24 meeting in Lawrence failed, another meeting, this time with officers of the American Woolen Company, would be arranged. Atteaux indicated that Wood suggested that the strike committee delegate a subcommittee of nine of its members, all employees of the American Woolen Company, to represent them in future discussions with the company. The Lawrence delegation agreed that both strategies would be taken under consideration by the strike committee, but, at the same time, Ettor made it clear that under no circumstances would he or the strike committee continue to negotiate with

---

[8]"Trial Testimony," 4:2181, 2242, 2351, 2488; Atteaux was the owner of Frederick E. Atteaux & Co., a firm that supplied dyes and other chemicals to textile corporations, *Boston Directory* (Boston, 1912), 174, 2723. The presence of Atteaux at the meeting of January 23 is particularly interesting since he was implicated as the supplier of the dynamite that was discovered in Lawrence on January 19, 1912. Strikers insisted that the dynamite was a "plant" from the very beginning, and in 1913 William M. Wood and Atteaux were tried for their alleged parts in the dynamite plot, "Three Lots of Dynamite Unearthed at Lawrence" *Boston Daily Globe*, Jan. 21, 1912, 1, http://search.proquest.com/docview/501902453 (accessed April 11, 2011); "Approval in Wood's Name," *Boston Daily Globe*, May 24, 1913, 1-2, http://search.proquest.com/docview/502229304 (accessed April 21, 2011). Parry C. Wiggin was the comptroller of the American Woolen Company and a member of the board of directors of the Cosmopolitan Trust Company in Boston that Max Mitchell had recently helped to establish, *The Directory of Directors in the City of Boston and Vicinity*, (Boston, 1911), undated clipping between pages 600-01, http://www.Googlebooks.com (accessed July 6, 2012).

American Woolen unless the corporation's president, William M. Wood, met with strike committee representatives in person.[9]

At its meeting in Lawrence the next morning, the strike committee agreed to follow through on both of the strategies outlined in Boston: the meeting at City Hall scheduled for that night (Wednesday, January 24) and, if that meeting failed to achieve anything, another meeting in Boston. Anticipating the possibility of a meeting with Wood, the strike committee elected nine members (the specific number suggested by Wood), with Ettor as their chairman, to negotiate on its behalf with the president of American Woolen.[10]

Contrary to the expectations of strikers for a face-to-face meeting with representatives of all the mills, Wednesday evening's meeting devolved into a pathetic attempt at mediation. While the 48-member strike committee met with members of the State Board of Conciliation and Arbitration in the Aldermen's Chamber in City Hall, agents of eight mills met in a separate room with other members of the state board. For about an hour, "Members of the Board went back and forth with messages between mill representatives and Strike Committee members" and both sides remained firm on their respective positions. Finally, the strike committee cut off the meeting with nothing accomplished. Nothing was accomplished because four of the city's textile corporations (the Kunhardt, Duck, Pemberton, and Arlington Mills) failed to send any representatives to the meeting at City Hall, and the agents of two of the mills that did show up left just as the discussion with the state board began. The remaining five mill agents claimed that they lacked authority to speak for their respective corporations, and any further discussion was pointless. Consequently, the strike committee walked out of the meeting, and Ettor reiterated, for the press, the strikers' original demand for direct talks between committees made up of representatives of all the strikers and all the corporations. Privately, members of the strike committee were not surprised that the City Hall meeting failed to resolve anything, and they awaited Max Mitchell's call to schedule the meeting with Wood tentatively set for Friday, January 26.[11]

Like the meeting in Lawrence on Wednesday evening, the meeting in Boston on Friday, January 26, was a complete failure. Max Mitchell, as he had on January 23, met the Lawrence delegation as they arrived in Boston, but this time accompanied them to American Woolen Company offices at the Shawmut Bank Building on Devonshire Street. According to reports that members of the Committee of Ten later made to the press and the strike committee, William M. Wood, Frederick E. Atteaux, and American Woolen Company attorneys spent

---

[9] "Trial Testimony," 4:2352, 2729; "Was Without Result," 1.

[10] "Trial Testimony," 4:2352, 2493.

[11] "Conference Not Held; Strike Breach Widens," *Lawrence Evening Tribune*, Jan. 25, 1912, 2; "Attempt to Settle Strike Fizzles Out," *Boston Daily Globe,* Jan. 25, 1912, 1, http://search.proquest.com/docview.501890505 (accessed April 20, 2011). Ebert, *Trial of a New Society,* 24, 65; "Trial Testimony," 4:2352, 2494-96.

most of the meeting exchanging verbal jabs with Ettor and the nine striking workers. In one exchange, when someone at the meeting asked the time, Annie Welzenback commented that she had no watch since she could not afford one on what she was paid. Atteaux told her that she would be able to afford one once she returned to work. At another point, Wood condescendingly slapped Ettor on the back and called him a "good little general." In the end nothing substantive was discussed, and the subcommittee suspected that Wood was using the publicity surrounding the meeting as a ploy to convince striking workers that the strike was over.[12]

While the strike did not collapse on January 29, it did take a new direction when Annie LoPizzo was killed that evening. With Ettor's arrest on January 30 on charges of being an "accessory before the fact" of the murder of LoPizzo, mill owners again expected matters would resolve themselves and the strike would collapse without Ettor's leadership.[13] To the disappointment, no doubt, of corporate executives, the strike continued.

In early March, a combination of circumstances finally forced William M. Wood to resume negotiations with the strike committee and their subcommittee, the Committee of Ten. First, state police exonerated strikers from any connection to the dynamite that was "discovered" in Lawrence on January 19, and John Breen, a member of the Lawrence School Committee, was arrested for planting the explosives. Then Wisconsin Representative Victor L. Berger (1860–1929) introduced a resolution in the United States' House of Representatives calling for an investigation into conditions in Lawrence. Finally, when strikers began to send their children out of the city, and police forcibly prevented strikers from sending more children out of Lawrence on February 24, the situation reached its tipping point, and Congress began its highly publicized hearings in early March with a dozen child workers from Lawrence testifying in Washington before the House Committee on Rules. Among the dignitaries who observed the children's testimony on March 5 was none other than the nation's First Lady, Helen Taft (1861–1943). Something had to be done to end the stalemate.[14]

It was also apparent that there was no alternative, if the strike was ever to end, to negotiations with the strike committee, despite its connection to the IWW. The

---

[12] "Trial Testimony," 4:2273, 2353-54, 2493; "Was Without Result," 1.

[13] "Dead Now Number Two: Ettor and His Right Hand Man Arrested on Murder Charge," *Boston Daily Globe,* Jan. 31, 1912, 1, 5, http://search.proquest.com/docview/501862405 (accessed April 21, 2011).

[14] "Foss Wants Strike Probe," *Boston Daily Globe,* Jan. 26, 1912, 4, http://search.proquest.com/docview/501884290 (accessed April 22, 2011); "Stops Exodus of Children," *Boston Daily Globe,* Feb. 23, 1912, 1, 4, http://search.proquest.com/docview/501913234 (accessed April 19, 2011); "U.S. Action to Be Urged," *Boston Daily Globe,* Feb. 25, 1912, 1, 6, http://search.proquest.com/docview/501922317 (accessed April 21, 2011); "Strikers Depart for Washington," *Lawrence Evening Tribune,* March 1, 1912, 1; "Mrs. Taft is Spectator at Washington Hearing," *Lawrence Evening Tribune,* March 6, 1912, 8.

only possible alternative, the trade unions affiliated with the Central Labor Union (CLU) and the American Federation of Labor (AFL), represented, at most, 2,500 of the city's striking textile workers. Despite joining the strike on February 4, the CLU followed their own leadership, not that of the strike committee, and on February 12, the CLU presented such a complicated schedule of demands, trade by trade and differing from one mill to the other, that any coherent negotiations through the CLU were impractical. The corporations never even bothered to respond formally to the demands of the CLU-affiliated trade unions, and simply announced an across-the-board five-percent wage increase on Saturday, March 2.[15]

Simultaneously, both local and state government officials pressured the American Woolen Company to renew its negotiations with the strike committee. On February 23, the Massachusetts Legislative Committee on Conciliation "urged" Lawrence mill owners to "meet the strikers represented by the Industrial Workers of the World." Mayor Scanlon and City Councilor O'Brien added to the pressure, and met with mill owners on February 28 in Boston appealing to them to consider the welfare of the city as a whole. An end to the stalemate came on March 1, when the Legislative Subcommittee on Conciliation finally forced the American Woolen Company to give formal recognition to the strike committee.[16]

Timed to coincide with the announcement that American Woolen officially recognized the authority of the strike committee, Max Mitchell once again arranged a meeting between the Committee of Ten and Wood on Friday, March 1. Now made up only of the nine local strikers with Edward Riley as their spokesman, the committee had a tense meeting with Wood and Frederick Ayer (1822–1918) which lasted about an hour. When Wood simply proposed the same five-percent increase that the other Lawrence corporations announced that day, the strikers were indignant. They described Wood as "dogmatic," and recounted for reporters how he rudely interrupted them as they spoke.[17] While it appeared that nothing significant was accomplished at the meeting, the simple fact that it took place publicly signaled a possible end to the strike, and certainly Wood hoped that news of the meeting and the five-percent increase would prompt workers to return to work in large numbers on Monday, March 4.

---

[15] Neill, *Report on Strike,* 14, 46-50; "Other Mills Grant Raise," *Lawrence Evening Tribune,* March 2, 1912, 1.

[16] "No Result from the Meeting," *Lawrence Evening Tribune,* Feb. 26, 8; "Confer with Mill Men," *Lawrence Evening Tribune,* Feb. 29, 10; "Strikers Hold to Old Demands," 5.

[17] "Lawrence Renews Hope of Peace in a Few Days," *Boston Daily Globe,* March 2, 1912, 1, 5, http://search.proquest.com/docview/501997831 (accessed April 20, 2011). Frederic Ayer was the original president of the American Woolen Company, a vice-president in 1912, and Wood's father-in-law, Bruce Watson, *Bread and Roses: Mills, Migrants, and the Struggle for the American Dream* (New York, 2006), 22; *Directory of Directors,* 26; "I.W.W. Strikers Firm," *Lawrence Evening Tribune,* March 2, 1912, 1.

Though roughly 1,100 workers returned to the city's textile mills that Monday, nearly 15,000 workers held firm, and the strike was still on. At the same time, the escalating bad press resulting from the Congressional hearings in Washington and renewed efforts to send more children out of Lawrence continued to embarrass the city and state. It was under these circumstances that the state legislative committee stepped in and took the initiative to shepherd both sides toward an end to the long standoff. After the failed meeting between the Committee of Ten and Wood in Boston on March 1, George H. Ellis, writing on behalf of the state legislature's Committee of Conciliation (a committee that was distinct from the State Board of Conciliation and Arbitration that had attempted to intervene to end the strike in January), sent a letter to the strike committee proposing yet another meeting in Boston, this time at the State House, not American Woolen Company offices.[18]

Another circumstance may have paved the way for meaningful discussions: William Haywood's highly publicized departure for Washington, D.C. The IWW's role in the Lawrence strike had been a source of aggravation for the city's corporations, as well as city officials and the Citizens' Committee. As Haywood left Lawrence on Tuesday, March 5, Ellis sent yet another letter to the strike committee inviting their delegation to Room 249 in the State House for a meeting with officials of the American Woolen Company at 10 a.m., Thursday, March 7.[19] On March 7, the strike committee sent the same nine-member delegation to Boston that had negotiated with Wood on Friday, March 1, but this time Haywood's absence from the city gave the appearance, despite the fact that eight of the nine members of the delegation belonged to the IWW, that the strikers' delegation was not representing the IWW, but representing the strikers as a whole. Perhaps Haywood's absence simply made the entire prospect of direct negotiations with strikers more palatable to Wood.

On March 7, Wood laid out a new position. This time, he and his attorneys told the strikers' delegation that the flat five-percent wage increase was the least amount returning workers would receive, and offered to work out a sliding scale of increases, varying according to the worker's job classification, that would be fully articulated in about two weeks. Meanwhile, Wood suggested at the meeting that workers return to their jobs to await the new wage schedule. To that proposal, one of the members of the strikers' delegation responded that "the strikers would prefer to loaf two weeks longer." The Committee of Ten came away from the Thursday meeting with the impression that they had been treated better than in the past, and that they were gaining ground in the negotiations. Returning to Lawrence, Edward Riley described that the committee had been "hailed with

---

[18] Neill, *Report on Strike*, 33; "Strikers Hold to Old Demands," 5.
[19] "More Children to Go Tomorrow," *Boston Daily Globe,* March 6, 1912, 1, 10, http://search.proquest.com/docview/501978325 (accessed April 20, 2011); "American Woolen Co. to Hear Strikers," *Lawrence Evening Tribune*, March 6, 1912, 1.

joy," and Annie Welzenback exclaimed, as she reported to the strike committee later that day, "I think we've got Billy's goat."[20]

Another meeting between the Committee of Ten and officials of the American Woolen Company at the State House followed on Saturday, March 9, but the schedule of wage increases still lacked the specificity the strikers demanded. When the Committee of Ten boarded the 1:17 p.m. train out of Lawrence on March 12, however, they were bound for their last meeting in Boston with American Woolen representatives. This time Wood laid out the increases, to the penny, for each wage class in the factory. More importantly, the Committee of Ten now had an offer they could bring to the entire strike committee and then bring to a vote before a mass meeting of strikers on the Lawrence Common on March 14. The strike was over, and nine ordinary textile workers had negotiated the conditions that ended it.[21]

Until March 2, the identities of the nine strikers who served on the Committee of Ten were not generally known. The Committee of Ten that met with Wood on January 26 included Joseph Ettor along with Thomas Holliday, Gilbert Smith, Edward Riley, John Bienkowski, William Born, Annie Welzenback, Joseph Bedard, Lorenzo Maroni, and Samuel Lipson. When the Committee of Ten next met with Wood on March 1, Ettor was in custody at the Essex County Jail in Lawrence. As a result, after January 30, the Committee of Ten functioned as a committee of nine with Riley as chairman. Maroni and Lipson were also absent from the Boston meeting on March 1 since both were in Washington, D.C., testifying before the House of Representatives' Committee on Rules that was conducting hearings on conditions in Lawrence. Samuel Lipson was a key witness at the hearing having chaired, as he termed it, "the children's 'vacation committee.'" Archie Adamson and Ettore Giannini replaced Lipson and Maroni on the Committee of Ten from March 1 through March 12 when the final settlement talks took place in Boston. Consequently, official photographs of the group, specifically identifying all the subcommittee's members, included Adamson and Giannini, and the roles of Lipson and Maroni in the first talks with the American Woolen Company on January 26 went unacknowledged.[22]

---

[20] "Settlement is Possible," *Boston Daily Globe*, March 8, 1912, 1-2, http://search.proquest.com/docview/501946511 (accessed April 21, 2011). *Globe* reporter Frank P. Sibley quotes "One of the women who went to Boston" as saying, "Mr. Wood's goat," "Settlement is Possible," 2; Annie Welzenback is quoted as specifically saying, "I think we've got Billy's goat," in "Early Settlement Belief of Riley," *Lawrence Evening Tribune*, March 8, 1912, 10.

[21] "To Bring Strike to a Close," *Lawrence Evening Tribune*, March 12, 1912, 1; "Vote to Work in Six Mills," *Boston Daily Globe*, March 15, 1912, 1-2, http://search.proquest.com/docview/501938048 (accessed April 21, 2011).

[22] "Trial Testimony," 2: 522, 531, 4:2184, 2258-59, 2352; U.S. Congress, *Strike at Lawrence*, 44-47, 121, 234-40. "Lawrence Renews Hope of Peace in a Few Days," 1; "Prominent Men as Witnesses," *Lawrence Evening Tribune*, Nov. 4, 1912, 2.

In addition to their service on the Committee of Ten, the eight men and one woman credited with negotiating the settlement that finally ended the dispute on March 14, contributed to every aspect of the Lawrence strike. Bedard, Smith, Holliday, and Giannini were members of Local 20 prior to the strike, and were, as such, at the center of strike committee activities from the first days of the labor conflict. Even before the strike, Bedard, at the request of the members of Local 20, unsuccessfully attempted to talk with the mill agents of the four American Woolen Company plants in Lawrence on January 3 in an effort to clarify whether the mills intended to cut wages as a result of the recently implemented 54-hour law. When the strike erupted on January 11, Bedard, Smith, Holliday, and Giannini were the nucleus of the strike committee with Bedard serving as its financial secretary and Smith as its recording secretary. Bienkowski and Born joined the strike early on and were soon elected to the strike committee by Polish and German strikers. As the strike continued into its second week, Adamson, Riley, and Welzenback joined the strike and the strike committee linking it to important skilled textile trades: warp dressers, perchers, and menders, respectively.[23]

As members of the strike committee, many of these local leaders also served on other subcommittees, in addition to the Committee of Ten. Bedard, Riley, Adamson, and Born all served on the relief committee, for example. After Ettor's arrest on January 30, Adamson and Riley jointly assumed Ettor's position as chairman of the strike committee, and Gilbert Smith took over as its spokesman. Ettor's arrest led to the creation of a "Defense committee" on which Bienkowski, Holliday, and Giannini served, and Gilbert Smith and Archie Adamson served on the six-person delegation that visited Governor Foss in Boston on Saturday, February 3.[24]

In their dealings with local and state officials, these strike leaders were direct and un-intimidated. When Mayor Scanlon assailed Ettor on January 15, as the cause of rioting in Lawrence that day, and told Ettor and other "outsiders" to go back to New York City, Thomas Holliday interrupted the mayor telling him that Ettor was in Lawrence at the invitation of Local 20, and that they wanted him

---

[23] "Textile Workers on Anxious Seat," *Lawrence Evening Tribune*, Jan. 5, 1912, 8; "Submit Demands," *Boston Daily Globe*, Feb. 15, 1912, 4, http://search.proquest.com/docview/501926809 (accessed April 20, 2011); warp dressers operated machines that sized the warp yarns, wound the warp yarns onto a warp beam, and then loaded the beams onto the looms, www.websters-online-dictionary.org/definitions/warp dresser (accessed July 30, 2012); as explained by Edward Riley, perchers looked over cloth for imperfections, marked the imperfections, and sent the fabric on to the menders, "Trial Testimony," 4:2170, 2173, 2227, 2229, 2245, 2443-44, 2481, 2485, 2565, 2568.

[24] "Submit Demands," 4; "Trial Testimony," 4:2186, 2249, 2449; Ebert, *Trial of a New Society*, 71, 86; "Strikers Call on Gov. Foss," *Boston Daily Globe*, Feb. 4, 1912, 2, http://search.proquest.com/docview/501925703 (accessed April 20, 2011); "Statement by G. Smith," *Lawrence Evening Tribune*, Feb. 3, 1912, 1.

to stay. Holliday was equally blunt with members of a state legislative subcommittee that interrupted a strike committee meeting in Lawrence on January 26. As Massachusetts House Speaker Grafton D. Cushing (1864–1939) walked into the meeting, just as Holliday was about to speak, Holliday turned to Cushing and told him, "We don't want to talk with politicians. We came here to do business." Later that day, Holliday sadly and passionately described for the legislators the unfair wages and sub-standard living conditions that had prompted the strike. He ended by reminding the legislators that "The textile workers of Massachusetts form a large part of the population and . . . the Legislature is supposed to look out for the interests of the population." Edward Riley was skeptical of the purpose of the legislative subcommittee inquiry as proposed by Speaker Cushing in Lawrence on January 26, and asked Cushing and Representative John F. Meany, "Is there any law, if we show by an investigation that one party is in the wrong—is there any law under which you can force it to do right?" Meany simply responded that there was no such law, only the force of "public opinion." At the meeting with Governor Foss at the State House on February 3, the six-member strike committee delegation clearly laid out the causes of the strike and the efforts of strikers to avoid violence, and Gilbert Smith complained to the Governor about Judge Jeremiah J. Mahoney's handling of strikers' cases that were brought before him in Lawrence.[25]

Solidarity was the only leverage that Lawrence's workers had over the corporations, and each local member of the Committee of Ten formed an essential link in the chain of worker solidarity that bound strikers in Lawrence together, regardless of their ethnicity or skill. So, despite the fact that all of these nine local workers were American Woolen Company employees, they nevertheless reflected the diverse make-up of the mass of Lawrence's 25,000 to 30,000 striking workers.

The newspaper and magazine reporters, along with sociologists who visited Lawrence, often remarked on the diverse make-up of the strike committee, and were impressed by the variety of ethnic groups in the city and their ability to work together. The *Boston Globe* claimed that no fewer than 17 ethnic groups were represented on the strike committee. The Committee of Ten, with seven nationalities represented on it, reinforced that picture of ethnic solidarity that the strike committee worked to maintain. The substitution of Ettore Giannini for Lorenzo Maroni after January 26, for example, preserved the connection between the Committee of Ten and Italian strikers. Giannini, William Born, and John Bienkowski linked their ethnic communities to the negotiations that eventually resolved the strike. In addition to their work on the Committee of Ten, they

---

[25] "Strikers Driven Back by Troops But Close Mills," *Boston Daily Globe,* Jan. 16, 1912, 3, http://search.proquest.com/docview/501868662 (accessed April 22, 2011); "Indifferent to Probe by State," 4; "Strikers Call on Gov. Foss," 2.

were also delegates to the strike committee who represented the perspective of their particular ethnic constituency. They also introduced Joseph Ettor and Bill Haywood to gatherings of Italian, German, and Polish strikers. When the names Giannini, Born, Bienkowski, as well as Bedard, Welzenback, Riley, Adamson, Smith, and Holliday appeared in the caption that accompanied their photo, it reinforced the image of ethnic solidarity and inclusiveness that was essential to the ultimate success of the strike.[26]

While mindful of the necessity of maintaining ethnic solidarity, the strike committee was equally determined to establish a sense of shared destiny between skilled and unskilled workers. Otherwise, differences in pay and working conditions were certain to be exploited by the corporations in order to drive a wedge between the strikers. Edward Riley, Annie Welzenback, and after January 26, Archie Adamson, were likely appointed to the Committee of Ten for that very purpose. Their inclusion on the Committee of Ten underscored in the public mind, and perhaps that of William M. Wood, that Lawrence's strikers, regardless of where they had been born or their particular job in the factory, were united. Edward Riley, the spokesman of the Committee of Ten, was a percher, Annie Welzenback was a mender reputed to earn as much as $20 a week, and Archie Adamson was a warp dresser and active in the warp dressers' union which was affiliated with the CLU and the AFL.[27] That Riley, Adamson, and Welzenback joined their fortunes with the mass of Lawrence strikers carried weight with the skilled, better-paid textile workers whose support was essential to keeping the mills from operating.

Welzenback's highly publicized wages, certainly reminded everyone of the shared cause of skilled and unskilled workers in Lawrence in 1912, but it was her particular skill, mending, that made her important to the strike, especially in its early days. Menders repaired flaws in the finished fabric, and made otherwise wasted fabric, saleable. It was estimated that the mills had such a vast backlog of fabric that needed mending that they could continue to fill existing orders for weeks. Consequently, it was essential to get the menders to leave their work and strike a blow at the ability of the mills to continue to sell goods. Thus, Welzenback, and the sway she held among menders, the vast majority of whom were women, was central to the ability of strikers to close the mills and force concessions from the corporations. In her first public speech on January 27, the day after the Committee of Ten's first meeting with Wood in Boston, she addressed the striking

---

[26] "Many Nationalities Represented Among the Strikers in Lawrence," *Boston Daily Globe*, Jan. 28, 1912, 9, http://search.proquest.com/docview/501908406 (accessed April 20, 2011); "Bottom out of Strike Trouble," *Lawrence Evening Tribune*, Jan. 13, 1912, 1; "Trial Testimony," 4:2446-47, 2572; Ebert, *Trial of a New Society*, 90.

[27] Harry Emerson Fosdick, "After the Strike—in Lawrence," *The Outlook*, June 15, 1912, 344-45; "Prominent Men as Witnesses," 2; "President Wood Meets Strikers Committee," 3.

menders of the Arlington Mills exhorting them to reach out to those menders at the Wood Mill who were still working.[28]

Adamson and Riley provided important connections to male-dominated skills. They often introduced Ettor and Haywood to meetings of warp dressers, burlers, and perchers. In early February, when unions affiliated with the AFL joined the strike under the leadership of John Golden (1862–1921) and the United Textile Workers of America rather than the strike committee, Adamson and Riley were instrumental in sustaining the loyalty of many skilled workers. Adamson and Riley, along with Thomas Holliday, signed a public letter on February 7 defending the IWW and industrial unionism against John Golden's attacks which warned workers against the dangers of industrial unionism which he characterized as inherently violent.[29]

Striker solidarity was maintained by constant picketing and large-scale parades, and as the strike progressed, Welzenback became famous among the strikers for the picket lines she organized. United States Commissioner of Labor Charles P. Neill (1865–1942), visiting Lawrence on March 6, witnessed one such picket line when police confronted Welzenback as she led 1,000 picketing strikers through the city's streets.[30]

Parades of as many as 10,000 strikers were organized on Sundays and Mondays. Holliday was credited with suggesting the strategy of organizing mass parades for Monday mornings at a strike committee meeting on Saturday, January 27. As he explained at the meeting, Holliday suspected that American Woolen Company president William M. Wood had timed the first conference with the Committee of Ten in Boston on Friday, January 26, in order to trick Lawrence workers into believing that a settlement had been reached.[31] Throughout that weekend local and Boston papers were filled with stories, floated by the corporations, that the strike was on the verge of collapsing. A report in the January 28 *Boston Daily Globe* was typical:

---

[28] "The Menders' Attitude," *Lawrence Evening Tribune*, Jan. 18, 1912, 1; "Put Emery Dust in the Oil Boxes," *Boston Daily Globe*, Jan. 28, 1912, 8, http://search.proquest.com/docview/501912575 (accessed April 19, 2011).

[29] "President Wood Meets Strikers Committee," 3; "Strike Committee," *Lawrence Evening Tribune*, Feb. 10, 1912, p. 1; "Mill Owners Are Slow About Making Answer," *Lawrence Evening Tribune*, Feb. 17, 3; "Prominent Men as Witnesses," 2; "I.W.W. Leaders Score A.F. of L. for Taking Hand," *Boston Daily Globe*, Feb. 7, 1912, 1, http://search.proquest.com/docview/501911444 (accessed April 21, 2011).

[30] "More Children Go Tomorrow," 1, 6; "Three Sisters Arrested," *Lawrence Evening Tribune*, Feb. 16, 3; "Threatened to Draw Away from Strikers," *Lawrence Evening Tribune*, March 5, 1; "Denies Kissing Defendant Ettor," *Lawrence Evening Tribune*, Nov. 6, 9; "I.W.W. Pickets Cause Trouble," *Lawrence Evening Tribune*, March 6, 1; "Trial Testimony," 4:2510-13; Fosdick, "After the Strike—in Lawrence," 344.

[31] Ebert, *Trial of a New Society*, 66-67.

> The representatives of the various mills sent out from their Boston headquarters a notification that 'The demands presented by Mr. Ettor were such that the mills could not possibly accede to them. Accordingly, no further attempts to settle the strike will be made through Mr. Ettor and negotiations along this line are at an end. An increasing number of operatives have returned to work and many more have signified their purpose to come in on Monday morning.[32]

Letter carriers distributed leaflets throughout the city over the weekend announcing the end of the strike, further confusing the status of the strike in the public mind. As a result, Holliday feared that strikers would be tricked into reporting to the mills on Monday (since people customarily applied for work on Monday mornings), and suggested organizing a parade to begin by 5:45 a.m., well before the mills opened at 6:30, in order to intercept anyone who had been misled by the press coverage and the leaflets. The pattern was repeated throughout the strike. On Fridays and Saturdays, newspapers reported hopeful stories with headlines such as "Conditions Look Good for End of Strike," "Report Progress with Mill Agents," and "Stampede of Workers to the Mills Monday," and strikers organized their largest demonstrations for Sundays and Mondays in order to dispel any impression that the strike was off.[33]

Joining the strike, choosing to serve on the strike committee and the Committee of Ten, and joining the IWW, all came at a price, as each striker appreciated. John Bienkowski joined the strike and the IWW the day after he was clubbed by police at the corner of Essex and Union Streets as he tried to make his way home on January 12.[34]

For most strikers, and certainly for those who served on the strike committee, their greatest fear was for their future livelihood. When the strike committee articulated its specific list of demands on January 15, they sought assurances that, along with the wage concessions, they would be protected from discrimination in employment after the strike. Indeed, at first, most strike committee members requested anonymity from the press out of their concern that when the strike was settled they would be denied employment.[35]

---

[32] "Put Emery Dust in the Oil Boxes," 8.

[33] "Trial Testimony," 4:2206, 2365; Ebert, *Trial of a New Society*, 66-67; "Lawrence Hears Strike Will Be Settled Today," *Boston Daily Globe*, Feb. 8, 1912, 9, http://search.proquest.com/docview/501943223 (accessed April 20, 2011); "Conditions Look Good for End of Strike," *Lawrence Evening Tribune*, Feb. 16, 1912, 1; "Report Progress with Mill Agents," *Lawrence Evening Tribune*, Feb. 16, 1912, 12; "Stampede of Workers to the Mills Monday," *Lawrence Evening Tribune*, March 2, 1912, 1.

[34] "Trial Testimony," 4:2563; "Two Clergymen Heard for Ettor," *Boston Daily Globe*, Nov. 7, 1912, 20, http://search.proquest.com/docview/502143799 (accessed April 21, 2011).

[35] Ebert, *Trial of a New Society*, 54; "Many Nationalities Represented Among the Strikers in Lawrence," 9.

Strike leaders also feared that they would be targets for arrest. At one strike committee meeting, the members discussed a conversation that had been overheard between Pinkerton detectives and officials at the Pacific Mill. The detectives advised that the way to "break the backbone of the strike" was to go after its leaders and the strike committee. Joseph Ettor and Arturo Giovannitti were arrested shortly after the discussion, and, as a precaution, strikers elected another strike committee of 60 in the event that the members of the original strike committee also were arrested.[36]

While not all Committee of Ten members were arrested, some of them were not long after their names first appeared in the newspapers. The *Lawrence Evening Tribune* described Ettore Giannini's speech at City Hall on January 13, and on January 19 he was arrested by a private detective (hired by one of the mills) for "interfering with women" and carrying a revolver. Annie Welzenback also seemed targeted. Her first public speech to striking menders was on January 27. She then began her work on the picket lines, along with her two sisters, and around midnight on February 15, she was "dragged" from her bed on Bailey Street in South Lawrence and brought to Lawrence jail. Her younger sisters, Emma and Lillian Steindl, were simultaneously arrested at their parents' home on Howard Street. All three were brought before Judge Mahoney the next day and charged with intimidating two menders who were still working at the Washington Mills. At their initial hearing, Judge Mahoney announced his intent to make an example of the three sisters. Up to that point, according to the judge, he had only sought to "admonish" strikers, but "now he would punish." Eventually they were all found guilty, but they refused to pay the fines, and their cases were continued into March.[37]

While apparently never arrested, Joseph Bedard endured the threat of legal action against him for more than a year. When the strike committee was formed on January 12, Bedard took on the responsibility, as its financial secretary, for the strikers' relief fund. As the relief fund grew and the controversy developed in February over the tactic of sending strikers' children out of the city, Bedard's handling of relief funds was challenged. As reported by the press, Bedard purchased the railroad tickets for the children who left, or attempted to leave,

---

[36] "Trial Testimony," 4:2184, 2485.

[37] "Bottom Out of Strike Trouble," 1; "New Troops Called in Lawrence Strike," *Boston Daily Globe,* Jan. 20, 1912, 1, 4, http://search.proquest.com/docview/501908469 (accessed April 19, 2011); "Gets Stiff Sentence," *Lawrence Evening Tribune,* Jan. 19, 1912, 1; "Put Emery Dust in the Oil Boxes," 8. "Three Sisters Appear in Court," *Lawrence Evening Tribune,* Feb. 16, 1912, 1, 3. "Skilled Help in Conference," *Boston Daily Globe,* Feb. 17, 1912, 4, http://search.proquest.com/docview/501910335 (accessed April 20, 2011). "Defense Scores," *Boston Daily Globe,* Feb. 21, 1912, 2, http://search.proquest.com/ docview/501910893 (accessed April 22, 2011); "Found Guilty with Sisters," *Lawrence Evening Tribune*, Feb. 20, 1912, 1.

Lawrence for New York City, Philadelphia, and Barre, Vermont. Presumably, out of concern for the safety of the children, Judge Frank Leveroni, a pioneering juvenile welfare advocate, launched an attack on Bedard in a letter that was published in the newspapers. Leveroni's letter was just the beginning, and for the remainder of the strike, and throughout the next year, Bedard was hounded by controversy and allegations that he had mishandled $18,000 of relief funds.[38]

When the strike finally ended on March 14, the corporations appeared to have honored their agreement to rehire the strikers, and most of the workers who served on the Committee of Ten returned to their jobs. Annie Welzenback, Thomas Holliday, and William Born returned to the Wood Mill, Gilbert Smith to the Ayer Mill, and Ettore Giannini, John Bienkowski, and Edward Riley to the Washington Mill. Riley even helped to smooth over post-strike complaints of discrimination by some workers who had trouble getting rehired at the Washington Mill. Bedard left Lawrence for Lowell, and Adamson also went onto Lowell, temporarily, as a paid full-time organizer for the IWW during the strike that followed there in late March. Like Bedard, the end of the strike in March did not mean the end of legal troubles for Ettore Giannini and Thomas Holliday. When a grand jury indicted Ettor and Giovannitti in Newburyport on April 18, 1912, Giannini and Holliday were also indicted on charges of conspiracy to intimidate.[39]

Adamson, as chairman of the Central Committee of IWW Local 20, worked once again with Holliday, Smith and Riley to organize the September 29, 1912, parade in Lawrence and the one-day general strike organized by the IWW on Monday, September 30, 1912. Both events were timed to coincide with the beginning of the trial of Ettor, Giovannitti, and Joseph Caruso in Salem, Massachusetts. When the parade on September 29 turned violent, and someone displayed a banner that read "No God, No Master," the IWW was put on the defensive, particularly Adamson. He was arrested in October when he

---

[38] "U.S. Action To Be Urged," 6; "Demands Full Account Today." Feb. 29, 1912, *Boston Daily Globe*, Feb. 29, 1912, 4, http://search.proquest.com/docview/501928230 (accessed April 21, 2011); "Finds Leaders Accountable," *Boston Daily Globe*, August 9, 1913, 14. http://search.proquest.com/docview/502333100 (accessed April 22, 2011).

[39] "Equal Treatment for All is Cry," *Lawrence Evening Tribune*, March 19, 1912, 6; "Trial Testimony," 2:522; "May Pave Way to End the Strike," *Boston Daily Globe,* April 1, 1912, 10, http://search.proquest.com/docview/501988690 (accessed April 21, 2011); "Prominent Men As Witnesses," 2. "Indicts Ettor," *Boston Daily Globe*, April 19, 1912, 9, http://search.proquest.com/docview/501955302; "Holliday Under Arrest," *Boston Daily Globe*, April 20, 1912, 10, http://search.proquest.com/docview/501955225 (accessed April 10, 2011).

attempted to distribute flyers explaining why the general strike had been called for September 30.[40]

Adamson was freed on bail, and as the trial of Ettor, Giovannitti, and Caruso unfolded in Salem, he and other Committee of Ten members were important witnesses. Eight of the nine provided testimony: Bedard was called by prosecutors, while Riley, Adamson, Holliday, Smith, Born, Welzenback, and Bienkowski testified for the defense. Riley was the first defense witness called and provided details of the make-up of the strike committee, and was important in establishing that the committee was not a committee of the IWW, but an independent committee made up of representatives of all the nationalities and textile crafts on strike.[41]

Born was Ettor's "alibi witness." At the very time that Annie LoPizzo was shot on January 29, 1912, near the corner of Garden and Union Streets, Born was with Ettor on Berkeley Court at a meeting of German strikers. But, since the prosecution of Ettor and Giovannitti was based on the premise that they had, through their words, set in motion the violent confrontation that had resulted in the death of Annie LoPizzo that January day, the state considered this alibi irrelevant.[42]

In order to support his theory of the prosecution, District Attorney Atwill used his cross examinations of defense witnesses to establish an image of the IWW as a secret organization whose purpose was the violent overthrow of capitalism. Members of the Committee of Ten, in particular, were grilled on the ideology of the IWW and their reasons for striking. They were also questioned as to why the strike committee held closed meetings after the conferences with Wood in Boston. Contrary to Atwill's implications that violent revolution was being hatched at these "secret meetings," each witness explained that it was at the request of Wood that the substance of their ongoing negotiations was kept a private matter between the strike committee and its subcommittee, the Committee of Ten. As the members of the Committee of Ten explained, only when the strike committee was satisfied that a reasonable deal had been struck

---

[40] "Police Stabbed and Beaten in Street Riot at Lawrence"; *Boston Daily Globe,* Sept. 30, 1912, 1, 5, http://search.proquest.com/docview/502064192 (accessed April 20, 2011); "To Resume Work After Wild Day," *Boston Daily Globe,* October 1, 1912, 1, 3, http://search.proquest.com/docview/502123105 (accessed April 20, 2011); "Truce to be Maintained," *Boston Daily Globe,* October 3, 1912, 1, 4, http://search.proquest.com/docview/502117135 (accessed April 20, 2011). "Prevent Parade," *Boston Daily Globe,* Oct. 27, 1912, 14, http://search.proquest.com/docview/502109378 (accessed April 11, 2011).

[41] Joseph Caruso was prosecuted for the murder of LoPizzo, and Ettor and Giovannitti were prosecuted as accessories before the fact, "Trial Testimony," 1:2. "Declare Ettor Against Force," *Boston Daily Globe,* Nov. 3, 1912, 39, http://search.proquest.com/docview/ 502161429 (accessed April 21, 2011).

[42] "Trial Testimony," 4:2446.

with Wood did they wish to bring the details of the proposed settlement before the strikers as a whole and the public at large.[43]

When Welzenback testified for the defense, Atwill explored these issues and others, and then finally attempted to humiliate her. In his cross-examination on November 5, Atwill, as characterized by a *Boston Daily Globe* reporter, "implied improprieties when he asked Welzenback 'Did you greet Ettor going out of the court room the other day?' she said yes. 'Did you kiss him?' 'I did not,' said the witness hotly." In its description of the exchange between Welzenback and the district attorney, the *Lawrence Evening Tribune* added that when Atwill accused Welzenback of kissing Ettor, "her eyeglasses nearly fell."[44]

The appearance of Committee of Ten members at the highly publicized trial appears to have been the last time they were linked together in public, but it did not mark the end of the trouble that many of them continued to deal with. Bedard struggled well into 1913 with the accusations against him for mismanagement of the strikers' relief fund, though there was little public mention of those allegations after William Wood's acquittal in June 1913 as one of the conspirators responsible for planting dynamite in Lawrence in January 1912. In the midst of the scandal, Bedard moved to Lowell, and eventually, on to Plymouth, Massachusetts. Annie Welzenback was fired from the Wood Mill on November 1, 1912, the day she was served the subpoena to appear in Salem for the Ettor-Giovannitti-Caruso trial. Her firing came in the aftermath of months of being, as she described it, "hissed and hooted every day since the strike." Welzenback left Lawrence in 1913 and moved to New York City and later Baltimore. There is no record of John Bienkowski in Lawrence after the Salem trial.[45]

After the November acquittal of Ettor, Giovannitti, and Caruso, District Attorney Atwill dropped the charges against Giannini and Holliday, and both continued to work in the mills. But there was little peace in the future for either Giannini or Holliday. In 1913, Holliday was arrested while organizing striking

---

[43] "Trial Testimony," 4:2180-84, 2208-13, 2494-95.

[44] "Operatives on Witness Stand" *Boston Daily Globe,* Nov. 6, 1912, 9, http://search.proquest.com/docview/502152713 (accessed April 22, 2011); "Denies Kissing Defendant Ettor," 9.

[45] "Wood Found Not Guilty by Jury," *Boston Daily Globe,* June 8, 1913, 2, http://search.proquest.com/docview/502270838 (accessed April 23, 2011); "Trial Testimony," 2:522; "World War I Draft Registration Card, Joseph Edward Bedard," http://search.ancestry.com/cgi-bin/sse.dll?h=16711706&db=WW1draft&indiv=try (accessed August 7, 2011); "Excluded by Court," 8; "World War I Draft Registration Card, Joseph Welzenback," http://search.ancestry.com/cgi-bin/sse.dll?h=15164197&db=WW1draft&indiv=try (accessed March 21, 2011); U.S. Census Bureau, 1930 Federal Census, Baltimore, Baltimore (Independent City), Maryland, Roll 870, 47B, Enumeration District 440, Image 320.0, www.Ancestry.com (accessed March 21, 2011).

textile workers in Ipswich, Massachusetts, and in July, 1914, he lost his job at the Sutton Mill in North Andover. Giannini was similarly fired from the Arlington Mill in 1914, and both Holliday and Giannini were blacklisted for their "radical" activities.[46]

Giannini never returned to the city's textile mills, working the remainder of his life as a mechanic and a painter, but his activist past remained a source of trouble for him. On September 28, 1917, Giannini was arrested at IWW headquarters on Oak Street, and the next day, both the offices of the IWW and Giannini's home were searched and "papers and pamphlets seized." Giannini was, in fact, one of 165 IWW members indicted in a federal court in Chicago on September 28, 1917, and later arrested in raids along the eastern seaboard. It is unclear if Giannini was among those eventually tried since he was back in Lawrence at least by 1923 and died in the city in 1931. Unlike Giannini, Holliday eventually returned to work in the mills and helped to organize the Amalgamated Textile Workers in 1919.[47]

Holliday, Adamson, Born, Riley, and Smith all worked in area textile mills through World War I and into the 1920s. Born worked in a cotton printing plant at least until 1920, and the others continued to work in woolen mills until the mid-1920s when the decline of the textile industry in the Merrimack Valley began to touch off cyclical unemployment. After 1925, Holliday worked only sporadically in the textile mills, making his living for the most part as a laborer "doing odd jobs for different people," until his death in 1946. Riley left the textile mills and Lawrence behind in the 1920s and moved with his family to Los Angeles. Adamson worked as a warp dresser at the International Worsted

---

[46] "Indictments Not Pressed," *Boston Daily Globe,* Feb. 14, 1913, 9; "I.W.W. Leaders Surrendered," *Boston Daily Globe,* July 24, 1913, 2, http://search.proquest.com/docview/502303063 (accessed April 21, 2011); Letter naming active IWW Central Committee members, December 14, 1914, Second Floor Stacks, Labor and Political Activities/IWW/F.14 (Lawrence History Center, Lawrence, Massachusetts).

[47] *The Lawrence Directory* (Boston, 1915), 234, http://search.ancestry.com/cgi-bin/sse.dll?h=2052107&db=US1890censusSubstitute&indiv=try (accessed July 28, 2011); *The Lawrence Directory*, (Boston, 1917), 239, http://search.ancestry.com/cgi-bin/sse.dll?h=3034020&db=US1890censusSubstitute&indiv=try (accessed July 28, 2011); *The Lawrence Directory* (Boston, 1928), 439, http://search.ancestry.com/cgi-bin/sse.dll?h=494694644&db=USDirectories&indiv=try (accessed August 8, 2012; "I.W.W. Literature is Seized Here by Officials," *Lawrence Evening Tribune*, Oct. 2, 1917, 1; "Leader of I.W.W. Is Arrested Here," newspaper clipping dated Oct. 1, 1917, in "IWW Materials, Box 4, "Political Activities Related to Unions," file 4 (Lawrence History Center, Lawrence, Massachusetts); *The Lawrence Directory* (Boston, 1931), 417, http://search.ancestry.com/cgi-bin/sse.dll?h=3045106&db=USDirectories&indiv=try (accessed July 28, 2011); "World War I Draft Registration Card, Thomas Holliday," http://search.ancestry.com/cgi-bin/sse.dll?h=17594525&db=WW1draft&indiv=try (accessed March 20, 2011); Dexter Arnold, "'A Row of Bricks': Worker Activism in the Merrimack Valley Textile Industry, 1912-1922" (Ph.D. diss., University of Wisconsin-Madison, 1985), 673.

Company in Methuen into the 1920s, and then went on to work as a gardener in Methuen, Brookline, and Danvers, Massachusetts. Smith remained in the Lawrence area, and was the only one of the Committee of Ten making his living in the textile mills, still as a fabric inspector, in 1940.[48]

IWW apologists and Progressive Era writers often romanticized the Committee of Ten. Justus Ebert's chronicle of the strike, *The Trial of a New Society,* written on behalf of the IWW in 1913, extols their nobility, wit, and determined socialism. In the pages of the *Outlook,* Harry Fosdick explains that Annie Welzenback joined the strike out of her outrage at the way Italian and Lithuanian workers were treated in Lawrence, but on the witness stand in Salem on November 5, 1912, she simply explained that she joined the strike because "I was reduced about a dollar in my pay."[49] History will never know whether she and the others came away convinced that it had all been worth it. Did she believe, for instance, that her triumphal exclamation to strikers in March, "This thing has got Billy's goat," had come back to haunt her by the summer of 1912 as she walked to the Wood Mill amidst the taunts and jeers that followed her?

For historians, the experiences of the local members of the Committee of Ten provide an opportunity to revisit some of the generally accepted conclusions

---

[48] "World War I Draft Registration Card, Thomas Holliday": "U.S. World War II Draft Registration Card, 1942 Record for Thomas Holliday," http://search.ancestry.com/cgi-bin/sse.dll?h=9031450&db=WWIIdraft&indiv=try (accessed March 20, 2011); *Polk's Lawrence City Directory* (Boston, 1948), 242; "World War I Draft Registration Card, Archibald Hossack Adamson," http://search.ancestry.com/cgi-bin/sse.dll?h=18039542&db=WW1draft&indiv=try (accessed March 18, 2011); *Lothrop's Methuen, Mass. Directory*, (Boston, 1926), 42, http://search.ancestry.com/cgi-bin/sse.dll?h=3416276&db=US1890censusSubstitute&indiv=try (accessed July 22, 2011); *W. A. Greenough Co.'s 1931 Brookline Directory* (Boston, 1931), 46, http://search.ancestry.com/cgi-bin/sse.dll?h=1745548&db=US1890censusSubstitute&indiv=try (accessed March 22, 2011); *Polk's Salem City Directory 1933-34, Including Peabody, Danvers, and Marblehead* (Salem, 1934), 771, http://search.ancestry.com/cgi-bin/sse.dll?h=1743083&db=US1890censusSubstitute&indiv=try (accessed July 20, 2011); *Lawrence Directory* (Boston, 1919), 132, http://search.ancestry.com/cgi-bin/sse.dll?h=474779498&db=USDirectories&indiv=try (accessed July 17, 2011); U.S. Census Bureau, 1920 Federal Census, Lawrence Ward 3, Essex Massachusetts, Roll T625_693, 14A, Enumeration District 104, Image 34, www.Ancestry.com (accessed March 31, 2011); *Lawrence Directory,* 1920, 132; "World War I Draft Registration Card, Record for Edward Riley," http://search.ancestry.com/cgi-bin/sse.dll?h=20126668&db=WW1draft&indiv=try (accessed August 5, 2011); *Methuen Directory 1920* (Boston, 1921), 172, http://search.ancestry.com/cgi-bin/sse.dll?h=512963340&db=USDirectories&indiv=try (accessed August 5, 2011); U.S. Census Bureau, 1930 Federal Census, Los Angeles, Los Angeles, California, Roll 153, 11A, Enumeration District 556, Image 728.0, www.Ancestry.com (accessed August 8, 2012); "World War I Draft Registration Card for Gilbert Graham Smith," http://search.ancestry.com/cgi-bin/sse.dll?h=23957853&db=WW1draft&indiv=try (accessed July 29, 2011), U.S. Census Bureau, 1940 Federal Census, Salem, Rockingham, New Hampshire, Roll T627_2296, 10A, Enumeration District 8-70, www.Ancestry.com (accessed August 8, 2012).

[49] Ebert, *Trial of a New Society,* 41-42; Fosdick, "After the Strike—In Lawrence," 344; "Trial Testimony," 4:2481.

about the Lawrence Strike of 1912. For instance, was the reaction to the strike in Lawrence as clearly determined by ethnicity as Donald Cole concludes in *Immigrant City: Lawrence, Massachusetts 1845–1921*? After all, by joining the strike and assuming leadership roles in it, Holliday, Riley, Adamson, Smith, and Welzenback, all of whom enjoyed valued positions within the textile hierarchy and were either American-born or naturalized, risked their economic security along with Giannini and Bienkowski who were recent immigrants with arguably less at risk and more to gain from the strike.

Similarly, as we continue to learn more about individual local strike leaders, we gain a greater understanding of the complexity of the forces that contributed to the victory of labor over the corporations in Lawrence in 1912. Would strikers have been victorious in Lawrence only on the strength of the public sentiment that the children's exile and the Congressional inquiry it elicited? If the local leaders who served on the Committee of Ten, as well as other strike committee members yet to be studied, had not maintained the solidarity of the mass of strikers through February, there would have been no strike force to leverage against the American Woolen Company and Lawrence's other corporations in March. Finally, the Committee of Ten "Met the Mill Bosses—and Won" an important battle in the history of the American labor movement, but they also provide historians an opportunity to appreciate the contributions that "local heroes" made to the labor movement in the United States.[50]

---

[50] Donald B. Cole, *Immigrant City: Lawrence, Massachusetts 1845-1921* (Chapel Hill, North Carolina, 1963).

CHAPTER 4

In Harm's Way: The Lawrence Textile Strike Children's Affair

Lawrence Cappello

The tactics of non-violent resistance are sometimes best served when met with naked brutality.

A February morning, Massachusetts, 1912. The group of mothers, children, and various chaperones from the Lawrence Textile Strike sat in the waiting room of their city's railroad station and considered the words of John Sullivan, their new city marshal, who had just been in to see them. The delicacy of the situation had Sullivan using terms like "assistance" and "misapprehension," but however placid his rhetoric the larger message was certainly clear: any attempt to send the children away would result in arrests. It's likely the group was unsurprised by the marshal's speech. He'd been saying as much publicly for days. But they were also aware of their diminished numbers. Only 40 of the originally scheduled 200 children had shown up. Some of those missing caught sight of militia on their way to the station and lost their nerve at the last moment. The rest were dissuaded by a common understanding in Lawrence, printed in the week's local and national papers, that they were "likely to meet opposition."[1]

As the 7:11 to Boston pulled into the station towing a special rail car reserved exclusively for the children and their escorts, Sullivan and his men took up positions directly between the waiting room and the train. While uncertainty flooded the depot one of the mothers, a Polish woman, took her child by the hand and broke for the platform. By the time the officers intercepted her it was too late

---

[1] United States, *The Strike at Lawrence, Mass. Hearings Before the Committee on Rules of the House of Representatives on House Resolutions 409 and 433*, 328-331; "Plan to Ship 100 Children—Lawrence Strikers Likely to Meet Opposition." *The New York Times*, Feb. 24, 1912.

to keep the rest of the group at bay; the remaining women quickly assembled the children into columns and followed suit toward the rail car. According to witness testimony, it was then that the police descended on the crowd and within moments "the women and children were being clubbed and beaten—deliberately clubbed and beaten." The *Boston Globe* reported, "The women shrieked and clung to their children." The *Philadelphia Inquirer* that "no discrimination was shown as [the] women were beaten." The *New York Times* that "to discourage any attempt on the part of the strikers to rescue the children, four companies of infantry and a squad of cavalry surrounded the railway station." Those unable to escape were herded into military convoy trucks and shuttled to the Lawrence police station. Not one child made it to the rail car. Amid the confusion the strike's leader, William "Big Bill" Haywood (1869–1928), powerless to stop the ordeal, stewed furiously as he watched the scene unfold from his seat on the train. If he had been thinking in a purely tactical sense he might have seen that the morning's events played out far better than he originally intended. In that moment, the children of Lawrence had won the strike.[2] (See Young Lawrence mill workers, Figure 10, p. 119.)

The Lawrence Textile Strike, known affectionately as the Bread and Roses Strike, is a watershed of the American labor movement. It gave the Industrial Workers of the World (IWW) a major win on the national stage and its climax at Lawrence station on February 24th had consequences beyond the moment. Headlines of police brutality captured the attention of the nation and sparked protests that reached into Europe. Massachusetts Governor Eugene Foss ordered an immediate investigation of the incident. Letters from constituents and labor organizations flooded the mailboxes of elected officials. A congressional investigation came to order the following week, and those Washington hearings sparked a broader inquiry by the Federal Bureau of Labor. President Taft later cited Lawrence as the cause for an investigation of industrial conditions throughout the nation. With public opinion so vehemently against them, the mill owners caved to almost all of the strikers' demands within two weeks.[3]

The confrontation on the platform, what Phillip Foner later called "the children's affair," was the outgrowth of a tactic employed numerous times at

---

[2]"Police and Strikers Clash," *Lawrence Evening Telegram*, Feb. 24, 1912; United States, *The Strike at Lawrence, Mass. Hearings Before the Committee on Rules of the House of Representatives on House Resolutions 409 and 433,* "Women Twice in Fights with the Lawrence Police," *The Boston Globe,* Feb. 25, 1912; "Women Clubbed, Children Seized in Lawrence Riot," *Philadelphia Inquirer,* Feb. 25, 1912; "Police Clubs Keep Lawrence Waifs In" *The New York Times,* Feb. 25, 1912.

[3]Melvin Dubofsky, *We Shall be All: A History of the Industrial Workers of the World* (University of Illinois Press, IL, 1969), 252. Philip Sheldon Foner, *History of the Labor Movement in the United States, Vol. 4* (New York: International Publishers, 1947), 327-328.

Lawrence under the banner of non-violent resistance. Less than a month into the strike, a lack of funds to maintain relief became the paramount concern of an IWW local struggling to feed thousands of workers who took to the picket lines. In early February, leadership decided to begin sending children from Lawrence out of the strike zone to stay with families in other cities who were sympathetic to the cause, issuing special appeals through the pro-labor press to any and all willing to take them in. The move served at least two purposes. First and most immediate, it meant fewer mouths to feed. But it was also a public relations gambit aimed at re-energizing an amenable socialist base and, in the process, possibly capturing broader sympathy from outsiders by calling attention to the abysmal conditions inside the textile city. The tactic was used decades before in labor struggles throughout Europe, but never to such avail in America. In less than three weeks, it had worked well enough to bring a squad of police officers to the railway platform, intent on taking drastic measures to keep more children from leaving.[4]

What makes Lawrence so alluring to labor historians is that there are so many aspects of the strike to choose from: the diverse racial and gender makeup of the strikers; the highly publicized arrest of two IWW organizers as accomplices to murder; the widespread use of music and song throughout the struggle; the role of the clergy; even a bona fide dynamite plot that turned out to be a botched "frame-up" on the part of employers. But it was the children's affair that won the strike, and it is the children's affair that remains a benchmark in the tactical history of non-violence in America.

More recently, Bruce Watson's work has filled many holes in the historical literature concerning both the removal of the children and the Lawrence Strike in general, but there remains an extensive discourse involving an interesting cast of characters that has yet to be completely fleshed out. Press coverage of the children's exodus sparked a sensationalized public debate wrought with poetry and vitriolic slander. The contours of this debate and the prodding of federal inquiries into the tactic's origins, novelty, and "twofold" purposes warrant closer examination. While there is no evidence suggesting the protest leaders sought the bloody outcome that turned the tables in their favor, they were certainly aware that the children were likely to encounter hostility and had every intention of repeating the move immediately following the incident. There is something provocative in this paradox of knowingly placing children in harm's way being, in some respects, the antithesis of moral behavior, while

---

[4] Foner calls attention to the Irwin fields coal miner strike of 1910 in which the Local No. 11, IWW, of Philadelphia recommended sending children to the homes of outside working class organizations for the duration of the strike. But, as he too contends, the scope and implications of the tactic were not intended to yield any outside impact.

simultaneously being the mechanism through which the strikers won the moral approval of the American people.[5]

On the afternoon immediately following the children's affair, William Trautman presided over a meeting of the IWW strike committee to denounce the police conduct. "Let them keep on arresting the women," he said, "until they have the jails filled." Familiar instructions to anyone casually acquainted with the Wobblies; not two years before Lawrence the union pioneered another non-violent tactic throughout the American West in response to ordinances prohibiting the making of public speeches by local organizers. In Missoula, Spokane, and Fresno, the "free-speech fights" found hundreds of union members intentionally getting themselves arrested with the aim of overwhelming the legal infrastructure of any locality that had such a law on the books, in many cases flooding the jails and courts until the authorities were forced to relent.[6]

The city of Lawrence recently marked the centennial of its great struggle. Part of our fondness for round numbers lay in the fact that they give us pause— occasion to reflect on an historical event against the backdrop of everything that has transpired since. When in the context of non-violent resistance we mention "flooding jails with protesters" and "children marched into police custody,"

---

[5] See Bruce Watson, *Bread and Roses: Mills, Migrants, and the Struggle for the American Dream* (New York: Viking, 2005), arguably the most complete work on the subject. Also Henry F. Bedford, *Socialism and the Workers in Massachusetts 1886-1912* (University of Massachusetts Press, Amherst, MA, 1966); William L. Cahn, *Lawrence 1912: The Bread and Roses Strike* (Pilgrim Press: 1977); Donald B. Cole, *Immigrant City: Lawrence, Massachusetts, 1845-1921* (Chapel Hill: University of North Carolina Press, 1963); Theresa Corcoran, "Vida Scudder and the Lawrence Textile Strike." Essex Institute Historical Collections 115, no. 3 (1979): 183-195; Dubofsky; Elizabeth Gurley Flynn, *I Speak My Own Piece* (New York: Masses & Mainstream, 1955); Foner; David Joseph Goldberg, *A Tale of Three Cities: Labor Organization and Protest in Paterson, Passaic, and Lawrence, 1916-1921* (New Brunswick, N.J.: Rutgers University Press, 1989); William D. Haywood, *Bill Haywood's Book: The Autobiography of William D. Haywood* (New York: International Publishers, 1929); James J. Kenneally "Catholic Clerical Quandary: The Lawrence Strike of 1912." *American Catholic Studies* 117, no. 4 (2006): 33-54; Joyce L. Kornbluh, *Rebel Voices: An I.W.W. Anthology* (Ann Arbor: University of Michigan Press, 1964); Lisa M. Litterio, "Bread and Roses Strike of 1912: Lawrence, Massachusetts, Immigrants Usher in a New Era of Unity, Labor Gains, and Women's Rights." *Labor's Heritage* 11, no. 3 (2001): 58-73; Stefano Luconi, "Crossing Borders on the Picket Line: Italian-American Workers and the 1912 Strike in Lawrence, Massachusetts." *Italian Americana* 28, no. 2 (2010): 149-161; John Bruce McPherson, *The Lawrence Strike of 1912* (Boston: The Rockwell and Churchill Press, 1912); Milton Meltzer, *Bread and Roses: The Struggle of American Labor 1865-1915* (New York: Random House, 1967); Lucille O'Connell. "The Lawrence Textile Strike of 1912: The Testimony of Two Polish Women." *Polish American Studies* 36, no. 2 (1979): 44-62; Robert L Tyler. "The Lawrence Strike of 1912: A View of Textiles and Labor Fifty Years Ago." *Cotton History Review* 2, no. 3 (1961): 123-131; Mary H. Vorse. "The Troubles at Lawrence," *Harpers Weekly*, 56, (March 1912): 10.

[6] "Women Clubbed, Children Seized in Lawrence Riot," *Philadelphia Inquirer*, Feb 25, 1912; Foner, 190-214; Kornbluh, 94-119.

America's historical memory is quick to align these tactics with the struggle for civil rights and the participants of a movement most contend was grounded in a markedly spiritual and pacifistic constitution. Let our pause for Lawrence remind us then, among other things, that these effective tactics of non-violent resistance first appeared on American soil less than two years apart from an anti-statist organization which repeatedly affirmed that violence was never off the table. "Any kind of tactics that will get results," explained Bill Haywood to a separate government inquiry years later. "The question of right and wrong is not to be considered."[7]

At Lawrence, the Wobblies were quick on their feet. They pioneered a complex arsenal of results-oriented non-violent tactics which reflect a growing sophistication in the ability of American protesters to communicate with the public at large.

*   *   *

Suffering strained living conditions and a reduction in wages the textile workers of Lawrence, Massachusetts, took to the streets in protest on the morning of January 12. Seamsters, dyers, machine operators, and runners poured in and out of seven of the city's 30 mills for hours, enjoining their fellow workers over the sounds of shattering glass and looms being smashed to pieces. By the end of the week, estimates place the strikers' numbers at between 15,000 and 20,000.[8]

The American Federation of Labor (AFL) had a presence in the city, laying claim to approximately 2,500 members, but its exclusive membership practices precluded most unskilled laborers from joining its ranks. What remained for the majority of workers was the small IWW Local 20 established not two years prior and boasting only 300 members—but open to all. Local member Angelo Rocco (1883–1984) sent word via telegram to IWW organizer Joseph Ettor (1886–1948) in Manhattan asking for assistance. Ettor jumped at the opportunity and arrived shortly in Lawrence with poet and secretary of the Italian Socialist Federation Arturo Giovannitti (1884–1959). Ettor's organizational success in Lawrence remains one the most impressive endeavors of its kind in American labor history. In a few short days, he assembled tens of thousands of workers spanning dozens of nationalities and speaking more than 14 different languages into an effective apparatus comprised of various committees, all centralized into one general strike committee (of which he was elected president).[9]

---

[7] The Birmingham protests, for example, were administered by the Southern Christian Leadership Counsel; *Testimony of William D. Haywood before the Industrial Relations Commission,* (Chicago: I.W.W. Publishing Bureau, [ca. 1915]) in Staughton Lynd, *Nonviolence in America A Documentary History* (Indianapolis: Bobbs-Merrill, 1966), 227.

[8] "Strikers Rush Mills; Battle with Officers," *Lawrence Evening Tribune,* Jan. 12, 1912; "Strikers Force Mills to Close," *Lawrence Telegram,* Jan. 12, 1912; Watson, 1-4, 17-19, 43-57; Foner, 316-317.

[9] *House Document No. 671,* 40-42, 120; U.S. Bureau of Labor, 14-19; Foner, 317-318; Dubofsky, 237; McPherson, 22.

The arrival of Haywood and Elizabeth Gurley Flynn (1890–1964) days later (fondly remembered as "Big Bill" and the "Rebel Girl," respectively) sent a clear message that the IWW and its resources were fully committed to the struggle in Lawrence. But in a battle for hearts and minds, such notorious figures were also easy targets for a hostile press.

To much of 1912 America, the term *Wobbly* was synonymous with *violent radical*. In some respects, this perception was correct. "We distain to conceal our views," wrote Lawrence strike organizer Ettor in the IWW organ *Solidarity* years later. "We openly declare that our ends can be attained only by the forcible overthrow of all existing conditions." The "ends" he refers to being the attainment of the syndicalist utopia; a somewhat unfledged vision of a future in which all governments are abolished following a worldwide general strike of the laboring class, after which control of global industrial production would come to the hands of a proletariat that would give rise to a new state of perpetual justice and harmony. Whereas most socialists sought the overthrow of capitalism through the ballot box, the syndicalist persuasion was more ideologically aligned with anarchism. Remarking on this impending day of reckoning, Haywood once told elected officials, "In that day there will be no political government, there will be no States."[10]

But there are words and then there are deeds, and it is here where pinning down the violent nature of the IWW (or non-violent nature with regards to the children's exodus, for that matter) becomes blurry. One "IWWism" condoned by Haywood before an inquiry by the Industrial Relations Committee reads: "The avenging sword is to be unsheathed, with all hearts resolved on victory or death." Yet in the history of the Wobblies we find no Haymarket bombings, no platoons of union riflemen, no storming of government offices, but instead a strict adherence to raw pragmatism—a *victory by any means necessary* kind of line. Aware of their reputation with the public at large, frequently outmanned and outgunned, the Wobblies did not turn to the "sword" to achieve their aims but to industrial sabotage and results-oriented non-violent resistance. In this regard, the IWW employed non-violent tactics not from some ideological conception of morality but because they were devastatingly effective; a stance Elizabeth Flynn experienced firsthand in the American West two years before arriving in Lawrence.[11]

---

[10] Unlike Communism, this Syndicalist utopia would have no governing body. There is a distinct lack of articulation within syndicalist literature (noted even by their authors) concerning how such a society would allocate resources and handle general day-to-day operations. For more on early 20th century syndicalism see Dubofsky, 146-170, and Foner, 110-147; Joseph Ettor, "A Retrospect on Ten Years of the IWW," *Solidarity*, 14 August, 1915; Dubofsky, 146-170; *Testimony of William D. Haywood before the Industrial Relations Commission, 1915* in Lynd documents, 226-228.

[11] *Testimony of William D. Haywood before the Industrial Relations Commission, 1915*, in Lynd documents, 227, 240.

The IWW "free speech fights" first picked up steam in 1909 Missoula when the Rebel Girl, still a teenager, along with husband Jack Jones attempted to organize lumber and mine workers despite a public ordinance outlawing such recruitment on grounds of conspiracy. When they were arrested, the IWW sent wave after wave of members "by freight cars—on top, inside, and below," to make public speeches and blatantly invite incarceration. "There were some humorous aspects to our efforts," Flynn later recalled. "Not all the IWW workers were speakers . . . they would read along slowly, with one eye hopefully on the cop, fearful that they would [be permitted to] finish before he would arrest them." Their actions burdened municipal resources and taxpayer dollars to the point where no other option was available but to drop all charges against the protesters.[12]

Flynn's speeches were like a firebrand to many workers. Energized by their victory in Montana, the IWW went on to employ the same measures in Fresno, Missoula, Spokane, Aberdeen, and San Diego. Though Haywood was temporarily absent from the IWW during this period, he marveled at the effectiveness and ingenuity of the new tactic. Years later, he would be playfully reluctant in conceding "non-violence" when asked about the free speech fights, remarking, "There is nothing more violent that you can do to the capitalist than to drain his pocketbook. . . . Those men were released from the prison in that face of the fact that they had been sentenced to jail by judges. That I regard as an action more violent than the discharge of bombs."[13]

By the end of January 1912, Lawrence was in a state of perpetual tension. Frequent skirmishes between strikers and police prompted Mayor Michael Scanlon to request a militia presence from the governor and cede command of the mill district to Colonel E. LeRoy Sweetser. Many of the soldiers were students from Harvard, excused from mid-term exams to participate in breaking the strike.

The arrest of Ettor and Giovannitti on murder charges on January 31st made matters worse. During an encounter between militia and workers two days prior, Anna LoPizzo, an Italian striker, was shot in the head by an unknown gunman. While neither Ettor nor Giovannitti was present at the scene, they were quickly arrested as accessories before the fact (the charges claimed they "incited the riot" which led to the shooting). With both men locked up, effective leadership of the strike fell into the hands of Bill Haywood, with Flynn as his chief

---

[12] Elizabeth Gurley Flynn, *The Rebel Girl; An Autobiography, My First Life (1906-1926)* (New York: International Publishers, 1973—first published 1955), 102-110; Foner, 190-214; Kornbluh, 94-119.

[13] *Testimony of William D. Haywood before the Industrial Relations Commission, 1915* in Lynd Documents, 237-239.

advisor. There was much to do, and among the most pressing concerns was the issue of strike relief.[14]

By February 1st, keeping the strikers fed and warm had become a serious problem. Contributions from the IWW coffers, outside sympathizers (many of them socialist organizations rallied by Haywood's frequent speaking engagements in New York), and Ettor's brilliant organizing had been enough to sustain them during the initial weeks of the struggle. A general relief committee was also established along ethnic lines on top of 15 separate relief stations. But the sobering fact remained that more than twenty thousand workers and their families were without a steady income and hunger has always been an asset to employers. While attending a meeting in New York, members of the Italian Socialist Federation told Haywood of a relief tactic employed in Italy and France where strikers' children were sent away to live with friends and family, thereby lessening the burdens of the embroiled workers. Seeing both risk and opportunity, in early February Haywood convinced the general strike committee to move forward with the unorthodox tactic and the children of Lawrence began preparing for their journey.

The little ones would need a place to go and patrons to look after them. Haywood turned to the socialist press in New York for help with the search for candidates and on February 7 the *New York Call* inserted a short 13-line statement immediately below a Lawrence-related headline. Set in a bolded rectangular border, the plea jumped from the front page:

TAKE THE CHILDREN

Children of the Lawrence strike are hungry. Their fathers and mothers are fighting against hunger, and hunger may break the strike. The men and women are willing to suffer, but they cannot watch their children's pain or bear their cries for food. Workers and strike sympathizers who can take a striker's child until the struggle ends are urged to send their name and address to the *Call*. Do it at once.[15]

The imagery is stark, but its undertones are what make the communiqué masterful. The children embody a certain singularity in their roles as victims. They are hungry, suffering, uncomplicated bystanders caught up in a struggle thrust upon them by the adult world. They are above any notion of *sides*; above the question of who is right and who is wrong. The strikers on the other hand are presented with duality. Hungry and downtrodden yes, but hungry by choice and by the strength of their character. They are sticking it out—simultaneously victim and hero.

---

[14] Most historians (Dubofsky, Foner, and Watson included) contend the move was intended mainly as a means to cut the head off the strike's leadership and bring about the inevitable demise of the protest. Both would be acquitted months later following a dramatic trial. Dubofsky, 228-229, 247-248, 254-255; Foner, 320-325.

[15] Take the Children, *New York Call*, Feb. 7, 1912.

The ad worked. Within hours after going to press hundreds of calls and letters poured in from New Yorkers eager to take in the seraphic refugees. "If you have a child to spare I am willing to receive one," wrote one Bronx man. "I can assure you of kind, loving treatment and a comfortable home . . . sex, creed, or nationality not mattering." Others wrote that they had no room for a child but were eager to help in other ways. One woman suggested: "Many of us working women have no home to take a child into, but many of us could pledge a small sum weekly, which would pay for the food for a child." The *Call* ran the same ad again the following day, this time under the triumphant headline "Workers Rally to Aid of Lawrence Textile Strikers." The paper pressed on with the imagery of destitution but now threw in a dash of hope: "And now the hunger of the children is to be stayed. Their tears are to cease to flow. Their shivering bodies are to be clothed. The keen anxiety of their parents is to be relieved."[16]

Logistical implementation of the first children's exodus was a joint venture conducted by the IWW, the women's committee of the Socialist party, and the Italian Socialist Federation. Over the next two days, operatives vetted hundreds of New York applicants through interviews and home visits in preparation for their arrival. The nurse Margaret Sanger, prior to being immortalized for her advocacy of birth control and voluntary motherhood, chaired the Socialist party's women's committee and volunteered to escort the children on their journey out of the strike zone. Flynn would join her. Back in Lawrence, parents were informed of the plan and children were selected by the "Strikers' Children's Vacation Committee."[17]

The first group of 119 children left the city with Sanger and a handful of chaperones on February 10. Estimates place over 1,000 spectators at Grand Central station waiting to catch a glimpse of the children, with some hoping to perhaps take home any little ones who might have remained unclaimed. Adding to the excitement, the delegation that was supposed to arrive at 3:30 that afternoon missed their connection in Boston and pulled into the station closer to 8:00 that evening. The children exited the train in columns two by two, and at a signal from one of the escorts suddenly announced their arrival with an orchestrated yell: "Who are we, who are we, who are we. Yes we are, yes we are, yes we are strikers, strikers, strikers!" (see Figure 9, p. 118). They were taken from Grand Central to the Socialist Party's Labor Temple on 84th Street, fed, given medical examinations, and distributed through the night to applicants previously approved by Sanger and the committee. What began as a small rectangular ad in a socialist daily had captured the attention of press outlets throughout the country. America's newspapers jumped all over the spectacle.[18]

---

[16] Letters and addresses of select contributors published in "Workers Rally to Aid of Lawrence Textile Strikers," *New York Call*, Feb. 8, 1912.
[17] *House Document No. 671*, 44.
[18] "Children Shout and Sing in New York For Strike," *Boston Herald*, Feb. 11, 1912.

The *Boston Herald* reported, "The enthusiasm seemed to be contagious. . . . Outside the gates and behind the ropes the men and the women and the children who had gathered to welcome the little ones yelled and yelled and when they got tired of yelling they jumped up and down and threw their caps into the air." the *New York Herald's* front page featured a large photo from inside the labor temple capturing dozens of children sitting at long wooden tables almost every inch of which were covered by half eaten plates and serving dishes. A caption below read, "Feeding strikers children in labor hall." The *Philadelphia Inquirer* announced that their city would be next, extolling on its front page "Philadelphia joins New York in taking part in caring for the babes of the striking textile workers." Coverage from the *Call* was of course the most sensational. Having laid the groundwork the day before in announcing the children's impending arrival, it went on to report the event as a resounding success.[19]

One Massachusetts paper was not quite so sympathetic. William Randolph Hearst's *Boston American* slammed the move, spreading its condemnation across three separate headlines on the following day's front page. The first drew a loose literary comparison which read: "Like the Acadian Exiles, Strikers' Babes Torn from Homes Half Clad in Zero Weather, With Many Never to Return." One article charged the children were taken against their parents' will and used as "mediums of advertisement to elicit sympathy" and seconded the "outrage" of Boston's Society for the Prevention of Cruelty to Children who also condemned the move as an exploitative stunt. Immediately to its left lay a five-paragraph editorial written by the Reverend and Professor A. A. Berle with the opening line, "I regard the exploitation of the Lawrence Children in New York as a piece of insane foolishness. . . ." A final piece expressed concern for the children's safety with the subheading: "Pathetic Spectacle as Lawrence Little Ones March Shivering in Cold."[20]

So whereas the *Call* and other papers framed the event as one where destitute children were mercifully rescued from the perils of a brutal struggle, the *American* proposed they were in fact being dragged into one against their will. Victims always—but who were their exploiters? On a conceptual level, the *Call* (acting as megaphone for the strike committee) seems to have relied on the assumption that by illustrating the privation of the Lawrence children the public would naturally come to infer that their kin and kind were also victims, thus leaving the employers as the only possible option to fill the role of villain. The *American* exposed the holes in this assumption, taking a rhetorical line which preserved the

---

[19] Ibid., "1,000 Clamor to Give Homes to Lawrence Strikers' Children," *New York Herald*, Feb. 11, 1912; "Philadelphia Will Take 200 Children From Mill Strikers—Joins New York in Relief of Lawrence Victims," *Philadelphia Inquirer*, Feb. 12, 1912.

[20] "200 Children Are Shipped to New York to Exploit Strike," "Exploiting Children Insane Foolishness, Says Dr. Berle," and "Strikers' Children Parade in New York" all in the *Boston American*, Feb. 11, 1912.

irrefutable hardship of the children and their parents, toned down any mention of the myriad grievances the workers had against their employers and the living conditions they were forced to endure prior to the strike, and effectively challenged the *Call's* follow-through by claiming instead that the IWW was exploiting their suffering.

So were the children exploited? To claim the strike committee acted entirely out of self-interest would be incorrect. Medical examiners at the Labor Temple found almost all the children to be malnourished, and throughout their stay in New York the historical evidence indicates the children were fed well, amply clothed, and had their ailments treated by physicians—a level of care they were clearly not receiving in Lawrence. But the dual purpose of the children's exodus as a tactic to also raise funds and garner public sympathy is strongly evidenced by what *did not* happen that day. The pageantry of the 10th had been drastically streamlined due to the group's late arrival. The original itinerary was to include a parade march down Fifth Avenue from Grand Central to Union Square where a mass public meeting would be held on the strike with the children as the guests of honor, then another parade back uptown to the Labor Temple on East 84th Street.[21] So the plan was to transport a group of malnourished children along a parade route that spanned more than 90 city blocks in the middle of a New York winter, all of whom had just been separated from their parents, to be put on public display at a strike rally taking place in an outdoor forum. Had the journey been made exclusively for the welfare of the children, an argument can be made that immediately feeding and placing them in new homes would have taken priority over pageantry.

Despite the vitriol of the Hearst paper, the committee considered the media attention to be a step in the right direction and immediately made plans to send another group as soon as possible. The *Call* continued to hold the line. Later that week, it published an editorial by Sanger entitled "The Fangs of the Monster at Lawrence." The nurse added to the now familiar imagery surrounding the impoverished children, writing, "Mothers in comfortable homes, whose own children are clothed and fed and housed, protected and loved, you all must come forward and do your share to care for the children of Lawrence!" But perhaps seeing those holes exposed by the *American* she also took pains to better illustrate what she and her associates believed to be the true enemy in Lawrence: the armed agents of the employers. "The fangs of despotism and murder," as she described them, "appearing upon the scene to protect its tottering structure with glistening bayonets and rapid fire guns to mow down the workers, if necessary, in order to cling to its stolen property."[22]

---

[21] *House Document No. 671,* 224; "Lawrence Strikers Send 250 Children—To Arrive at Grand Central Station at 3 o'Clock Today, Whence Huge Multitude Will Parade to Union Square," the *New York Call,* Feb. 10, 1912.

[22] "The Fangs of the Monster at Lawrence," the *New York Call,* Feb. 15th, 1912.

More and more the *Call* tried to keep the press discourse centered on the grievances of the workers, juxtaposing images of the harsh reality Lawrence children called home with ones of state-sanctioned violence waiting for them behind every corner. It printed a lengthy statement by the New York Lawrence Strike Committee that sought to return law enforcement in Lawrence, not the IWW, as the sole perpetrators of violence, charging the children had "come from a city held in the grip of an armed terror. These children have seen the gleam of edged weapons on the streets. They have heard their parents tell of the terror of steel and lead. These children of Lawrence are fresh from a battlefield stained with the blood of your fellow workers." This blending of the children as helpless to a "starvation, poverty, degradation" reinforced by the bayonets of threatening soldiers became the heart of the children's exodus tactic. Circumstance would eventually serve to legitimize this imagery through the confrontation at Lawrence Station.

The *Call* also employed poetry when making its case to the public. Snippets from the February 15th issue by Jane Roulston and Sydney Greenbie:

Two hundred homeless babies crying went –
   Our times indeed are trying babies souls
 While parents suffer plagues most flagellant
   Their babies are marching toward their parents' goals
	Ye tyrants tremble! For never yet
	   Since ye set your mark on this planet fair
	 Have hosts so mighty your path beset
	   For the workers' children are everywhere

But the *American* was relentless. First it printed and applauded a statement issued by John Golden of the AFL's United Textile Workers (whose conservative craft-based union in Lawrence had been upstaged by the IWWs endurance, numbers, and organizational accomplishments) in which he protested "against the sinister motives of the leaders of the IWW in tearing children away from their home ties to exploit them to raise funds to maintain their revolutionary organization."[23]

The vanguard of the attack was a week-long campaign of public denouncements by religious and social leaders coupled with frequent accusations of the children being sent away from their homes without the consent of their parents. The banner headline of the *American's* February 12 issue shouted, "Force Strikers to Give Up Children." An interview with Mayor Scanlon told of parents being notified that if they did not give up their children to be sent away, they would no longer receive strike aid from the relief committees. On the 13th, it reported "many of the mothers are complaining of the methods employed in securing the children, several claiming to have been told that they would be unable to secure any further aid unless they were willing to lend their children to the cause." The article goes on to relay that Flynn herself told the mothers their children were "simply being paraded to advertise the strike and raise funds to carry on the fight." By the 14th a

---

[23] "Mill Strikers Forced to Part With Children," the *Boston American*, Feb. 12, 1912.

casual glance at the Hearst paper's front page might give the impression that it was dedicated exclusively to combating the removal of the children. Interviews with mothers told of confusion and regret at having sent their children away. One Central Labor Union member was quoted: "It was the most disgraceful and inhuman act that was ever committed in Lawrence or any other city." Yet for all of its accusations the *American* offered nothing in the way of actual evidence, claiming in every instance that the mothers would only speak on the condition of anonymity.[24]

It is understandable in the face of such attacks to form an impression that the *American* was simply anti-labor and thus took any available rhetorical line that would benefit the employers. But a close reading of the paper's coverage throughout the strike finds space made for IWW tracts appealing "to the world for justice" and reports of how Ettor and other speakers cautioned against violence and rioting. An article ran on January 13 whose first line asked, "What could this man do with his family on $6.30 a week? . . . Think what [the] children will become in such an atmosphere." Many other sympathetic accounts are found with regard to the plight of the strikers and there is much in the way of praise for relief organizations. No, the *American's* problem was with the IWW and the children's exodus itself. It was certainly a pro-employer paper, but characteristic of its owner's reputation, the potential for sensationalism was too irresistible. Children being wrested from their beds, their exploitation by syndicalists along the streets of New York, the breaking up of families—it all makes for good reading.[25]

What then of the accusation that the children were sent against their parents' will? While the claims are unsubstantiated, it is important to take an objective look at the atmosphere on the ground in Lawrence to better understand how it was possible for the *American* to consider such an indictment. Worker solidarity is essential to the success of any strike. From the onset, laborers were constantly on the offensive to root out "scabs" by any means necessary, a practice which ranged from intimidation to bloodshed. During the first walk-out at the Washington Mill, many workers were "removed from their looms at knifepoint, two women beaten, and a foreman stabbed in the hand." In the coming weeks, trolley cars carrying replacement workers were shattered to bits by rocks, ice, and bottles; the homes of scabs had their front doors smeared with red paint while the families inside were threatened; assaults with knives and clubs were frequent. As

---

[24] Ibid., "Round Up 1,000 Strike Exiles," the *Boston American,* Feb. 13, 1912; "Mill Strikers' Children Lured From Home," the *Boston American,* Feb. 14, 1912.

[25] See "Boston Women Aid in Raising Funds for Mill Strikers," the *Boston American*, Jan. 15, 1912; "How Strike Spreads Hardship Among Poor," the *Boston American,* Jan. 13, 1912; "Lawrence Strikers Appeal to the World for Justice," the *Boston American,* Jan. 16, 1912; and "Pathetic Scenes Witnessed Around Lawrence Mill Tenements," the *Boston American,* Jan. 16, 1912.

Ettor himself put it, "Make life miserable for the scabs and they will have to line up with us."[26]

Practices like these rarely play out with total clarity, and at times manifest to a point where the meaning of "scab" not only applies to someone crossing the picket line but to anyone who does not wholeheartedly comply with the orders of union leadership. It is important to stress here that the IWW and the strikers were two distinct entities. One could speculate that in such an environment striking parents felt at least a modicum of psychological pressure to comply with requests that they send their children away, and that in certain instances operatives may have threatened to cut off relief to those who were reluctant. So while the strike committee was careful to place an identification card around the neck of every child leaving the city which contained the expressed consent and signature of both parents, it is possible that such consent was given in a climate that fostered a large measure of duress. Employing its typical flair, the *American* likened the cards to the way one might "tag" cattle.

But this interpretation is problematic for a number of reasons. Most glaringly, the *American* failed to name even one of its sources directly, and nowhere in any of the subsequent inquiries (some conducted well after the strike was over) did any parent claim that a child was sent away without their permission, save one quickly remedied mix-up. There is also the matter of numbers. Statistical analysis of the city's under-14 population puts the most conservative figure at more than 10,000. The IWW needed only a few hundred, a rather small percentage of those eligible, making any need for coercion less likely when one considers the level of solidarity demonstrated by most striking families.[27]

A second children's exodus took place on February 17, this time to two separate destinations. A small group of 35 was sent to the mountains of Barre, Vermont, where they were met by "three brass bands and a large crowd" before marching to the Barre Socialist Hall. Flynn accompanied another group to New York where the previous week's foiled parade went off with all intended enthusiasm. Images from the visual record show hundreds either following or walking hand in hand with the children as drummers and a trumpeter lead the procession. Banners held by children and adults pervade the photos reading: "THEY Asked for Bread—THEY Received Bayonets," "We Came From Lawrence To Find A Home," and "A Little Child Shall Lead Them." Men and women tasked with soliciting strike funds moved steadily on the flanks of the procession. Finally arriving at the Temple, the children were fed and distributed to their caretakers.

---

[26] A survey of anti-scab tactics can be found in Foner, 320-325 and Watson, 69, 89, 130, 149, 167, 202.

[27] Eleven-year-old Mary Sullivan sneaked into the first New York-bound group and was promptly retrieved by her parents (see Watson, 146-147); U.S. Bureau of Labor, 14-19, 266-80.

The *Herald* again chose to go with a large photo of the children eating, this time with the better tagline: "Huh! Meat!"[28]

The *American* exploded the next day as if personally insulted, sprawling five negative articles across the same page. Three were what was by then the usual variety of organizational denouncement and depictions of mothers made "hysterical" at the loss of a child. A fourth reported the proposal of a bill in Congress by Representative Martin Hayes from Brighton prohibiting "the transportation or exhibition of children under the age of 18 for the purpose of soliciting contributions or of exciting sympathy or of advertising or calling attention to any matter of public or local interest." The fifth headline likely puzzled some contemporary readers given the weekend's events: "Exiling of Children is Stopped By Col. Sweetser."[29]

With the benefit of hindsight, this Sunday edition of the Hearst paper shows us two things. The Hayes resolution confirms that during the Lawrence Textile Strike the IWW, by pushing the limits of non-violent resistance, had reached a level of tactical sophistication significant enough to capture the attention of the federal government even before the confrontation on the platform. The Sweetser article foreshadows the end game. Mostly a reprint of a letter sent by the colonel to the strike committee, the author proclaimed, "I will not permit the sending of little children away for any such purpose . . . these children are not starving." The officials at Lawrence were sticking with the Hearst rhetorical line; they were protecting the American home from exploitative anarchists. With both sides firmly committed to the role of paternalist, things quickly reached a breaking point.

Just days before the climax at Lawrence Station, each party pressed hard to reaffirm the conflicting images they tried so desperately to carve out for themselves in the public eye. On February 22, the *Lawrence Evening Tribune* printed an order from the new city marshal, John Sullivan, officially outlawing the removal of any more children. "To stop this making a show of the children on the public streets to collect money for anybody or for any purpose" read the order, "I will not hesitate to use all the force, power, and authority I possess or may summon to my aid." That same day, 11 children heading to Bridgeport, Connecticut, were stopped on the platform by two policemen and told they would not be allowed to leave. Those parents who explained they were accompanying their own children on the journey were allowed to go on; the six children unable to make such a claim were promptly arrested (though shortly thereafter released). The *American* painted the detainment as a triumph for the solemnity

---

[28] Photos in Kahn, 181, 187; "Real Food and Plenty of it Delights Hungry Children of Lawrence Strike," the *New York Herald,* Feb. 18, 1912.

[29] "Dr. DeNormandie on Lawrence Strike," "Boy Fights Hard to Escape But Loses," "Strikers' Children Parade in New York," "Hayes Bill Prevents Traffic in Children," & "Exiling of Children is Stopped by Col. Sweeter," the *Boston American,* Feb. 18, 1912.

of the home and "the first real step taken by the Lawrence authorities to put a stop to the exploitation of children."[30]

Haywood took aim at critics of the tactic with a vicious contempt in that week's *Sun*: "With crocodile tears flowing down their painted cheeks these gentile ladies bemoan the loss of these 'exiles' who have been sent to 'wicked New York.'" Just as that found in the *Call*, Haywood's illustration was an amalgam of poverty-stricken children and a violently oppressive police state. He went on to challenge Sweetser directly, charging:

> The colonel in maudlin mockery says that it is inhuman to take the children from their happy homes. But we'll not discuss the question of inhumanity with the colonel, as he really doesn't know the definition of the word, or he would apply it to the militiamen under him, who with wheel spokes and loaded rifles with fixed saber bayonets, are prepared to carry out all orders issued by the doughty little champion of 'law and order.'[31]

Undeterred, Haywood and the committee approved another exodus to Philadelphia for the 24th, this time with more than 200 children. Special preparations were made with the Boston and Maine railroad to secure a rail car for their exclusive use. The actual number of children that morning dwindled closer to 40, but thanks to the police and their clubs, it would be enough.

The national press whipped itself into a frenzy after the confrontation on the platform. Headlines across the country recounted the scene with such titles as: "Police Clubs Keep Lawrence Waifs In," "Women Clubbed, Children Seized in Lawrence Riot," and "Mothers Fight with Teeth and Hatpins." A few papers such as the *American* did their best to downplay the incident by claiming the reports of abuse were false, but the tide was simply overbearing. Public figures openly expressed their consternation. Professor Vida Scudder of Wellesley College wrote, "I would rather never again wear a thread of woolen than know my garments had been woven at the cost of such misery." Senator William Borah called the assault "an invasion of Constitutional privileges." Journalist William White charged, "There was no excuse for the violence by police." Whispers of a Congressional investigation accompanied even the earliest news reports, and within days unions, social groups, and private citizens overwhelmed their representatives with letters decrying the outrage. Congressman Victor Berger of the Socialist party led the charge, and hearings before the Committee on Rules opened in Washington to a packed audience on March 2. Helen "Nellie" Taft, the First Lady of the United States, would later attend.[32]

---

[30] "Children to be Kept at Home," *Lawrence Evening Tribune*, Feb. 22, 1912; "Lawrence Child Exiling Stopped By Authorities," the *Boston American*, Feb. 22, 1912.

[31] "Haywood Flays Colonel's Order," the *Lawrence Sun*, Feb. 22, 1912.

[32] Kahn, 194-196; Dubofsky, 234; *House Document No. 671*, 4-17.

Ultimately, in the realm of public discourse, the tactic of removing the children was a battle between two separate renderings; each thoroughly rooted in sensationalism, each somewhat rooted in truth. The IWW's contribution to the history of non-violent resistance in America reached a high point in the success of the "children's affair," but it had been maturing for years. Reporting on the free speech fights two years prior to Lawrence, the union's organ *Solidarity* prophetically lectured that, when properly executed, non-violence "has a tremendous moral effect; it puts the enemy on record; it exposes the police and city authorities as a bunch of law breakers." By effectively publicizing and maintaining the imagery of destitute babes and oppressive bayonets, the only thing missing was an event such as the children's affair to unleash this "moral effect" upon the entire nation. The confrontation was the tipping point. Once circumstance had legitimized one rendering, it was simply impossible for the other to remain. The *American* had lost.

But is the "moral effect" we find in Lawrence somewhat ill-deserved? This is an area where the historical literature, perhaps understandably, chooses not to delve. When we take into consideration prior knowledge of the marshal's order, Haywood's frequently voiced estimations of the police as violent, and the fact that so many chose to stay home—those searching for a sinister conclusion could argue that the strike committee acted irresponsibly. But we must also consider that Haywood, Flynn, and the strike committee were walking a tightrope. None of those arrested two days prior were beaten. It is likely the leadership predicted the worst-case scenario to be mass arrests, and thus a potential opening for the flooding-of-the-jails tactic which had served them so well in the past. After all, not one child on the platform that day sustained any serious injuries, and keeping them at home would have meant relinquishing precious momentum. Regardless of viewpoint, that afternoon the strike committee unanimously approved another children's exodus to Philadelphia set to leave the following Monday.

Because conditions in Lawrence were always central to the struggle, the congressional hearings held weeks later focused predominantly on the destitution of the city's living quarters and the dangerously exploitative working conditions inside the mills it housed (see Figure 5, p. 116). But as it was the tactic of removing the children that had brought everybody there that morning, the transcript appropriately contains sporadic inquiry into its origins, novelty, and implementation.

The proceedings opened with a statement from Representative William Wilson of Pennsylvania expressing the sentiments of "an entire country startled" by newspaper reports of police brutality. Wilson and others went on to explore the constitutional implications of the marshal's intervention within the contours of "freedom of travel" and interstate commerce (because tickets were purchased from a railroad operating in multiple states). Over time, Berger continued the assault, producing letters and witnesses from the platform who corroborated the reports of police brutality and testified to the necessity of sending the children away on grounds that they were starving.[33]

Congressman Thomas Hardwick sensed the situation was not quite so cut and dried. When Golden later took the stand to be questioned by Berger and reiterated his claims of "an ulterior motive for sending the children away" (and added that police violence was unjustified and should be "thoroughly investigated"), Hardwick quickly interjected—"What ulterior motive?" Berger did his best to deflect the line of questioning, asking "What difference does the motive make?" Replied Hardwick: "I do not care; I want to know." Seeing his opening, Golden took the old Hearst paper rhetorical line: "We believe the real motive for sending the majority of these children away was for nothing but to keep up the agitation and further the propaganda of the Industrial Workers of the World."[34]

Later in the day, Simon Knebel, a Philadelphia Socialist and designated escort for the failed exodus to Pennsylvania took the stand. Hardwick dove right in, "It is a system that has been imported here from Europe, is it not?" "Yes, sir" replied the witness, "and it works out very well." The congressman continued his line: "Speaking about the exploitation business, were these children that were sent to New York used in any way in a mass meeting to aid the strike?" Knebel sensed where Hardwick was headed and replied vaguely, "I am informed that it was not done."[35]

Hardwick fully comprehended the IWW's adroitness in using non-violence as an effective means of messaging with the public despite its reputation for violent radicalism. Skillfully demonstrating his grasp of the tactic's finer points:

> Mr. HARDWICK. I am going to ask you a question which merely calls for an expression of your own opinion: Do you not really think that even if it be true that the carrying away of these children from localities where strikes are in progress is for a double purpose, the lessening of the expenses of the strikers and exciting sympathy elsewhere for the strikers, that it is a better weapon to employ than violence?
> Mr. KNEBEL. Well, it is for these purposes, possibly; but the main purpose is to try . . .
> Mr. HARDWICK (interposing). Well, the purpose is twofold; let us be candid.
> Mr. KNEBEL. But the main purpose is that which you did not mention.
> Mr. KNEBEL. Yes; and it is the main purpose; if possible to uncover, to take the lid off of conditions as they exist among the working people.

---

[33] Wilson was a strong supporter of the labor movement throughout his career, and before being elected to Congress helped found the United Mine Workers of America in 1891; *House Document No. 671*, 2-23.
[34] Ibid., 89-91.
[35] Ibid., 207-208.

Mr. HARDWICK. That is exactly what I meant by saying the purpose was that of exciting sympathy.
Mr. LENROOT. I do not think it is quite clear that the witness fully understood the question. Mr. Hardwick asked him if he did not believe these methods were better than violence.
Mr. HARDWICK. Do you not believe it is better to adopt these methods than to use violence and dynamite and go around fighting?
Mr. KNEBEL. Why, of course, yes; dynamiting and things like that are not used by good labor organizations.
Mr. HARDWICK. The appeal for sympathy is infinitely stronger by the use of these other things?
Mr. KNEBEL. Yes, of course.[36]

Following Margaret Sanger's testimony that the condition of the Lawrence children was "the most horrible that I have ever seen," Hardwick continued his inquiry into what he called "this new departure in American strike warfare." Asked if the idea was meant to excite sympathy, Sanger replied, "I think it is having a great deal to do with it." Hardwick pressed the nurse: "I thought you would answer frankly. I am not expressing any opinion one way or the other." Sanger relented, "I think it has."[37]

The hearings carried on for six days, in effect a preliminary exposé of the brutal living and work conditions of a Massachusetts textile city. Marshal Sullivan, cool under pressure, would go on to testify that no assault in fact took place that day—playing the role of slandered lawman which, in the face of recent developments, had become somewhat obsolete. But the damage had been done. By the time the hearings adjourned, numerous official and private investigations had been launched into the conditions at Lawrence. The public's attention was fixed. Even the *American* took notice, with one headline reading: "Seeing Lawrence Now the National Pastime."

At the basest of levels, the tactic that prompted the "children's affair" warrants our attention because it was efficacious and novel, but its greater significance comes into focus when placed in a broader context. Lawrence was one of the first strikes in American history to attract sympathetic coverage from mass circulation publications outside the usual pro-labor organs. The spectacle of removing the children helped inch the national press toward a cross-class sympathetic portrayal of a group of strikers aligned with the vocally syndicalist and anti-statist IWW. The "children's affair" was the tipping point, the product of a novel non-violent tactic that paved the way for a primed American press—even family magazines such as *Harper's*, *Collier's*, and the *American*—to take up the cause. "The Lawrence strike touched the most impervious," wrote Walter Lippmann the following year. "Story after story came to our ears of hardened reporters who

[36] Ibid., 216-218.
[37] Ibid., 226-229.

suddenly refused to misrepresent the strikers, of politicians aroused to action, of social workers become revolutionary."[38]

Students of American History will perhaps find it fitting that a tactic such as the children's exodus would be pioneered in the Progressive Era. Haywood, Flynn, and the strike committee were maneuvering in a period of pronounced social reform, one where historians have traced a steady trajectory toward sparing children experiences such as those they endured in Lawrence leading up to the First and Second Child Labor Acts of 1916 and 1918 (and also doing much toward alleviating such working conditions for all American laborers).[39]

This trend is evident throughout the press discourse surrounding the removal of the children. Two columns over from the *Philadelphia Inquirer's* reporting on the exodus of the 18th, the reader finds an article announcing the observance of "Child Welfare Day," sponsored by the Washington-based National Congress of Mothers. In mid-February, the *Boston Herald's* society pages announced rave reviews for Elizabeth McFadden's new play "The Product of the Mill," which, according to critics, had finally answered the question of "how to make the horror of child labor real to play-goers?" Even the pages of the *American* gave voice to the urging of the World Federation of Mothers, whose president Mrs. Merryman of Boston, urged "united work in work of aiding mothers among the poorer classes."[40]

On March 30, after singing the "Star Spangled Banner," more than 200 children waded through the morning commuters at Grand Central Station and boarded the 8 o'clock train to Boston. By that afternoon, "with happy and contented faces scrubbed to a picturesquely healthy glow," the Lawrence exiles were home—participants all in a growing tradition of non-violence in America.[41]

---

[38] Walter Lippmann, *A Preface to Politics.* (New York: Mitchell Kennerley 1913); Ray Stannard Baker. "Revolutionary Strike," *American Magazine*, May 1912, 18-33; Mary H. Vorse. "The Troubles at Lawrence," *Harpers Weekly*, March 16, 1912, 10; also Christine Stansell's "Response to 'Cleansing History'" *Radical History Review* 65 (1996):103-107, which takes notice of this shift in her engagement with Gerald M. Sider's review of Paul Cowan's 1979 *Village Voice* article, "Whose America Is This?" over historical memory and class-consciousness in 1970s Lawrence.

[39] See Stephen B. Wood, *Constitutional Politics in the Progressive Era: Child Labor and the Law.* (Chicago: University of Chicago Press, 1968); an excellent portrayal of the Progressive mood on this issue can also be found in Jane Adams, *Must Heed the Cry of the Children: Awakened Public Conscience Under Standard of Progressivism at Last Moves Society to Do Its Duty Towards the Helpless Little Ones.* ([S.l.]: Central Press Association, 1912).

[40] "Child Welfare Day is Observed in City," the *Philadelphia Inquirer*, Feb. 18, 1912; "Lifting the Curtain on Child Labor," the *Boston Herald*, Feb. 11, 1912; "World Federation of Mothers is Urged for Children's Sake," the *Boston American*, Feb. 19, 1912.

[41] "Children of the Strikers Return," the *Lawrence Evening Tribune*, Mar. 31, 1912.

CHAPTER 5

Why Labor Won: Tactical Innovation, Failed Repression, and Turning Points in the Bread and Roses Strike

Robert Biggert

In mid-March of 1912, the Bread and Roses strike in Lawrence, Massachusetts, ended after about nine weeks. The key demands of the striking textile workers included a wage increase, more overtime pay, an end to a bonus system, and protection from retaliation against strikers.[1] Each of these demands was met completely or substantially, led by the concessions of William Wood (1858–1926) and the American Woolen Company. William "Big Bill" Haywood (1869–1928), a leader of the strike and the Industrial Workers of the World (IWW), addressed the strikers at a mass meeting. He said:

> I want to say that this is the first time in the history of the American labor movement that a strike has been conducted as this one has. You, the strikers of Lawrence, have won the most signal victory of any organized body of working men in the world. You have demonstrated that there is a common interest in the working class that can bring all its members together.[2]

So ended one of the most significant strikes in American labor history.

Why did the workers win this surprising and decisive victory? The chapter begins by overviewing past research analyzing strike outcomes and considering some important drawbacks to this work. A key factor identified by most accounts of the Bread and Roses strike is the children's campaign. This phase of the

---

[1] Bruce Watson, *Bread and Roses* (New York: Viking, 2005).
[2] Philip S. Foner, *History of the Labor Movement in the United States* (New York: International Publishers, 1965), 342.

strike changed its macro-trajectory producing a turning point and altered the micro-dynamics shifting the balance of power between the strikers and mill owners. Key is the innovative tactics used by the strikers and the habitual repression used by the police surrounding the use of violence by both sides. The goal is to situate the children's campaign within a larger theoretical framework to better understand these events.

Most research on strike outcomes falls into two categories, the "macro-explanatory" and "micro-descriptive." The former analyzes larger samples of strikes over longer time periods with statistical techniques at the institutional level and the latter examines smaller samples for shorter time frames with historical methods at the narrative level. These two approaches are neither mutually exclusive nor incompatible. One exemplar of the macro-explanatory approach is research by Geraghty and Wiseman who offer a comprehensive analysis of strike outcomes in the United States from 1880 to 1945.[3] Although they focus on strike compromises, as opposed to labor victories and defeats, their framework is more generally applicable. They claim five sets of factors are important. The first is labor strength. When more workers are unionized, strike compromise is more likely. Union density is a signal to business of the organizational strength of labor. Second are macroeconomic conditions. Strike activity is related to the business cycle with workers more likely to strike and win during economic expansions and less likely to do so during contractions. The reason is simply if they were to lose their job during a strike, permanently or temporarily, they are better able to find another job during a cyclical peak.

The third factor is industrial organization. Competition is central within industrial sectors. If a particular market is more competitive with a profit upside, strike success is more likely. A more competitive sector is more likely to make concessions to labor to avoid profit loss and less able to achieve inter-firm coordination to oppose the strike. Fourth is the role of government intervention through mediation. Geraghty and Wiseman argue that, absent mediation, labor and business are unwilling to reach an agreement because an early offer to settle might indicate weakness to the opposition and trigger an unwillingness to negotiate.[4] With the negotiation option in play, the costs of willingness to settle decrease if a third party intervenes. Finally, the global economy is important, especially immigration and foreign trade. Regarding immigration, they believe lower immigration rates are more likely to produce strike compromises. The larger the number of immigrant laborers, the bigger the pool of potential strike-breakers. For foreign trade, Geraghty and Wiseman say decreased tariffs and

---

[3] Thomas M. Geraghty and Thomas Wiseman, "Conflict and Compromise: Changes in US Strike Outcomes, 1880–1945," *Unpublished Manuscript* (2010).
[4] Ibid.

increased exports promote compromise strikes.[5] Lower tariffs stimulate international trade expanding the economic pie beneficial to both business and labor through higher profits and higher wages, respectively.

On the micro-descriptive side, much labor history as it pertains to the Bread and Roses strike falls in this category and provides rich and detailed accounts.[6] Tripp identifies a range of factors accounting for the success of the Bread and Roses strike, comparing it to the failed IWW strike by silk workers in Patterson, New Jersey in 1913.[7] A centralized woolen industry, especially American Woolen Company, provided a useful, practical, and symbolic target. An emerging critique of unregulated capitalism focused on the monopoly power of industrial "trusts." Less economic competition within the industry created the perception and reality that the mills had the resources to meet the workers' wage demands. The industry was also less able to shift production away from Lawrence and less likely to lose it to out-of-state competitors. The IWW with its roots in the West was an unknown and under-estimated union adversary in the East. The union's adherence to a more revolutionary approach consistent with its historical origins was different from the conventional unionism of the woolen industry and more threatening to business. The industry was unprepared to react to this deviation from the business unionism of the AFL. The IWW benefitted from the support of the Socialists through strike relief and their support of the children's campaign. The incompetence, infighting, and miscalculation by Mayor Scanlon and the Lawrence City Council played into the hands of the IWW. These missteps created a more favorable "political opportunity structure" for the strikers.[8] A series of "flashpoints," including the botched dynamite "frame-up," bayoneting of John Ramey (1894–1912), shooting of Annie LoPizzo (1878–1912), arrests of Joseph Ettor (1885–1948) and Arturo Giovannitti (1884–1959), and most importantly the mishandling of the children's campaign, discussed below, marked the strike.[9] After these flashpoints were framed and processed by stakeholders, each event benefitted the strikers and hurt business and government.

While both kinds of research are useful and insightful, they do have important limitations. As is often the case, the strengths of one approach are the weaknesses

---

[5] Ibid.

[6] Foner, *History of the Labor Movement in the United States*; Melvyn Dubofsky, *We Shall Be All* (Chicago: Quadrangle, 1969); Watson, *Bread and Roses*.

[7] Anne Huber Tripp, *The IWW and the Paterson Silk Strike* (Urbana, IL: University of Illinois Press, 1987).

[8] Charles Tilly and Sidney Tarrow, *Contentions Politics* (Boulder, CO: Paradigm Publishers, 2007).

[9] David P. Waddington, Karne Jones, and Chas Critcher, *Flashpoints: Studies in Public Disorder* (London: Routledge, 1989)/ David P. Waddington, "Applying the Flashpoints Model of Public Disorder to the 2001 Bradford Riot," *British Journal of Criminology* 50, no. 2 (2910): 342-359.

of the other. Moreover, both frameworks suffer from an important shortcoming. Following Franzosi and Biggs, strikes by definition are interactions between labor and business through time.[10] Yet much work ignores this essential character. It focuses on environmental conditions which produce opportunities and threats (business cycle, economic competition), on the characteristics of actors identifying strengths and weaknesses (union density, union ideology), and on action by one actor or another (factory occupation, police crackdown). What research neglects is viewing a strike as actors engaged in interaction. An action by labor or business is significant to understanding a strike. What is more important is how action is met with reaction to form sequences of interaction. To extend this "strategic interaction" approach, this analysis will introduce a third actor—government, especially the police, which is essential to the conflict.[11] It will focus on the interaction between the strikers and the police around the protest/repression nexus.

To do so, this chapter will concentrate on the children's campaign central to most accounts of the strike. Simply put, the children's campaign entailed the strikers sending their children outside of Lawrence to host families for the partial or full duration of the strike. The campaign moved through three phases.[12] On February 10, 119 children left Lawrence via Boston for New York City (see Figure 9, p. 118). A week later a second wave of 150 children departed, one group again going to New York City and a second to Barre, Vermont. In neither instance did the police, militia, or city officials interfere in any way. Following the second exit though, Colonel E. Leroy Sweetser (n.d.), head of the militia in Lawrence, notified the strikers of his intent to prevent additional groups of children from leaving the city.[13]

The final phase is most remembered. On February 22, strikers attempted to put 11 children on a train to Bridgeport, Connecticut. The local police allowed children traveling with parents to leave but detained children unaccompanied by parents. Two days later, 46 children were prepared to leave. However, the police prevented the parents and adults from boarding the train. Accounts of what happened next differ but the encounter was contentious and violent. Foner writes:

> Many of the mothers, including some who were pregnant, and children were pushed, beaten, choked, and clubbed. Fifteen children and eight adults were arrested, thrust into patrol wagons, and taken to the police station.[14]

---

[10] Roberto Franzosi, *Puzzle of Strikes: Class and State Strategies in Postwar Italy* (Cambridge: Cambridge University Press, 2006). Michael Biggs, "Strikes as Sequences of Interactions: The American Strike Wave of 1886," *Social Science History,* 26 (2002): 583-617.

[11] Biggs, Ibid.

[12] Foner, *History of the Labor Movement in the United States*; Dubofsky, *We Shall Be All*; Watson, *Bread and Roses*.

[13] Watson, Ibid., 160.

[14] Foner, *History of the Labor Movement in the United States*, 326.

Later that afternoon, the mothers arrested were charged, convicted, and fined for child neglect and/or disturbance. All the children were taken into the care of the city.

Why was the children's campaign so important? At the macro level, the children's campaign marks a turning point.[15] Abbott argues many social phenomena are processes, a series of social states linked with transitions. Any process is necessarily historical, encompassing a trajectory with regularity and directionality. A trajectory contains a narrative involving actors, plots, and scenes. Regular and recurrent processes can be seen as sequences. A turning point is a significant change in trajectory. In other words, what comes after is very different from what came before. Turning points occur through the interaction between structure and process. Abbott advocates pattern-based, rather than variable-based, methods to analyze trajectories and turning points.

A strike is a social process. It begins when the workers strike or are locked out. Each side then employs a repertoire of tactics. This involves two sub-processes. One is collective bargaining, which is a more formal discussion among the two sides regarding the issues of the strike. Another is more informal, involving protest and repression. Business, labor, and government interact through time and at some point the process ends with a strike outcome. There are three possibilities: labor victory, labor/business compromise, or labor loss.

While compromise is the most common outcome, occasionally labor or business wins decisively. Why? It usually involves the presence of a turning point. By turning point, I mean an event which significantly redirects the social process outside of its bounds. So to explain why labor won in this particular case, we search for a turning point which changed the strike trajectory.

Turning points also involve shifts in power (see Figure 1). Critical to understanding a strike is the power positions of both labor and business. The "rules of the game" are defined by the parameters of capitalism. One of the fundamental properties of capitalism is power asymmetry, business has more power and labor less. It is primarily, but not solely, a function of labor's resource dependence on business. Workers must sell their labor power to business. Labor cannot hire business under capitalism. If it could, the economic "game" would cease to be capitalism. This reality is represented by the upper and lower bounds in the diagram. The vast majority of strikes occur within these two bounds. It would be unusual to go outside them.

To understand these events at the micro level, the focus will be on the strikers and the police, their respective tactics, and the interaction between these two actors

---

[15] Andrew Abbott, *Time Matters* (Chicago: University of Chicago Press, 2001).

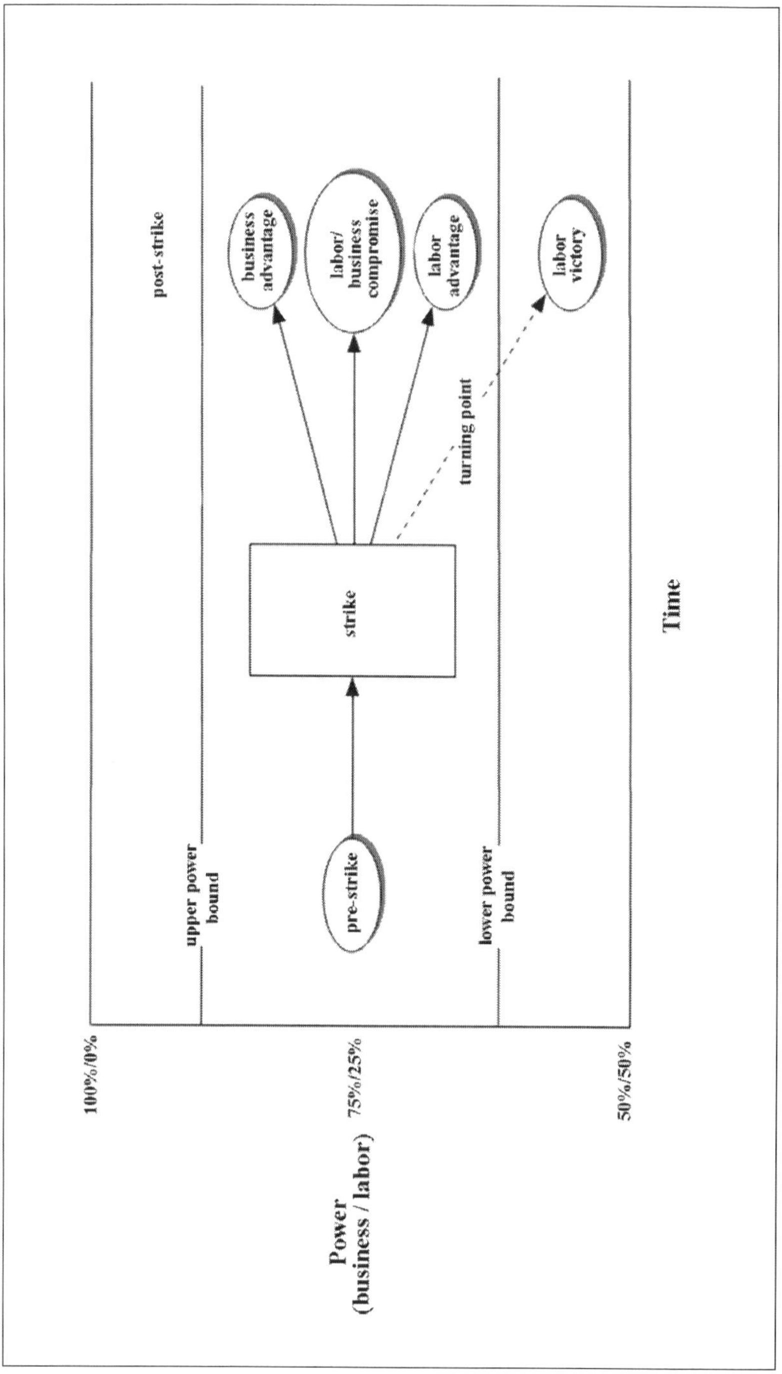

Figure 1. Possible strike trajectories.

within the larger context of the strike. This interpretation will draw from contentious politics theory and game theory.[16]

For the Bread and Roses strikers, as with all strikers, their overarching objective is to get business to meet their demands through collective action, most importantly withholding their labor power. However, strikes are more complicated affairs in at least two ways. First, labor as a political contender does not limit its collective action to a simple refusal to work. Its "repertoire of collective action" is broader and more complex.[17] During the course of the Bread and Roses strike, the workers engaged in walk-outs, occupations, picketing, meetings, rallies, marches, speeches, boycotts, and other forms of collective action (see Figure 8, p. 117). Different tactics were used at different times and in different ways. Second, the obvious target of the strikers is business. Because strikers engage in protest though, their more proximate and concrete target often is the police. The police serve the dual role of enforcers of public laws and defenders of private property, serving sometimes as a neutral third party and others as a hostile adversary.

For the police, responding to strikes and protests ranges from facilitation at one extreme to repression at the other.[18] The former positively affects the power position of the protesters and the latter negatively influences it. The decision to facilitate or repress or how vigorously to repress is shaped by multiple interests. They are charged with enforcing the laws and maintaining public order, thus protesters breaking laws and producing disorder triggers intervention. What constitutes crime and disorder and guides policing strategy is shaped by political control over police agencies and their organizational location within the state. Further, government's dependence on business for a range of resources (tax revenues, expertise, campaign contributions) creates a political asymmetry in its dealing with labor/business conflicts.

The role of violence is important for both actors. For the strikers, research suggests violence is useful in some circumstances but unproductive in others. Two classic social movement works, one by Piven and Cloward and the other by Gamson, indicate violence does pay off for protesters.[19] More recently,

---

[16] On contentious politics theory, see Charles Tilly, *From Mobilization to Revolution* (Reading, MA: Addison-Wesley, 1978); Doug McAdam, Sidney Tarrow, and Charles Tilly, *Dynamics of Contention* (Cambridge: Cambridge University Press, 2001); Tilly and Tarrow, *Contentious Politics*. On game theory, see Biggs, "Strikes as Sequences of Interactions: The American Strike Wave of 1886." James M. Jasper, *Getting Your Way: Strategic Dilemmas in the Real World* (Chicago: University of Chicago Press, 2006).

[17] Tilly, *From Mobilization to Revolution*.

[18] Tilly, Ibid.

[19] Frances Fox Piven and Richard Cloward, *Poor People's Movements,* Second Edition (New York: Vintage, 1979); William Gamson, *Strategy of Social Protest,* Second Edition (Belmont, CA: Wadsworth, 1990).

Chenoweth and Stephan, looking globally and historically, conclude nonviolence is more successful than violence.[20]

Similarly, violence is a key variable in the calculus of the police.[21] Assuming police repress rather than facilitate repression can vary from using coercive "hard" techniques to negotiated "soft" strategies.[22] The decision to use violence depends on the internal organization of the police, the external threat posed by protesters, and the context of police/protester interaction.

Moreover, we should more carefully specify the interaction between strikers and the police considering the role of violence. A useful method to do so is with game theory. Game theory in essence is simple and straightforward.[23] It involves two (or more) actors choosing rationally (more or less) between two (or more) alternatives by assessing their own interests and those of their counterpart. This interaction is specified with payoffs contingent upon the choices of both actors.

Applying game theory to strikes, Biggs conceptualizes them broadly as an "iterated game of chicken."[24] Strikers can be provoked by business though lock-outs or started by workers walking out. Regardless of the beginning, what ensues is a series of offers and counteroffers. Each side's ability to gain advantage in a settlement is a function of its power position, the "ability to inflict costs" on the other side.

To analyze the children's campaign more narrowly, a second, more focused game is useful. Chong points out that interaction between protesters and police is a "public relations game" (see Table 1).[25] The protesters have a dominant strategy in this game. They will be peaceful regardless of the actions of the police because their first choice strategy is preferable to their third choice in the first column and second choice is preferable to fourth choice in the second column. The police do not have a dominant strategy. Their response will be contingent upon the action of the protesters. Nonviolence is preferred if the protesters are non-violent (strategy 2 is better than 4 in the second row) but violence is preferred if protesters are violent (strategy 1 is preferable to 3 in the first row). This produces instability and provocation

---

[20] Erica Chenoweth and Mana J. Stephan, *Why Civil Resistance Works: The Strategic Logic of Nonviolent Conflict* (New York: Columbia University Press, 2011).

[21] Donatella Della Porta and Olivier Fillieule, "Policing Social Protest," in *The Blackwell Companion to Social Movements*, ed. David A. Snow, Sarah A. Soule, and Hanspeter Kriesi (Blackwell, 2004), 217-241.

[22] Jennifer Earl, "Political Repression: Iron Fists, Velvet Gloves, and Diffuse Control," *Annual Review of Sociology* 37 (2011): 261-284.

[23] Ken Binmore, *Game Theory: A Very Short Introduction* (Oxford: Oxford University Press, 2007).

[24] Biggs, "Strikes as Sequences of Interactions: The American Strike Wave of 1886."

[25] Dennis Chong, *Collective Action and the Civil Rights Movement* (Chicago: University of Chicago Press, 1991).

Table 1. Tactics and Repression as a Public Relations Game

		Police	
		Violent	Peaceful
Protesters	Violent	3 / 1	4 / 3
	Peaceful	1 / 4	2 / 2

(In each cell the ranking of the protester strategy, with 1 high and 4 low, is on the left and the ranking of the police strategy is on the right.)

becomes important. The protesters want the police to react violently to highlight their nonviolence. The police want the protesters to act violently so they can react violently.

Barkan's work on the civil rights movement confirms what non-violent protesters know.[26] His essential conclusion is that when the authorities responded to non-violent protest with violent repression, the civil rights movement was more successful. For example, in Albany, Georgia, a "pack-the-jails" strategy derailed a broad-based campaign to fight desegregation. Conversely, when the response to nonviolence was violence, the movement was more successful. In Birmingham, Alabama, the heavy-handed tactics of Bull Connor handed the movement a decisive victory.

This game theoretic analysis only serves to set the stage for the children's campaign. It does not explain the proximate cause of this violent episode. The question then becomes what is the solution to the game or, perhaps better, which side will "blink" first. Again, what was the turning point?

With these theoretical insights, we can re-visit the narrative of the children's campaign. First, the children's campaign was an innovative tactic adopted by the strikers. As previously noted, the strikers engaged in a range of tactics during the strike. Some tactics were used continuously while others selectively. Some were more successful and others less so. But the children's campaign was new, different, and perhaps never before used in an American strike.

Several characteristics made this tactic novel. For the strikers, the campaigners were non-workers and hence non-combatants. At the forefront were mothers and their children. The campaign unfolded in a public space, the railway station, which they could lay claim to as citizens. Their actions, mothers simply trying

---

[26] Steven Barkan, "Legal Control of the Civil Rights Movement," *American Sociological Review* 49 (1984): 552-565.

to board children on a train, were legitimate and lawful. The children's departure was secondary to the central issues of the strike. Most importantly, the tactic was non-violent with the actors not armed in any way by all accounts. In sum, the campaigners posed little threat to the police.

Two questions are relevant. How did this innovation come about? It was done for practical and strategic reasons. As Cameron notes, workers' families engaged in a variety of arrangements to take care of their children.[27] As the strike wore on, the welfare of the children became paramount. Further, it was a tactic used in Italy, France, and Belgium and was suggested by Italian socialists to Bill Haywood on a visit to New York City.[28]

How do we understand the timing of the innovation? Context is relevant. The Bread and Roses strike was a long strike lasting nine weeks. The children's campaign began midway through the strike and lasted for two weeks. This suggests the relationship between duration, innovation, and success is relevant. Research on the association between duration and success indicates a negative correlation. Systematic analysis of strikes indicates the shorter the strike, the greater the chances of a worker victory.[29] This finding underscores how anomalous the Bread and Roses strike was: a longer strike and a worker victory.

Perhaps more important is the linkage between duration and innovation. As the strike continued, it began to approach a war of attrition. The strikers faced two constraints. Following the LoPizzo shooting, Ettor and Giovannitti were arrested, creating a leadership void. Fortunately, Bill Haywood assumed a more prominent leadership position in the strike. As Watson notes, the IWW could not let the strike go on much longer, given their resource disadvantage vis-à-vis business.[30] Five weeks into the strike, the leaders were concerned with at best slow progress and at worst a possible tipping point. The combination of new leadership and slow progress set the stage for the emergence of the children's campaign and other novel tactics as well. Further, the children's campaign was met with more violent repression by the police and militia. That is not to say that repression prior to the children's campaign was non-violent. Threatened and actual violence were a constant reality of the entire strike. The events of February 24 marked a distinct escalation by the police though.

The most important question is why the police were more restrained through the first and second phases and obviously less so on February 24. There was a

---

[27] Ardis Cameron, *Radicals of the Worst Sort* (Urbana: University of Illinois Press, 1995).
[28] Watson, *Bread and Roses*, 142-143.
[29] David Card and Craig A. Olson, "Bargaining Power, Strike Durations, and Wage Outcomes: An Analysis of Strikes in the 1880s," *Journal of Labor Economics* 13, no. 1 (1995): 32-61; Biggs, "Strikes as Sequences of Interactions: The American Strike Wave of 1886"; Geraghty and Wiseman, "Wage Strikes in 1880s America: A Test of the War of Attrition Model," *Explorations in Economic History* 45, no. 45 (2008): 303-326.
[30] Watson, *Bread and Roses,* 149.

confluence of factors which were relevant.[31] There was growing public pressure on Governor Eugene Foss (1858–1939), a long shot to become the Democratic presidential nominee, to more effectively resolve the strike. Disputes over the funding and jurisdiction of the militia boiled over. Doubts lingered about the competence of the police to manage the strike, particularly given their handling and perhaps involvement in the LoPizzo shooting. The city marshal, or police chief, was replaced amid this controversy. Questions regarding the welfare of the strikers' children grew with their separation from their parents. And all these issues spilled over into the Lawrence newspapers.

Most importantly, as the public relations game would indicate, the police took the strikers' bait in the end. In this particular episode, the strikers changed to a less violent tactic and the police shifted to more violent repression. This increased the endemic instability of the game. We may never know the precise action which instigated the melee on February 24. It is difficult to know whether the actions of strikers and their families were perceived as threats to the police or whether the police simply overreacted to the situation. Most evidence would suggest the latter. At any rate, the outcome was to shift the balance of power away from the police and toward the strikers.

What Chong neglects to consider in his conceptualization of the public relations game is its resolution. In most game theoretic accounts, the identification of the winner and loser is immediate and clear cut. It is not the case in this situation. In the immediate aftermath, both strikers and police sought to blame the other side. Resolution of the game is a function of framing of the event by not only the two contenders but other stakeholders. Those stakeholders shifted the balance of power away from business and toward the strikers. The national press began to pay more attention to the strike and their assessments were largely negative.[32] The federal government began hearings on the strike in Washington, DC, on March 1. Also, on March 1, following pressure from politicians, mill owners led by William Wood indicated their willingness to raise wages, albeit significantly below the increase sought by strikers. A "Committee of Ten" was chosen to represent the strikers and to confer with mill owners. By Tuesday, March 12, the basic agreement for settling the strike had been reached.

In essence then, the children's campaign ended the Bread and Roses strike transforming a potential defeat into a pivotal victory for labor. The use of a non-violent, groundbreaking tactic by the strikers had an energizing effect on a strike which had begun to languish. Caught off guard, the police over-reacted, violently discrediting the department, city government, and mill owners. The strikers won the public relations game. This small but critical action/reaction

---

[31] Watson, Ibid.
[32] Watson, Ibid., 175.

sequence at the Lawrence train station on February 24 defined a larger turning point in the strike.

Although the overarching dynamic in any strike is between labor and business, also important is the protest game played by strikers and the police. Going beyond simply considering these two actors, their actions, and the environment within which they operate is important. A more careful consideration of the strategic interaction between them yields a fuller understanding of the strike and helps to explain this positive but anomalous strike outcome. This insight is central to better explaining one of the most significant strikes in American labor history, a strike which still resonates today in its centennial year.

CHAPTER 6

The Parades: Evolving Views of God and Country and the IWW in Lawrence

Ken Estey

> If all good citizens unite on this matter we could have a parade thousands strong (sic). It would have a demonstrative effect to eclipse all demonstrations seen here for years. It would be a glorious and inspiring sight going down Common Street around Union Street and up Essex Street with thousands of the most beautiful and best loved emblems of nationhood, THE AMERICAN FLAG, floating in the breeze. Patriotic songs could be sung. The American Flag carried in such numbers through those streets would also cleanse the air there recently befouled with anarchistic rags and sacrilegious (sic) banners. – City Council Resolution, October 2, 1912[1]

Municipal and religious authorities in Lawrence, Massachusetts, used the God-and-Country parades of 1912 and 1962 to repudiate the Industrial Workers of the World (IWW) and what they stood for as a threat to the peace and security of Lawrence (see Figures 3 and 4, p. 115). The preamble to the IWW Constitution declared the fundamental rift to mill owners in Lawrence: "The working class and the employing class have nothing in common." For industrialists unmoved by a statement they probably also believed, the third sentence spells out the consequences: "Between these two classes a struggle must go on until the workers of the world organize as a class, take possession of the earth and the machinery of

---

[1] Paul Hannagan, Alderman, City of Lawrence, City Council Resolution, October 2, 1912. As quoted directly from the framed version found on the front left-hand wall of the City of Lawrence, City Council chambers.

production, and abolish the wage system." But one did not have to be versed in the historic text from the founding convention in Chicago in 1905 to know what the IWW and its red card-holding members were about. The IWW had already organized textile workers at Marston Mills in Skowhegan, Maine, in April 1906 to reinstate fired workers, organize a shop committee, and secure more equitable pay. Even in March 1907, the IWW organized a strike in Paterson, New Jersey, against silk dye-houses which had fired IWW workers. As a result, 6,000 dye-house workers gained a dollar a week increase in pay. By 1908, also in Paterson, the General Executive Board of the IWW founded the National Industrial Union of Textile Workers. Other textile industry actions occurred in Chicago, St. Louis, and New York. In 1906, the IWW organized Lawrence Local 20. By 1910, they had their own union hall and hosted the third convention of the National Industrial Union on Labor Day later that year. In the summer of 1911, they conducted a successful strike against Atlantic Mills. The story of Lawrence in 1912 has this extensive preface and authorities there already had many reasons to dislike the IWW.[2]

The Shattuck Flagstaff (1914) and a recently discovered time capsule from 1962 are reference points for the parades to track Lawrence's evolving view of the scope of this perceived threat over that half century. Similarly, the meaning of God and Country shifted, enabling this phrase to meet new needs in 1962 with reference to the events of the Lawrence Textile strike in 1912.[3] The God-and-Country parades in Lawrence are central to the story of the Lawrence Textile Strike of 1912 and the city's characterization of the IWW. Tempting as it might be to diminish God and Country and their supporters as only implacable opponents of the IWW, one does so at the peril of missing the wider meaning and the consequences of the strike for Lawrence and elsewhere. The vociferous counterattack that the 1912 strike engendered is actually a useful way to gauge the influence that the strike and the IWW had on its opponents. The God-and-Country parades also partake of the larger national story about the relationship of religion and state. In Lawrence, the issue was not at all whether the two should be conjoined but about *how* religious and civil authorities worked together to ward off perceived threats to municipal security. The working people of Lawrence and the assertion of their agency as workers became deeply contested territory;

---

[2] This account of early IWW textile organizing is a summary from Fred W. Thompson and Jon Bekken, *The I.W.W.: Its First One Hundred Years, 1905-2005* (Cincinnati, 2006), 27-28, 46-47.

[3] The phrase – God and Country – will be used without quotations throughout the chapter as it appears to have been a common phrase in use before 1912. The phrase "For God and Country" in quotations is used by some authors as a direct reference to the wording suggested by Father O'Reilly for the banner on October 12.

the forces of religion and state in this city served as a formidable weapon against the workers who resisted injustice.

The God-and-Country parade of 1912 cemented mounting opposition to the IWW in many quarters and contributed, through the parade of 1962, to continued marginalization within Lawrence of the strike and the mill workers' resistance. An examination of two examples of the material culture of the parades, the Shattuck Flagpole (1914) in the Lawrence Common and a recently discovered time capsule from 1962 that contained documents from the planning process for the parade that year, makes it possible to see how perceptions of the IWW and the 1912 textile strike evolved over time. By 1962, when the God-and-Country supporters rallied a massive display of opposition to the Soviets at the height of the Cold War, the focus was less on the IWW as an anarchist organization and much more about the IWW as an early source for worldwide communism. The parade featured a Hawk Missile float, courtesy of Raytheon, and a "Smash Khrushchev" display on a car. These were powerful visual representations of the threat that the IWW had supposedly set in motion a half century earlier. Then too, the meaning of the phrase God and Country had evolved since the 1912 parade which enabled it to meet new needs on the basis of old battles. The God in question was no longer specifically Christian (and largely Roman Catholic) but had shifted to include a more general Judeo-Christian orientation enabling wider participation in the struggle against the Soviets. This nuanced understanding of the God-and-Country phenomenon helps explain how the official opposition to the Lawrence textile strike endured over time.

It is tempting to view the original God-and-Country parade of 1912 and its municipal and religious sponsors solely as a new formation to oppose the threats represented by the IWW. Yet Lawrence, from its founding, had been built on the conjunction of municipal and industrial interests with religious authority serving as the bulwark. One representation of the identity of industry, state, and church is the large painting of the 1853 city seal, in the lobby of the Lawrence City Hall, which depicts the mills on the Merrimack River with a church tucked in among the mill buildings. This tight unity of interests served as the foundation for the planning, construction, and maintenance of the nation's largest and most complex industrial city. Therefore, the concerted response of Lawrence's elite to the challenge posed by the IWW and the striking mill workers in 1912 cannot be a complete surprise if a challenge to the mills is essentially equal to an assault on fundamental civic order. Speeches supporting the first parade in 1912 referred to the Revolutionary War and the Civil War as relevant historical antecedents. While such references might be rhetorical inflation to deflate public support for the strikers, recollection of past wars also reflect deep concerns that elite circles had over threats to their prosperity and sense of security, a sensibility with roots in the very founding of the city.

REVIEW OF EVENTS LEADING TO THE GOD-AND-COUNTRY PARADE ON OCTOBER 12

The Lawrence Textile strike (Jan. 11–March 14) was just one phase of an extended struggle that consumed most of 1912. Important tasks remained after the mill owners conceded to the strikers' demands. The shooting death on January 29 of Anna LoPizzo (1878–1912), an Italian striker, and a militia member's bayonet slaying on January 30 of John Ramey (1895–1912), a Lebanese boy, served as a pretext for the authorities to jail Joe Ettor (1885–1948), the key IWW organizer of the strike, and Arturo Giovannitti (1884–1959), an organizer for relief efforts in Lawrence. Authorities accused both of them of being accessories to the murder of LoPizzo.[4] Arrest and the Essex County jail followed thereafter. Joseph Caruso, arrested a few weeks later, also faced indictment for conspiracy to kill LoPizzo.[5] Their incarceration during the strike, the prospect of the death penalty, and the agitation for their release well after the end of the strike are the essential story elements leading up to the October 12th parade.

The IWW debated vigorously over the merits of the legal process versus direct action to free Ettor and Giovannitti from their jail cells. Giovannitti suggested that Carlo Tresca (1879-1943) come to Lawrence and take the lead to build a mass movement.[6] When Tresca arrived at the beginning of May, he thought he would be preparing for a general strike to coincide with the trial date at month's end. However, the trial was postponed until September. Even when summer ended, debates persisted over the merits of a general strike to gain the release of the three men. After a series of funeral processions to LoPizzo's grave earlier in May, Tresca organized yet another parade honoring LoPizzo on Sunday, September 29—the eight-month anniversary of her death and the day before the trial of Ettor, Giovannitti, and Caruso began.[7] During this 4,000 person-strong procession to the cemetery, Carlo Tresca stood backward on a one-horse buggy and looked on at how "one big banner, when all the others had given away to the force of the persistent downpour, remained intact. On it was a red, challenging motto, 'No God, No Master.'"[8] Elizabeth Gurley Flynn (1890–1964) claimed that it was Boston anarchists who unfurled the banner. The failure of the IWW to control their message, according to Flynn, "was worth a million dollars to the employers and may have been a deliberate act of provocation. Some of us believed that it was."[9]

---

[4] Bruce Watson, *Bread and Roses: Mills, Migrants, and the Struggle for the American Dream* (New York, 2005), 114.
[5] Ibid., 220.
[6] Elizabeth Gurley Flynn, *The Rebel Girl: An Autobiography; My First Life, 1906–1926* (New York, 1973), 147.
[7] Watson, *Bread and Roses*, 224.
[8] Nunzio Pernicone, *Carlo Tresca: Portrait of a Rebel* (Oakland, 2010), 54. This is a quote from *The Autobiography of Carlo Tresca* which Pernicone also edited (New York, 2003).
[9] Flynn, *Rebel Girl*, 150.

THE ORIGINAL CONTEXT FOR GOD AND COUNTRY IN LAWRENCE

Flynn completed the manuscript of her autobiography in the mid-1950s, and with the clarity that 40 years of hindsight afforded, observed that:

> We had pursued a correct labor policy during the strike of confining our remarks to answering Father Reilly and others only on strike issues. We did not discuss religion and warned all speakers, regardless of their personal views, not to offend the religious feelings of the people. Now came this banner in an IWW parade, unsigned and with no reference to the IWW on its face. But the full impact of its appearance was used against the IWW in Lawrence.[10]

It was not just any banner. The words "No God, No Master" happened to be a concise parallel negation to the God-and-Country doctrine held dear by Father James T. O'Reilly (1851–1925) and his followers in Lawrence for quite some time. On Memorial Day in 1890, at a speech marking the placement of a flagstaff on St. Mary's School building, featuring a gathering of 1,200 children dressed in white and each holding an American flag (prefiguring similar displays 22 years later), O'Reilly offered a lengthy defense of Roman Catholic patriotism. His central argument was built on the inseparable union of religion and patriotism. Pushing back against the claim that Roman Catholics are politically beholden to a foreign power in Rome, a preoccupation of many Protestants at the time, he argued that the "truest of patriotisms" is loyalty to God and country.[11] Education such as that offered at St. Mary's provides religious principles to students forming their lives and readying them for good citizenship. Reaching out across religious lines, O'Reilly argued in conclusion that "My fellow-citizens of all creeds, the truer we try to be to the principles of Christianity, the nearer we have the Cross to our hearts,—the stronger will be our devotion to our flag, the more secure in our hands will be the destiny of our country."[12] About three years later, Father O'Reilly founded a local Knights of Columbus council – Lawrence Council No. 67 – formally instituted on January 8, 1893.[13]

A remarkable aspect of Father O'Reilly's theological tutelage is that, in 1912, he was able to parlay his earlier conception of God and Country, rooted as it was to

---

[10] Ibid.

[11] Alice L. Walsh, *A Sketch of the Life and Labors of the Rev. James T. O'Reilly, O.S.A., Pastor of St. Mary's Church, Lawrence, Mass. Since 1886 to 1924* (Lawrence, no date supplied), 12.

[12] Walsh, *Sketch of the Life and Labors of the Rev. James T. O'Reilly*, 14.

[13] Susan H. Brosnan, Archivist, Knights of Columbus Museum, to Ken Estey, e-mail, Jul. 9, 2012 (in Ken Estey's possession). O'Reilly's founding of Lawrence Council No. 67 occurred seven years before the Knights of Columbus included patriotism as a fourth degree of membership in 1900.

meet the needs of a Roman Catholic constituency, into a broader civic context. The emphasis was not about proving that Roman Catholics could be remarkably loyal citizens on the basis of their religious beliefs. Now, the theme of God and Country could be deployed as a direct refutation to a new alien people and doctrine—the anarchists and the anarchy that they spawned. The Roman Catholic community, through O'Reilly, came into its own. No longer need Catholics be on the defensive, but could join with others. Diverse religious and ethnic groups in Lawrence had a shared interest to join ranks against a common threat.[14]

BATTLE OF THE BANNERS: GOD AND COUNTRY 1912— A CASE OF CHURCH AND CITY

On Wednesday, October 2, Alderman Paul Hannagan successfully introduced a resolution to the Lawrence City Council, citing recent appeals in the press for the same, that called for approval to have a parade "of all the residents who believe in this country, its constitution and its institutions, who love and honor its flag."[15] Designating October 12 as a good day for a parade "on account of its being a holiday," the American flag "carried in such numbers through those streets would also cleanse the air there recently befouled with anarchistic rags and sacreligious (sic) banners."[16] On Thursday, October 3rd, a follow-up mass meeting ensued at City Hall. As the Friday *Lawrence Telegram* headline blared: "Patriotism of the Citizens Aroused: Anarchistic Attack on American Flag and All Religion by the I.W.W. Leads to Spontaneous Indignation Mass Meeting in City Hall—Plans Made for Parade October 12."[17]

> Not for decades has such an enthusiastic meeting been held in the city hall as was the protest meeting against lawlessness Thursday evening. Men and women of all classes and creeds, all imbued alike with patriotic fervor and the desire for peace and security in this city, cheered the speakers till the bell rang and reverberated, and twice the national anthem arose at once

---

[14] Daniel Guérin, in the foreword to his compilation, *No Gods, No Masters: An Anthology of Anarchism* (Oakland, 2005) provides a short history in which he concurs that the phrase "might be an adaptation of a 15th century German proverb to be found in Act I, Scene II of the 1659 tragicomedy, *Peter's Feast*, or the *Atheist Confounded*, written by Devilliers, a sort of fore-runner of Molière's *Don Juan*," 1.

[15] Lawrence, Massachusetts City Council Resolution, Oct. 2, 1912. These quotations are from the original, framed, large-format version of this resolution (in calligraphy with accompanying artistic designs) that has been hanging in the City Council chambers for an indefinite period of time. It is located at the front of the room on the left wall near the row of city, state, and U.S. flags.

[16] Ibid.

[17] "Patriotism of the Citizens Aroused," *Lawrence Telegram*, Oct. 4, 1912, 1.

a sacred paeon and a song of defiance to those who would threaten the safety of the land.[18]

The accompanying photographs for this article—one of Mayor Michael A. Scanlon (1874–1914) and the other of Rev. O'Reilly—represent clearly the conjunction of city and church on the urgency of this matter. Charles E. Bradley, who was later to become the chair of the Citizens Association, an organization to promote patriotism in Lawrence, situated the struggle there in the hallowed lineage of war and struggle.

> We have read of the soldiers of '76. We have with us still some of the heroes of '61. No more serious duty devolved on them than does on us now. The Revolution was fought that this country might have a beginning. The war of '61 was fought that these United States of America might be perpetuated. The war of 1912 will be fought to determine whether this country will continue to be a land of the free and a home for the oppressed or whether anarchy and misrule will prevail.[19]

At least eight other speakers followed Bradley, including Father O'Reilly and George E. Lovejoy (1843–1916), the minister of South Congregational Church and, as the *Telegram* noted, the national chaplain of the G.A.R., the Grand Army of the Republic.[20] The Columbus Day parade committee appears to have been formally announced that evening as well.

On Saturday, readers of the *Lawrence Telegram* evening edition observed the headline that the Columbus Day Parade would be a "rebuke to the IWW and its red flag."[21] Cities such as Boston, Lowell, and Haverhill also were joining the movement.[22] As for Lawrence: "In the schools yesterday the national hymns were sung and the pupils were given talks of patriotism. . . ."[23] "Reverence to the flag will be one of the teachings in the schools now for the next few weeks."[24] For the following week, adult citizens of the city also had homework assignments. The first was Mayor Scanlon's appeal that everyone wear a

---

[18] Ibid.

[19] Ibid., 4.

[20] George Lovejoy actually had been recently elected the chaplain in chief for the Forty-Sixth National Encampment held in Los Angeles (September 9-14, 1912). This is an elected position in which the officer serves for the year until the next encampment or the annual meeting for the Grand Army of the Republic, the organization for Civil War veterans. See the web site of the Sons of Union Veterans of the Civil War National Headquarters and their "Complete Roster of Commandery-in-Chief Officers, Grand Army of the Republic, 1866-1949." http://suvcw.org/garcinc/officers1866-1949.pdf.

[21] "Columbus Day Parade Plans," *Lawrence Telegram*, Oct. 5, 1912, 1.

[22] Ibid.

[23] Ibid.

[24] Ibid.

miniature American flag until Thanksgiving Day.[25] The second, from the *Lawrence Telegram,* urged everyone to learn the *Star Spangled Banner* and *My Country 'Tis of Thee* to sing with marchers at the parade.[26] On Sunday, the churches in Lawrence featured "forceful sermons" preached on "patriotism and law and order."[27] George Lovejoy, pastor of South Congregational Church, in attendance at the mass meeting on Thursday, made the connection between church and city explicit.

> The only safeguard for personal liberty, and the sacred time-honored institutions for which other men labored is an intense conviction that God is at the helm of government, that He the Great Almighty Admiral is on the ship of state and that He expects even Americans to be loyal and do his duty.[28]

The United States is a free republic though it is an ongoing and unproven experiment, with no sure outcome. The issue is not only about foreign foes who might challenge the country. The problems for a free republic are also on the home front:

> This we have been made sadly conscious of in these opening years of this 20th century for in the great industrial centers of New England we have learned that the menace to government and the peril of our social order is meeting us from the enemies within the gates, we are having a fulfillment of the Master's prophetic words, "A man's foes shall be those of his own household."[29]

Lawrence turned out in force on October 12, Columbus Day, to meet those internal foes. At this point, the parade had not yet fully coalesced into a God-and-Country parade. The City Council resolution on October 2nd did not refer to it as such and even the *Lawrence Telegram,* a champion of everything to do with the events of those weeks, the day after headlined with "*Protest Parade A Grand Success*" (emphasis added).[30] As part of their description of the events, they deemed it a "'Flag Day' in every sense of the word. . . ."[31] Only in the editorial did they claim that the banner under which everyone marched "For God and Country, The Stars and Stripes Forever. The Red Flag Never. A Protest Against the I.W.W., Its Principles and Methods" in fact was "the purpose of

---

[25] "Mayor Issues Appeal to Patriotic Citizens," *Lawrence Telegram,* Oct. 3, 1912, 1.
[26] "Learn the Words," *Lawrence Telegram,* Oct. 4, 1912, 6.
[27] "Clergymen Appeal to Lawrence Citizens," *Lawrence Telegram,* Oct. 7, 1912, 2.
[28] Ibid.
[29] Ibid.
[30] "Protest Parade a Grand Success," *Lawrence Telegram,* Oct. 14, 1912, 1.
[31] Ibid., 5.

the parade."[32] Mayor Scanlon, in his appeal on October 3 for everyone to wear miniature American flags noted that "their creed is 'No God, no Master. Let ours be 'For God and Country'."[33] Yet this was in reference to wearing the flag, not to the parade itself. While the parade got the most attention, the event to which everything had been leading that day was the subsequent gathering of 60,000 on the Lawrence Common when two Grand Army veterans hoisted the American flag up a new 75-foot flagpole while a band played the *Star Spangled Banner*.[34] The *Lawrence Telegram* concluded in an editorial flourish that everyone in attendance was "impressed with a new sense of duty, of power, of dignity, of civic responsibility and pride. The latent spirit had inevitably reached its height and the step of every one was firmer and heads were carried higher."[35]

This vigorous city-sponsored display of patriotic fervor became very personal. Even before the parade, IWW members had buttons ripped off their clothing; a couple of days afterwards, they were fined for passing out leaflets in downtown Lawrence. The aggressive anti-IWW mood reached into a Lithuanian neighborhood a week later on the 19th when IWW member and Arlington mill worker Jonas Smolskas was caught in a bar wearing an IWW button instead of an American flag pin. He left the bar but didn't survive the subsequent fight in his own back yard. Even his funeral procession the following Saturday was subject to police harassment.[36]

The parade, in its planning, execution, and subsequent evaluation, is an instructive case study that demonstrates how a major public event takes on additional layers of meaning even as it is being planned and in the course of its occurrence. Calling it the "God-and-Country Parade of 1912," in retrospect, has been a widely accepted summation of its theme and purpose. Then, it was a parade which occurred on Columbus Day and also included a local Flag Day. Two years later, the *Lawrence Daily American* referred back to the events of that day as a "Flag day demonstration [on] Columbus day."[37] That both days could be observed simultaneously was not viewed as a problem since it was four years before Woodrow Wilson proclaimed that June 14 be observed as Flag Day and 37 years (1949) until a joint resolution by the U.S. Congress officially designated this date as Flag Day for the whole nation. For the parade on October 12 to fully become the "God-and-Country Parade of 1912" would have to wait. And when it did become what it is known as today, the meaning of God and Country would change as well.

---

[32] Ibid.
[33] "Mayor Issues Appeal to Patriotic Citizens," *Lawrence Telegram*, Oct. 3, 1912, 1.
[34] "Protest Parade a Grand Success," *Lawrence Telegram*, Oct. 14, 1912, 5.
[35] Ibid.
[36] Watson, *Bread and Roses*, 232.
[37] "Patriotic Exercises at Flagstaff Dedication," *Lawrence Daily American*, Apr. 21, 1914, 7.

THE SHATTUCK FLAGSTAFF: THE MEMORIALIZATION OF GOD AND COUNTRY IN LAWRENCE

For all the rhetorical flourishes that characterized the reporting by the *Lawrence Telegram* on this story, maybe the newspaper had it right in the case of one possible bystander observing the events that day. Joseph Shattuck (1827–1913), a long-time resident of Lawrence, was moved to contribute. He was a member of the Unitarian Church that once faced the Lawrence Common and fifth in a line of Joseph Shattucks. It was a distinguished family tree; his grandfather had served in the Revolutionary War, Bunker Hill and Valley Forge. By 1878, he was director of the Bay State National Bank and president of the Essex Savings Bank, serving as well on the Board of Aldermen.[38] In a letter to the mayor and city council written just six days after the October 12 parade, Shattuck wrote the following:

> Having learned that a new flagstaff is needed for Lawrence common, I hereby respectfully request the privilege of erecting one there, with a granite base, on which will appear my name in some appropriate form. All to be at my expense, but transferred to the city as its property. I am unable to furnish details at this time, but assure you that the complete structure will be a credit to the city, in which I have resided for nearly 70 years, and will be worthy of the flag.[39]

On November 1, Alderman Michael S. O'Brien met with Shattuck's representative to discuss details about the gift. At this point, the location had not been decided upon although, according to the *Lawrence Daily Eagle*, the spot where the temporary flagpole was located (presumably the one raised in place on October 12) "finds favor with many."[40] Shattuck expressed his willingness "to have only the best that money can buy."[41] Two months later, Shattuck wrote back to the city and said that, due to his advanced age, he would turn the responsibility for its design and construction over to the city, along with a $4,000 check to the city treasurer to construct the flagstaff and $1,000 to Essex Savings Bank as an endowment fund for replacement flags in the future. The City of Lawrence dutifully met on January 6, 1913 and appointed a commission that included George Lovejoy, Joseph McCarthy, James D. Horne and Fred H. Eaton (who went on to become the president of Essex Savings Bank, a descendent of

---

[38] H. A. Wadsworth, *Quarter-Centennial History of Lawrence, Massachusetts with Portraits and Biographical Sketches* (Lawrence, 1878), portrait page between pages 66 and 67.
[39] "Patriotic Exercises at Flagstaff Dedication," *Lawrence Daily American*, Apr. 21, 1914, 7. The text of Shattuck's letter is from this newspaper account (which appears to be a transcription) of Alderman Alfred Bradbury's speech who, in turn, quotes Shattuck.
[40] "Flag Pole Conference," *Lawrence Daily Eagle*, Nov. 1, 1912, 8.
[41] Ibid.

William Eaton who settled in Watertown and became its proprietor in 1642).[42] Other commission members included William T. Kimball, Lawrence native and a city clerk, as well as another son of Lawrence, Alderman Michael S. O'Brien, also known as "Father" of playgrounds.[43] James R. Menzie and Alderman Alfred Bradbury also were commission members. The donor and these commissioners illustrate that those involved in the emergence of a God-and-Country tradition in Lawrence were not solely restricted to Father O'Reilly and the theological and ecclesiastical interests of St. Mary's, but had the imprimatur of long-time figures in the Lawrence establishment.

The base upon which the flagpole is mounted is an example of Beaux Arts architecture and sensibility, the work of Richard Clipston Sturgis (1860–1951) of Boston who designed the Perkins School for the Blind in Watertown, Robbins Memorial Town Hall in Arlington, additions to the Massachusetts State House, as well as the Old Federal Reserve Building in Boston. The granite base for the bronze sculpture commands attention for its solidity and historical sensitivity. Roman fasces, bound rods surmounted by an axe, reminiscent of the reverse of the Mercury dime then in circulation, are carved out of its four corners, projecting the message of power, law, and discipline. The four faces of the base under the bronze showcase various coats of arms and the 13 stars refer to the original colonies. Upon this foundation is the elaborate bronze sculpture which commences with four cogs, one at each corner, suggesting movement and dynamism. Continuing in bronze, above the cogs, in soft relief, are wavy skeins featuring an occasional measuring knot to showcase Lawrence's textile industry. Resting on top of this depiction of industriousness, on four sides, the bronze softens as if into hanging cloth drapes upon which inscriptions are set, though now fading, for the passerby to read and to receive instruction. They include verses from the New Testament, quotations from Plato, Montaigne, Thomas Jefferson, Daniel Webster, Ralph Waldo Emerson, Abraham Lincoln, James Russell Lowell, and Herman Hagedorn. Weaving shuttles surmount the inscriptions continuing the representation of industry; the bronze base becomes circular with bands of oak, acorn, fruit, and a weave of wheat surmounted by a cornucopia of fruit and plenty. Yet above this, is a repeating pattern of bee and butterfly referring perhaps to the transformation that comes through industry, or the life made possible through human work. The bee is also depicted on the seal of the City of Lawrence. The result is a sumptuous table in bronze, signs of the blessings of work from which the pole arises to hold aloft the American flag.

Lawrence officials had hoped that the Shattuck Flagstaff could be erected on the anniversary of what Alderman Alfred Bradbury himself called the "memorable Flag day parade" but "circumstances beyond our control compelled the

---

[42] "Atty. Fred H. Eaton, President of Essex Savings Bank, Is Dead," *Lawrence Evening Tribune*, Apr. 28, 1948, 1 and 11.

[43] Maurice B. Dorgan, *Lawrence: Yesterday and Today, 1845–1918* (Lawrence, 1918), 214.

postponement of the exercises."[44] Shattuck himself died at the age of 86 on May 31, 1913. But in time for Patriots Day on April 20, 1914, Lawrence had yet another impressive display of civic pride. About 10,000 people, featuring school children, local militia companies, veterans from the Civil War, and city officials gathered for the unveiling of the flagstaff which was performed by Miss Dorothy Shattuck, the granddaughter of the donor, who pulled a battle-scarred "Old Glory" covering the bronze sculptural elements and the granite base.[45] A photograph shows the young Dorothy undertaking this official duty with the old Lawrence Common bandstand in the background.[46] The flagstaff assumed the center of the stage for civic attention that day, and not the bandstand which had been the platform for the speakers and the point around which many striker and IWW gatherings had occurred.

Once the flag was raised on the new pole and the singing of the *Star Spangled Banner* was over, Bradbury, the chair of the flagstaff commission, spoke about the donor Joseph Shattuck as well as details about the architect and the design of the flagstaff.[47] His remarks then shifted to invocations of the Mayflower, the events at Lexington, and the firing on Fort Sumter on April 12, 1861. Similar to speakers two years earlier who invoked a larger narrative of national strength and character out of the crucible of local struggle and controversy, Bradbury was able to present the events in 1912 as a story of character formed through conflict surmounted. After Bradbury formally presented the flagstaff to the city of Lawrence, a 21-gun salute from members of Battery C punctuated the gravity of the day. Then, Mayor Scanlon in a supposedly extemporaneous speech added his thoughts.

> Liberty is understood by some to mean that they have the right to do as they please. Liberty to us means obedience to law and unless we obey the law of the land then life and property are not safe and we have no liberty. If those

---

[44] Remarks of Alderman Alfred Bradbury, "Patriotic Exercises at Flagstaff Dedication," *Lawrence Daily American*, Apr. 21, 1914, 7.

[45] "Patriotic Exercises at Flagstaff Dedication," *Lawrence Daily American*, Apr. 21, 1914, 7.

[46] "Memorial Flagstaff on the Common Dedicated," *Lawrence Telegram*, Apr. 21, 1914, 1.

[47] Richard Clipston Sturgis's handwritten notes about his work with the Lawrence flagstaff commission offers insight into the design process. In the single page entry for May 7, 1913, Sturgis reports that he showed the commission the model for the flagstaff which they approved but that it "must be kept within the appropriation. . . ." Sturgis comments that "they would all like that done"—apparently referring to a desire to match the 70-foot height of the flag raised on October 12, 1912. He notes that commission member George Lovejoy "raised question of lights on it" but Sturgis argued it "will be sufficiently illuminated by the pole"—Sturgis also pointed out that "I don't want this" with respect to a fence to be built around it. R. Clipston Sturgis Architectural Sketchbooks, no. 54, April to Oct. 1913, May 7, 1913, Manuscript Collection (Boston Athenæum, Boston, MA.).

who come from other countries do not like our institutions or our laws and customs, and if they cannot learn to love and respect our flag and all that it represents to us, then they have the privilege of leaving and going where they can find conditions that will suit them.[48]

The Shattuck Flagstaff is a significant artifact that, for Lawrence, presents the events of 1912 worth remembering—certainly not the strike—but the events that occurred afterwards. That it remains nearly fully intact a century later on the Lawrence Common is a remarkable accomplishment of the original goal to memorialize and instantiate a counter-narrative in which the precipitating story is completely erased. The plaque on the Shattuck Flagstaff (on the side of the granite base facing City Hall) acknowledges the donor and recalls succinctly the participants, the parade, and the purpose: "The gift of Joseph Shattuck to the people of Lawrence as a perpetual reminder of October 12, 1912 when 32,000 men, women, and children marched under the flag for God and Country."

FATHER O'REILLY'S GOLDEN JUBILEE, 1924: EVOLUTION OF THE IWW

The events marking the Golden Jubilee of the 50th anniversary of Father O'Reilly's ordination offers a chance, 12 years after the 1912 strike, to observe various public characterizations of his civic work. One can also gain a sense of the official public viewpoint about the nature of the IWW in that year. The festivities of the four-day celebration between May 4 and 7 have been captured in Alice L. Walsh's hagiographic *A Sketch of the Life and Labors of the Rev. James T. O'Reilly*. In the outline of his "life and deeds," the entry for 1912 is unambiguous: "Originated idea of I.W.W. Protest Parade of Oct. 12, in which 40,000 marched under Roman Arch at Amesbury and Essex streets, also his idea, and personally supervised by Father O'Reilly."[49] Deeming him the "leader of the entire movement," she averred that the "citizens of the city gratefully acknowledged that their redemption in the eyes of the world was due to the foresight and fearlessness of the pastor of St. Mary's, Father O'Reilly."[50] Mayor James M. Curley of Boston spoke to the members of Division 8, Ancient Order of the Hibernians, at their reception for O'Reilly and said that this "splendid citizen organized his people into an army of loyalty and righteousness and led them 30,000 strong, bearing American flags, to give testimony of their allegiance

---

[48] "Patriotic Exercises at Flagstaff Dedication," *Lawrence Daily American*, April 21, 1914, 7.
[49] Walsh, *Sketch of the Life and Labors of the Rev. James T. O'Reilly*, no page number. See "Outline of Rev. James T. O'Reilly— His Life and Deeds" at beginning of book.
[50] Ibid., 19.

to God and country, to right and religion, to peace and principle; and lo, the forces of evil and their allies fled."[51]

On May 7, the city closed shop in the afternoon for a civic parade for O'Reilly in which 25,000 people marched. Later that evening, a public testimonial banquet provided more occasions to recognize O'Reilly. Mayor Rochefort of Lawrence deemed O'Reilly to have been "the moving force to stem the tide of Bolshevism in this community," echoing Curley's description of the threat facing Lawrence.[52] Dr. Jeremiah E. Burke, superintendent of Boston Public Schools, referred to the events of 1912 and said that not just for Lawrence but for the whole country, it was the "funeral knell of communism, of anarchy, and of rebellion against constituted authority."[53] Judge Charles A. DeCourcy of the Massachusetts Supreme Court also spoke of the events of 1912:

> That period seems like a nightmare when we look back upon it, and for a time it almost shook our confidence in the future of Lawrence. But that parade, followed by the inspiring Thanksgiving gathering in the City Hall, demonstrated that the old time American spirit of Lawrence was still in control. And the man most entitled to credit for the survival of that spirit is our guest of tonight.[54]

It is not clear what DeCourcy had in mind with the reference to the "old time American spirit." Perhaps he was thinking of what he considered best about the mutually reinforcing character of government, God, and gain in the United States. Lawrence officials, no doubt, felt that all three were under attack, ideologically and on the streets, not just 12 years earlier but also two years prior in 1922 with additional struggles forged against the mill owners.

FOR GOD AND COUNTRY, 1962:
A TIME CAPSULE FOR A PARADE

Municipal authorities in Lawrence have been adept at recalling and deploying history for purposes of state. Evidence for this skill was abundant during 1912 and certainly at the dedication of the Shattuck Flagstaff in 1914 situating then current events in terms of the past through a process of purposeful tradition-making. In 1962, Lawrence took on the task of official recollection once more, this time, producing history anew by referring to its own history-making with the 50th anniversary of the "For God-and-Country" parade.

As a result of a transfer of library holdings to the main Lawrence library building, a time capsule came to the attention of Louise Sandberg, archivist for the

---
[51] Ibid., 155.
[52] Ibid., 193.
[53] Ibid., 197.
[54] Ibid., 201-202.

Lawrence Public Library.⁵⁵ The contents, now organized into two archive boxes, comprise selected paperwork from Mayor John J. Buckley's (1916–1997) office that documents the planning process for the parade. These papers provide direct insight into the thinking and motivation of the parade planners. Similar to the Shattuck Flagpole of 1914, the time capsule is a source in its own right. A galvanized metal box featuring bold black lettering on its cover and one side, it was designed to be visible and handy for use a half century later. Remarkably, it worked. What could have been easily filed away in a file cabinet, and just as easily never found again, the metal box and the contents therein survived as an entire entity for nearly five decades. The papers were clearly intended to be a message to those who would read the contents in 2012—not to marvel at what it contained, but to take instruction thereby. On the box lid, it reads: "—Material—God and Country 50th Anniversary Parade 1912 1962 " On the side where the lid opens, it instructs: "Hold for 100th Anniversary Anno Domini 2012." Among the papers are two small note-card sized sheets, stapled together, on which hand-written instructions appear that specify the dimensions for the metal box and also how the contents should be handled a half century later. In a subtle shift of words, instead of instructing that one "hold" the documents for 2012, the note sheets instruct: "for use—in year 2012."⁵⁶ The message is clear. The City of Lawrence should conduct a 100th anniversary commemoration of the 1912 God-and-Country parade in September 2012. Overall, the documents provide an excellent view of the planning process by Mayor Buckley's office and the work of his dedicated secretary, Peter Hewett.⁵⁷

PLANNING FOR THE GOD-AND-COUNTRY PARADE

One key point in 1962 is that the parade's purpose was explicitly about God and Country from the very outset of its planning. The handwritten minutes indicate that "The initial meeting for making plans for the 'God + Country' parade" was held on Friday evening, April 27, 1962.⁵⁸ Eighteen were in attendance in the City Council chamber, including Mayor Buckley, his secretary Peter

---

⁵⁵ An image of the "time capsule" can be viewed at "Timecapsule," photograph, *Eagle-Tribune*, http://www.eagletribune.com/communitynews/x101445372/capsule-jpg.

⁵⁶ God & Country Parade 1962 Papers. Box 1. Folder 3. (Lawrence Public Library, Local History Room, Lawrence, MA.)

⁵⁷ While there is no direct evidence that conclusively documents that Peter Hewett assembled the materials, as the secretary to Mayor Buckley, he was well-placed to undertake such a project. Also, the papers contain a preparatory speech for the parade that he delivered to the Lawrence Exchange Club on August 21, 1962. The speech and its placement in the archive suggest Hewett as the archive's compiler. A recent article reports that two of Peter Hewett's children recall that he also talked about the time capsule: Yadira Betances, "A Box of History," *Eagle Tribune*, Apr. 20, 2012. See http://www.eagletribune.com/local/x2086602130/A-box-of-history.

⁵⁸ "Meeting Minutes for April 27, 1962," God & Country Parade 1962 Papers. Box 1. Folder 1. (Lawrence Public Library, Local History Room, Lawrence, MA.)

Hewett, and other municipal and civic leaders. Assignments for outreach to the various constituencies were made to "insure 100 percent participation" in a parade that all agreed "should be organized in a manner worthy of the city of Lawrence and of the event which it will commemorate. It was stressed that the parade should not be a commercial or a religious program but secular in the sense that all components of society be represented!"[59] The notes deemed that the "meeting was most successful" and the next one was scheduled for a week later on May 4 "to keep the enthusiasm running."[60]

The use of the word "secular" to describe a *God*-and-Country parade has particular import. A God-and-Country parade that is not a "religious program" shows just how far the meaning of this phrase had evolved by 1962 since O'Reilly's articulation of it on Memorial Day in 1890 in defense of his Roman Catholic constituency. As noted above, by 1912, God and Country had a broader reach in which Protestants could also appeal to the unity of church and state to fend off atheists and anarchists. However, by 1962, God and Country in Lawrence could be secular or "non-religious" insofar as anyone of any faith or religion could participate. This was a classic expression of civic religion in the United States in the post World War II era in which appeals to God could be generic and devoid of specific religious content.

Still and all, while the event planners at the first meeting designated that the parade be secular as defined by widespread participation, there is no question that Lawrence officially sponsored an event with significant religious content. Fifty years after 1912, the conjunction of city and church was revived in substantial fashion. That Father Edward Carney, the pastor of St. Mary's church no less, was named the honorary chairman of the event underlines this detail and situates this event in continuity with James T. O'Reilly and his activity in 1912. The parade featured a substantial number of marchers affiliated with St. Mary's. Nonetheless, bringing up the back of Division 3, were marchers from Congregation Temple Emmanuel, so that in Lawrence, even adherents of Judaism could be in on the God-and-Country celebration.[61]

Mayor Buckley's invitations to participate in the parade provide his account of how a local textile strike in 1912 led to consequences of world historical importance a half century hence. A narrow reading of the invitation would be to focus on the parade's "sole purpose"—American solidarity against the Communist

---

[59] Ibid.

[60] Ibid.

[61] But it should be recalled that, even in 1912, a Jewish synagogue in Concord, MA., during services on Oct. 5, had a large American flag carried to the rostrum—those present "enthusiastically saluted it." President Wiener of the synagogue addressed everyone on patriotism and they voted to participate in the forthcoming parade. "It was stated that they were not responsible for the part the Hebrews took in last Sunday's 'red-flagged' parade." "To Participate in Parade," *Lawrence Telegram*, Oct. 5, 1912, 1.

threat using the occasion of the 50th anniversary of the parade in 1912 as an excuse to show this unity. Still, the implication is clear that the Communist threat in 1962 had its ancestry in the IWW of 1912. Thus, it was not just a "hook" to celebrate the half-century mark but a chance to acknowledge the historical lineage of the threat. In his letter to Commanding Officer T.C. Ondrechen of the U.S. Naval and Marine Corps Reserve Training Center in Lawrence, Buckley wrote:

> Fifty years ago, The City of Lawrence experienced an industrial upheaval in its textile industry which was historic in its social implications. Into Lawrence came the I.W.W. – Industrial Workers of the World – with its host of organizers urging every kind of violence and destruction. Its slogan was "No God-No Master." It was the first overt showing in the world of what is now identified as Communism. On Sunday, September 23, 1962, the City of Lawrence will celebrate the 50th Anniversary of the famed "For God and Country" parade which was held on October 12, 1912 as a refutation of the Anti-God-Anti-Democratic slogans. A large civic group is presently engaged in making plans for a parade on that date which in and of itself should prove to be a historic event. May I request the cooperation of your good offices to enlist the participation of your Reserve Units. The sole purpose of this parade is intended to be indicative of American solidarity in the face of present day Communism.[62]

The Cold War had a long history featuring numerous points of conflict but the events of 1962 remain noteworthy. The Bay of Pigs invasion had occurred a year prior in April 1961 and was a backdrop for the mood in Lawrence and elsewhere. In April 1962, the U.S. military had made operational the Jupiter missiles aimed at the Soviets in Turkey. This provocation led Khrushchev and his advisors, in late April and May, to contemplate the response of stationing nuclear missiles in Cuba.[63] The Cuban missile crisis did not boil over in full public view and anxiety until after the parade, yet the chain of events that led to the crisis was well under way.

While God and Country took on an ever-widening scope in the history of its use in Lawrence, so did the perception of the nature of the IWW and the threat that it posed. In 1912, the IWW was identified with anarchism and atheism. By 1924, given the revolutionary activity in Russia in 1917 and 1918, the IWW had been transformed into the equivalent of Bolshevism. In 1962, with the Cold War in full swing, the mayor's office deemed the IWW as the first instance of the world-wide threat of Communism. The *Lawrence-Eagle Tribune*, which ran the parade entry forms for free and also purchased 10,000 flags to distribute

---

[62] Mayor John J. Buckley to T. C. Ondrechen, May 2, 1962. God & Country Parade 1962 Papers. Box 1. Folder 2. (Lawrence Public Library, Local History Room, Lawrence, MA.)
[63] Laurence Chang, Peter Kornbluh, eds., *The Cuban Missile Crisis, 1962: A National Security Archive Documents Reader* (New York, 1992), 351.

along the parade route, had one moment of consistency.[64] In an editorial the day of the parade, they declared that atheistic Marxism was the problem in 1912 and that a mightier form of atheistic Marxism continued in 1962.[65] Then too, above their masthead was another banner "God and Country—Lawrence's Answer to Anarchy." It almost didn't matter what the IWW actually stood for as long as people understood that it was nothing more than an enemy of the city, indeed, the entire country.

It is tempting to regard the 1962 God-and-Country parade as only a municipal response to the Soviets at the height of the Cold War and not really at all about the events of 1912. After all, the mayor's proclamation on September 21 (just two days before the parade) that September 23 be called "For God and Country Day" appears to plainly support the contention that this was about the Soviets and not about the IWW. The ninth "whereas" of the Proclamation says, "Fifty years ago, Lawrence refuted the 'No God—No Master' concept of the Communist doctrine now prevalent in the world and only ninety miles off our shores. . . ."[66] The reference to Cuba underlined the proximity of the threat and the preoccupation with the Soviets. To contend that the parade was directed against the Soviet Union respects the surface meaning of this part of the proclamation, yet it neglects the larger story which is the clear line of continuity that the city itself had drawn from the IWW of 1912 to the Soviets of 1962. For Buckley, Hewett and others, the Soviet Union was not a difference of kind from the IWW but a difference of scale and might. And just as Lawrence faced down the threat of Godless anarchy within, so it was prepared to face that threat without— a threat that Lawrence had "defeated" but one that somehow managed to regroup and repurpose itself to afflict good and God-believing people everywhere. The end of the Proclamation is a clear affirmation that however secular the parade of 1962 was to be, it would still be a parade with deep roots in monotheistic belief and culture:

> WHEREAS, This year of 1962 marks the fiftieth anniversary of the famed 'For God and Country' parade which restored the reputation of the City of Lawrence in the eyes of the world as a truly American and religiously conscious municipality, and
>
> WHEREAS, We, the people of Greater Lawrence today re-affirm these religious beliefs and tenets of true democracy, . . . [67]

---

[64] Handwritten memo, "For God and Country File," God & Country Parade 1962 Papers. Box 1. Folder 3. (Lawrence Public Library, Local History Room, Lawrence, MA.)
[65] "For God and Country!," Sept. 22, 1962. *Lawrence Eagle-Tribune*, 1.
[66] "Mayor John J. Buckley Proclamation," Sept. 21, 1962, God & Country Parade 1962 Papers. Box 2. Folder 8. (Lawrence Public Library, Local History Room, Lawrence, MA.)
[67] Ibid.

Moreover, the 1912 parade became fully a God-and-Country parade exactly because the 50th anniversary in 1962 made it so – by mayoral proclamation. And perhaps there was a little help, too, from a woman in Minneapolis who wrote to the City of Lawrence asking about the Shattuck Flagstaff, given their interest to undertake a similar initiative. An undated newspaper clipping tucked into the time capsule describes the effort of Mayor Buckley's staff, specifically naming Peter Hewett, to describe this history. As the article relates, the lengthy letter that he prepared about the flagstaff is interesting also because it recalls "the strike itself and, more important, the 'God and Country' parade held here. . . ."[68]

CONCLUSION

The gatherings in 1912 and in 1962, not only the spectators but the sheer number of marchers in division after parade division of participants, are remarkable examples of the capacity of municipal and religious leaders in Lawrence to mobilize mass displays of civic allegiance. The parades showed their creativity in deploying a common vocabulary to serve diverse ends in different times to meet distinct challenges. There was simply no way that an anniversary solely dedicated to the repudiation of the IWW, the red flag, and a banner they were accused of sponsoring in 1912 would have attracted the attention of the 200,000 reported to have turned out and the 25,000 who marched representing businesses, churches, civic groups, politicians, the U.S. military, and aspiring politicians such as the future Senator Edward Kennedy.[69] But a parade that leveraged the events of a half century ago to meet the concerns of the present day certainly worked.

Mayor Buckley's office undertook a very ambitious effort on a very short timeline in 1962. The first planning meeting occurred only five months before the day of the parade. The success of the mobilization effort is undeniable but the schedule of the planning process suggests that the anniversary of the parade in 1912 was not long in the minds of many but maybe something of a last-minute effort, perhaps even the brain child of the historically minded secretary to the mayor, Peter Hewett. But in a letter written six days after the parade in response to Andover resident Beulah Dennison's letter (and an enclosed pamphlet by Protestant fundamentalist leader Carl McIntire), Hewett claimed complete accord with her letter and that of McIntire and went on to emphasize that:

> My duties in the preparation of plans for the "For God and Country" Parade which was so successful last Sunday was not a spur of the moment

---

[68] God & Country Parade 1962 Papers. Box 2. Folder 7. (Lawrence Public Library, Local History Room, Lawrence, MA.)

[69] George J. Gelineau, "200,000 Watch Lawrence's 'God and Country' Parade," *Lawrence Eagle-Tribune*, Sept. 24, 1962, 1.

participation as secretary to the Honorable John J. Buckley, Mayor Lawrence. For long years I have felt as a "voice crying in the wilderness" of apathy and indifference to the growing threat which seeks to engulf and submerge our God-given democratic way of life.[70]

Perhaps they were never more than courtesy letters, but it is not surprising that the likes of President John F. Kennedy and FBI director J. Edgar Hoover could not accept Mayor Buckley's last-minute invitations to join him at the official parade reviewing stand.[71] The *Lawrence Eagle-Tribune*, an enthusiastic supporter of the 1962 parade, did its part to help readers brush up on the main details (from its perspective) on the key events and personalities in 1912. Earning a goodly sum, one could suppose, from the sponsorship by the Greater Lawrence Chamber of Commerce of a "Tribute to the Patriots of 1912," this eight-page supplement featured short articles and pictures along with the advertisements of 37 local businesses offering commentary on the events of 1912. Citing "Americanism in action," standing up against "advocates of anarchy" and "creators of chaos," the lead article noted that "Truly, it can be said that one of the first bloodless battles against godless groups was fought and successfully won right in the heart of Downtown Lawrence."[72] Lawrence could take its place right alongside Lexington, Concord, and Bunker Hill.

In the face of the nuclear weapons mounted on intercontinental ballistic missiles, a billy club seems a bit quaint. But Joseph T. Tremblay wanted to participate too. He wrote to Mayor Buckley in response to a newspaper article seeking people who marched in 1912. As a parade participant, he begged off on marching given his 80-year-old legs. Perhaps he was a member of the state militia, given his point that "And more over I still have a club that the Archibald Wheel Co. turned out for use of, at that time, the State Militia (now Nat. Guard) probably the only one left."[73] Even as the meaning of God, Country, and the IWW evolved over time, unfortunately, so did the weapons. Tremblay hung on to his even as 50 years whisked by. Lawrence kept theirs too in 1962, namely, the capacity to continually reimagine their foe and to keep the spirit of God and Country alive and growing.

In 2012, the City of Lawrence did not organize any efforts to mark the anniversary of the parades in 1912 or 1962 despite the hopes of those who

---

[70] Peter A. Hewett to Miss Beulah Dennison, Sept. 28, 1962. God & Country Parade 1962 Papers. Box 1. Folder 6. (Lawrence Public Library, Local History Room, Lawrence, MA.)

[71] Mayor John J. Buckley to J. Edgar Hoover, Sept, 7, 1962. God & Country Parade 1962 Papers. Box 1. Folder 6. (Lawrence Public Library, Local History Room, Lawrence, MA.), Mayor John J. Buckley to The President, Sept. 18, 1962. Ibid.

[72] "History Was Made in Downtown Lawrence on Columbus Day 1912," Lawrence, Mass., *Eagle-Tribune* "For God and Country" Edition, Sept. 22, 1962, 17.

[73] Joseph T. Tremblay to Major John J. Buckley, Sept. 15, 1962. God & Country Parade 1962 Papers. Box 2. Folder 6. (Lawrence Public Library, Local History Room, Lawrence, MA.)

assembled the time capsule. Instead, the Lawrence Textile strike itself was central. On Labor Day, within sight of the Shattuck Flagpole and across from City Hall, the 1912 Strikers' Monument Committee, a group of volunteer citizens, formally gifted to Lawrence a new 50-foot Centennial Flag Pole and the 1912 Strikers' Monument. The monument, a 30,000-pound boulder and bronze relief, depicts the striking workers marching through the streets of Lawrence. In the very park where the major rallies took place for the strike, this memorial is the first permanent and public acknowledgment of events that many in Lawrence had once wished to forget.

ACKNOWLEDGMENTS

For identification of resources, research assistance, and orientation to Lawrence, this author wishes to thank Jim Beauschesne, Visitors Services Supervisor Lawrence Heritage State Park; Amita Kiley, Assistant to the Director, Lawrence History Center; Louise Sandberg, Archivist, Special Collections at the Lawrence Public Library; Jonas Stundzia, City of Lawrence Historical Commission; Jennifer Williams, Archivist, Lawrence History Center; and Susan Grabski, Executive Director, Lawrence History Center. A thank you to the Leonard and Claire Tow Faculty Travel Fellowship Fund that made this research possible.

Figure 1. Panoramic of the City of Lawrence, Massachusetts, 1910. View shows canal at left and the Merrimack River, the source of power for the mills first built in the city in the 1840s. There was over one mile of mills stretched along the river. Courtesy of the Lawrence History Center, Lawrence, Mass.

Figure 2. Union Franco Belge, 1912. Franco-Belgians had a cooperative store and meeting hall in place before the 1912 strike. They used existing contacts with area farmers to help feed thousands. The soup kitchen run by the cooperative opened on January 22 and fed 1,300 workers twice a day without regard for nationality. Courtesy of the Lawrence History Center.

Figure 3. For God and Country. On October 12, 1912, the parade proceeded down Common Street. Strike opponents organized the massive demonstration to try to drive the Industrial Workers of the World (IWW) out of the city. Led by Father O'Reilly, the parade received support from local business, churches, and mill owners. For decades to come local memory of 1912 was dominated by the God and Country version of events: that IWW members were outside agitators and "godless communists" who had duped the immigrant millworkers; and that participation in the strike was shameful. Courtesy of the Lawrence History Center.

Figure 4. For God and Country. In 1962, the 50th anniversary of the 1912 strike saw a reenactment of the God and Country Parade, with little mention of the actual strike. In a letter to the students and staff of the Lawrence Public Schools preparing for the reenactment, Lawrence Superintendent of Schools James F. Hennessey wrote: "Their (IWW) methods and thinking were forerunners of many tactics used by modern Communism. They inflamed our working people; there were riots, bloodshed, and even deaths in our streets. The news of this violence in Lawrence gave our city a black name all over the world." Courtesy of the Lawrence History Center.

Figure 5. Two children in a typical alleyway between tenements. By 1911, living conditions were challenging. The White Fund published *The Report of the Lawrence Survey* (1911) in which was stated: "These houses are so situated that an uncontrolled fire in them would sweep the whole center of the city." Photograph from *The Report of the Lawrence Survey*. Courtesy of the Lawrence History Center.

Figure 6. Bayonets and Workers. A tense standoff between the heavily armed militia and strikers in Lawrence. Courtesy of the Lawrence History Center.

STRIKE IMAGES / 117

Figure 7. The *Committee of Ten*, nine Lawrence textile workers and Joseph Ettor of the Industrial Workers of the World. The group had the responsibility for making certain its strike meetings were translated into numerous languages and for conducting negotiations directly with the American Woolen Company's president, William Wood. Ettor was in jail at the time the photograph was taken, charged with complicity in the death of a striker; he was acquitted in November 1912. Courtesy of the Lawrence History Center.

Figure 8. Women Marchers. Lawrence's district attorney lamented, "One policeman can handle 10 men, while it takes 10 policemen to handle one woman." A horrified boss described women activists as full of "lots of cunning and also lots of bad temper. They're everywhere, and it's getting worse all the time." Courtesy of the Lawrence History Center.

Figure 9. The Children's Exodus. A parade of strikers' children in New York City, mid-February 1912. As the strike wore on, hundreds of young children were sent from Lawrence to be cared for by supporters in other cities. Library of Congress.

STRIKE IMAGES / 119

Figure 10. Lewis Hine photograph, September 1911 of Lawrence mill workers. At the time of the 1912 strike, children as young as age 10 worked in the city's mills. Library of Congress.

Figure 11. Lewis Hine photograph, September 1911, of Eva Tanguay, 15 years old in a spinning room in the Ayer Mill. Leaves home at 6:00 A.M. every workday and returns at 6:30 P.M. Library of Congress.

120 / THE GREAT LAWRENCE TEXTILE STRIKE OF 1912

Figure 12. Final strike meeting on March 14th on the Lawrence Common. Before votes were taken ending the strike, proceedings were translated into several langages. Courtesy of the Lawrence History Center.

http://dx.doi.org/10.2190/BRSC7

CHAPTER 7

The "American Dream" and the 1912 Lawrence Textile Strike

Frank Fletcher

Between January and March 1912, the textile strike in Lawrence, Massachusetts (also known as the Bread and Roses Strike) captured the nation's attention. An estimated 25,000 mostly immigrant and unskilled workers struck for nine weeks against powerful economic, political, and social interests and won. The strike, which occurred during the unusually cold and snowy winter of 1912, was a reaction of people pushed to the extreme through the constant degradation of their living and working conditions.

At the time of the strike, journalist Mary K. O'Sullivan explained:

> . . . It must be understood that the Lawrence strike was not caused by the Industrial Workers of the World or by the reduction of the working week from fifty-six to fifty-four hours with the ensuing loss of pay. The reduction was only the last straw in a situation that the workers could not endure any longer. The many injustices of the section boss with his personal discrimination against men and women who refuse to submit to his standards helped to bring on a rebellion. The rise in cost of living during the last two years, including increased rents, had reduced the mill hands to an extremity where the loss of a few cents weekly in their wages became a calamity in hundreds of homes. At the turn of the year, then, the strike began spontaneously without recognized leadership.[1]

Underlying this worker upsurge was the convergence of three versions of the American Dream. Although societal and personal interpretations of the American

---

[1] Mary K. O'Sullivan, "The Labor War at Lawrence." *Survey*, April 6, 1912.

Dream have shifted over time, its essentials still encompass core political, economic, and social beliefs. Using the concept of the American Dream as a prism for analysis, one is able to better understand why these events occurred in this textile center 100 years ago.

While the basic tenet of the American Dream is a belief that individuals are capable of improving their lives through their own efforts; how that is best achieved varies. In January 1912, these three paths to the American Dream collided. The first path was the Puritan/Merchant, represented by Francis Lowell and Nathan Appleton who created the original business model used to organize the Lawrence mills. The second path was the Gilded Age American Dream, based on *The Gospel of Wealth*. This perspective influenced mill management at the time of the strike. The third perspective was the immigrant's path to the American Dream, a long search for opportunity, economic security, and dignity.

THE PURITAN/MERCHANT'S AMERICAN DREAM

Two Boston merchants, Francis Lowell and Nathan Appleton, developed what came to be known as the Waltham/Lowell manufacturing model. This business model was used from the time after the War of 1812 to manage the larger corporate textile mills throughout New England, including those built in Lawrence starting in the 1840s. It also became a common business model for most early manufacturing in America.

Direct descendants of the original Massachusetts settlers, these merchants-turned-manufacturers were grounded in the Puritan's sense of "piety."[2] Piety was the belief that enterprise should be operated for both spiritual and economic gain, while promoting the betterment of the larger society. Ken and Will Hooper explain that for Puritan society, the purpose of life was the creation of God's kingdom on earth, which included using mechanical skills, morality through subordinating the interest of the individual to the group, and marshaling material and human resources into a single purpose.[3]

Lowell and Appleton were in England, prior to the War of 1812 where they saw the negative effects of British industrialization, including pollution, corruption, crime, and the generally poor conditions of the working classes. The workers' suffering and the social upheaval that resulted from the rise of the factory system particularly appalled Appleton. He wanted an American manufacturing system capable of successfully competing with the British, but with none of the negative effects on the workers and society. Appleton was determined to protect the United States from exploitative forms of capitalism and, with the start of their first factory in Waltham, Massachusetts, Lowell and Appleton

---

[2] Lawrence G. Lavengood, "American Piety and the Piety of Profits," *Harvard Business Review*, 37, November-December (1959), 47-55.

[3] Ken Hooper and Will Hooper, *The Puritan Gift* (London: I. B. Tauris & Co. Ltd., 2007).

established an important idea "that corporations should have souls, and should exercise a paternal influence over the lives of their operatives."[4]

By 1820, their Waltham factory was a great success and a bigger operation was soon needed. Essential to the operation was waterpower. Appleton and Lowell found a suitable site on the Merrimack River, now the City of Lowell, Massachusetts. Francis Lowell died prior to the project fully getting underway, but Appleton and the original investors, later dubbed by historians as the *Boston Associates*, set out to build a model factory town with decent working and living conditions. Their corporate paternalism represented social and technological innovation.[5]

To meet their labor needs, they innovated by recruiting "Mill Girls" who were young women from rural areas of New England. These women worked for months or a few years before returning home—most often, to get married. Appleton and Lowell attempted to reconcile their new production methods with traditional social values. "The company provided boarding houses, schools, churches, stores, and banks; required the workers to attend church (of any denomination); and dismissed anyone whose behavior did not comply." More than any of his associates, Appleton was also concerned with the moral and social effects of manufacturing. He hoped that paternalistic management, combined with wages well above subsistence level, would prevent the development of a propertyless and degraded working class.[6]

THE WALTHAM/LOWELL SYSTEM'S ECONOMIC REALITIES

R. G. Voorhees[7] observes that as early as 1827, the mills began responding to competitive pressure by increasing productivity through speeding up production. An operator, who previously ran one loom, now ended up tending four looms. In 1834 and again in 1836, reducing women employees' pay cut fixed labor costs. The working conditions were difficult, and few women stayed for very long, even if they did not leave to get married. High turnover plagued their operations, but rather than raise wages the company's response was to recruit immigrants whenever vacancies occurred.

---

[4] Lynn Gordon Hughes, "Nathan Appleton," *Unitarian Universalist Dictionary of Biography*, Web. March 18, 2013. http://www25-temp.uua.org/uuhs/duub/articles/nathanappleton.html>.

[5] Daniel Walker Howe, *The Political Culture of the American Whigs* (Chicago: University of Chicago, 1984), 103.

[6] Hughes, "Nathan Appleton," *Dictionary of the Unitarian Universalist Dictionary of Biography*.

[7] R. G. Voorhees, "Finance in History: Labor Days the Lowell Mills offer a lesson in the perils of focusing on labor costs at the expense of technology." CFO.com, August 30, 2007. http://www.cfo.com (accessed October 10, 2010).

In 1850, General C.T. James, a prominent engineer and specialist in the construction of textile factories, reported that since 1835 textile workers produced more, but they derived no gains from it, as their wages were not enhanced. In the decade between 1840-1850, output per worker in Lowell had increased 30 percent. An economist studying this factor a century later found that daily wages of cotton textile workers during 1832-1850 had risen by only one cent.[8]

The original group of investors capitalized the Lowell project at previously unheard of sums of money. Mills were capitalized at $600,000 in 1821 (almost $10 million today); the figure had doubled in just two years. As the number of stockholders increased through inheritance and public sales, newer investors were far less concerned about the founders' paternalistic vision.[9] Unwilling to forgo dividends, the new investors wanted an annual payout regardless of the financial health of the enterprises.[10]

Ultimately, dividends consumed every dollar of earnings leaving little cash on hand for future capital needs.[11] This situation created a dichotomy between capital required for reinvesting in the firms and the desire to avoid long-term debt. It also forced short-term borrowing or withdrawals from working capital, which constrained further growth. In turn: "up to the 1830s the mills at Lowell had been in the forefront of development in the American textile industry; after that date, the pace of innovation slowed considerably."[12]

By 1850, mill workers in Lowell made less money and worked longer hours than when the mills first opened. In less than 30 years, by the constant search for more dividends, the textile mills became uncaring behemoths. Their factories were soulless organizations. Their managers and stockholders forgot that they were morally responsible for the poor wages of those who labored in their mills and thus were the source of their wealth.

LAWRENCE: THE LAST OF THE BOSTON ASSOCIATES' PROJECTS

By the mid 19th century, corporation-style textile mills had assumed a set of fixed characteristics and relatively uniform policies. There were 340 establishments and 900,000 spindles in New England; of them, the Boston Associates operated 35 mills with 750,000 spindles, about three-fourths of the region's

---

[8] Meyer Weinberg, in *A Short History of American Capitalism* (New History Press, 2003), 68.

[9] "Capital and the Agents House," Lowell National Historical Park, http://www.nps.gov/lowe/planyourvisit/upload/Agents_05.pdf (accessed on January 15, 2012.)

[10] Betty Farrell, *Elite Families: Class and Power in Nineteenth-Century Boston* (Albany: State University of New York Press, 1993).

[11] Robert F. Dalzell, Jr., *Enterprising Elite: The Boston Associates and the World They Made* (Cambridge: Harvard University Press, 1987).

[12] Ibid. 55.

spindles.[13] The Boston Associates had operations in Manchester, Nashua, and Dover, New Hampshire, Chicopee and Holyoke, Massachusetts, and Saco, Maine, in addition to their Lowell operations. The final and most ambitious of the Boston Associates' planned textile cities was 11 miles downriver from Lowell, in what became the City of Lawrence (see Figure 1, p. 113).

Although Nathan Appleton, who was then 66 years old, played a key role in financing the venture, Abbot Lawrence was the prime mover behind it.[14] For the 14 original investors, who provided $1 million in capital, this venture was an opportunity to use the Waltham/Lowell formula for success.[15] However, in the 20 or so years since the establishment of Lowell, many of the favorable conditions that had allowed those investors to gain sizable profits from previous enterprises of the Boston Associates had changed.

The market for mass-produced coarse cloth products had become saturated. Acquiring ready capital got harder as more attractive alternatives to investing in textiles appeared. Frances Gregory, in a biography of Nathan Appleton, explained that the Lawrence venture had a rocky history. After paying dividends in the early years, between 1856 and 1860 none were awarded to stockholders. Stock consistently sold below par, many mills became insolvent, and an associated machine shop was a financial failure.[16]

However, Lawrence started an economic turnaround at the beginning of the Civil War. While the Civil War did cause some dislocation by losing access to cotton supplies from the South, with war came new contracts from the U.S. government. With a stockpiled supply of cotton and the shifting of production from cotton to woolens or worsteds, recovery got underway. New factories were constructed, population growth began again, and the growth continued through the end of the century.[17]

THE BOSTON ASSOCIATES' FINANCIAL LEGACY

By the time of Nathan Appleton's death in 1861, the Boston Associates oversaw an extensive network of financial interests. They owned and operated textile mills across New England and controlled one-fifth of the industry's total U.S. capacity. Seventeen Boston Associate directors served on various Boston bank

---

[13] Saul Barkin, "Management and Ownership in the New England Cotton Textile Industry," *Journal of Economic Issues*, XV. no. 2 (1981), 463-475.

[14] Frances W. Gregory, *Nathan Appleton Merchant and Entrepreneur 1779-1861* (Charlottesville: University Press of Virginia, 1975).

[15] D. E. Hay, "The New City on the Merrimack: The Essex Company and Its Role In the Creation of Lawrence, Massachusetts" (PhD diss., University of Delaware, 1986).

[16] Frances W. Gregory, *Nathan Appleton Merchant and Entrepreneur 1779-1861* (Charlottesville: University of Virginia Press, 1975).

[17] Nathan Beaudoin, "Altering the immigrant city: the rise, fall, and emergence of the City of Lawrence, Massachusetts 1845–1972." (Thesis (M.A. Tufts University, 2007).

boards representing 40 percent of that city's banking capital. Likewise, they had substantial influence on the railroads and insurance companies in the state.[18] Their efforts provided the wealth for many leading Boston Brahmin families.

This economic concentration, as Dexter E. Arnold points out, created a continued "community of interest" well into the 20th century. A large number of corporations made up the textile industry with none strong enough to dominate, although the management in control of these New England mill towns "create[d] a favorable political environment, stabilize [d] and regulate [d] the price of the cloth as well as the market, and coordinate [d] regional wage adjustments."[19] Industry coordination came about because of organizations like the National Association of Wool Manufacturers, the Cotton Claims Bureau, and the Arkwright Club in Boston (whose membership was limited to chief executives of New England mills). Almost all directors and treasurers of the Boston Associates' operations lived in Boston, attended Harvard, and socialized in clubs reserved for the elite of the city.

THE AMERICAN DREAM AND THE GOSPEL OF WEALTH

Following the Civil War, American businesses grew significantly through an unparalleled increase in factory production and mechanization. Business organizations expanded in size and scale. At the beginning of the 20th century, the major sectors of the economy were dominated by a small number of large corporations. This consolidation came about as businesses worked to control competition. Also, transportation improvements increased the distribution to markets and financial institutions increased the availability of capital.

Before the Civil War, most industrial capital was self-generated. After the Civil War, personal savings increased and new methods and institutions were created to make those funds available to business borrowers. At the end of the 1800s and early into the 1900s, economies of scale drove business concentration leading to large combinations requiring vast amounts of capital and human resources.[20] By the 1890s, overproduction, competition, and poor management had all taken a toll on the New England textile industry.

The first and largest consolidation in the wool-manufacturing industry was the American Woolen Company (AWC), and it was a by-product of the depression in the middle 1890s. The depression was peculiarly severe for wool manufacturers because of the Wilson-Gorman Tariff of 1894. For the first time, in

---

[18] Ibid.

[19] Dexter E. Arnold, "A Row of Bricks: Worker Activism in the Merrimack Valley Textile Industry" (University of Wisconsin Madison, 1985), 47.

[20] Stanley Buder, *Capitalizing on Change* (Chapel Hill: University of North Carolina Press, 2009).

more than 30 years, the importation of wool was duty free, and as a result, the "incidental" protection that manufacturers had been receiving from the so-called compensatory duties was eliminated. This facilitated the rise of worsted manufacturing.

Frederick Ayer, a successful Lowell businessman, purchased the Washington Mills in Lawrence and hired his future son-in-law, William M. Wood to run it. Wood had already successfully turned around a bankrupt mill in Fall River. With Ayer's financial backing, Wood brought together various underperforming mills with the aim of reducing competition and increasing prices. He convinced investors to permit profits to be reinvested into new plants and machinery.[21] In 1905, the AWC built the largest mill in the world, the Wood Mill in Lawrence. It "symbolized the era's commitment to maximized production, intense competition, and corporate consolidation."[22]

AWC was initially capitalized completely on stocks with the first issue being $25 million worth of preferred stock and $40 million of common stock. While overall, AWC was far from a monopoly, it did specialize in product lines that gave them quasi-monopolies in some areas. Arthur H. Cole, in a study of the AWC, believed that the consolidation was "noteworthy" because of its "growth in size, improvement in methods of operations, influence on the cloth market, labor policy, and its financial progress."[23]

In sheer numbers, the consolidation of the initial 26 mills gave them the production capacity that was 85 percent of the spindles in the United States and 25 percent of the looms. In addition to adding new machinery, equipment could be easily moved between mills and consolidated operations doubled their manufacturing capability. As the "big company" in the industry, they were able, according to Arthur Cole, to set the "tone and price levels" direction for the industry.

Economic power of this kind was facilitated by a supportive national culture. Horatio Alger, Andrew Carnegie, and others would transmit a mix of economic, intellectual, and religious beliefs reinforcing this newer concept of the American Dream. Carnegie, a financial giant of this era (or as some considered him, one of the "Robber Barons"), published his essay entitled *The Gospel of Wealth* in 1889. In his publication, he argued that the accumulation of wealth was beneficial to society and the government should take no action to impede it.

Alger, a Harvard graduate and the son of a Unitarian minister, published more than 100 short novels depicting rags-to-riches stories of common men rising to positions of wealth and prominence. Both William Whitman, head of the Arlington Mills (who came from Nova Scotia and worked his way up from a

---

[21] Sam Warner Jr., *Province of Reason* (London: Belknap Press, 1984).

[22] Ardis Cameron, Radicals of the Worst Sort: Laboring Women in Lawrence, Massachusetts, 1860–1912 (University of Illinois Press, 1995), 74.

[23] Arthur H. Cole, "A Neglected Chapter in the History of Combinations: The American Wool Manufacture." *The Quarterly Journal of Economics*, Vol. 37. no. 3, 1923, 436-475.

clerk's position), and William Wood, head of the AWC at the time of the strike (and son of poor Portuguese immigrants), were self-made industrial giants who made Horatio Alger's tales plausible.

Ray Baker contends that both Whitman and Wood misused their economic power to engage in a race to build or acquire mills and equipment that created excess capacity and production. This newly acquired economic power was created through excessive profits resulting from the protective tariffs and cheap labor. This race for new mills or equipment resulted in frequent shutdowns at great cost to the workers since "such exigency of intermittent employment as well as for sickness or injury, the mill owner takes not the slightest responsibility."[24]

LAWRENCE REALITIES AND THE IMMIGRANT'S AMERICAN DREAM

According to historian Donald B. Cole, despite poverty, declining wages, lost jobs, and anti-immigrant feelings, immigrants in Lawrence were able to find some security in their family, their ethnic groups, and in their Americanism. He contends, that at the "end of the 19th century, Lawrence was an "ardently American city." One in which both native and immigrant shared a common faith in the United States."[25] In other words, for many workers in Lawrence at the start of the 20th century, a version of the American Dream remained a possibility. Coming to the U.S. offered an opportunity for a better life than what existed in "the Old Country," especially for the children.[26] For this chance, they put up with hardships and uncertainty. Cole offers that these first generation immigrants believed that if they were not as successful as they had first hoped, in time and with the arrival of newer immigrants, their position would improve; they would move up. If not them, then certainly their children would succeed economically and socially.[27]

At the time of the strike in 1912, Lawrence led all other U.S. textile centers in the production of woolen and worsted products and almost half of the city's population (over age 14) worked in the mills. The majority of the work force was unskilled and first-generation immigrants, recruited with the promise of an expanding textile industry. Immigrants had completely replaced the original work force of young women from rural New England.

Both management and conservative labor unions felt that immigrant workers were impossible to organize. In Lawrence, the majority of the workers were young

---

[24] Ray Baker, "The Revolutionary Strike." *The American Magazine,* May 1912, 27.

[25] Donald B. Cole, *Immigrant City: Lawrence, Massachusetts, 1845-1921* (Chapel Hill: The University of North Carolina Press, 1993), 154.

[26] Vincent N. Parrillo, "The Immigrant Family: Securing the American Dream." *Journal of Comparative Family Studies.* XXII. no. 2 (1991): 131-145.

[27] Cole, *Immigrant City.*

female immigrants, kept apart by a dozen languages. Also, as new machinery was utilized, jobs were subdivided into more limited and repetitive movements, making mill workers easily replaceable.

In 1917 Melvin T. Copland, characterized union activity in the woolen industry as happening at the local level and said that a "strong union spirit, therefore, has not been manifested among the cotton mill employees, except in rare instances."[28] He goes on to explain, even when there was widespread dissatisfaction and a strike did happen, workers, including women and children, would join in, but once it was settled—union membership usually didn't grow. Also, strikes generally failed.

In 1912, there were three unions in Lawrence, two of which were local and the third, the mule spinners union was affiliated with the national United Textile Workers of America (UTWA). In 1898, the national UTWA union was affiliated with the American Federation of Labor (AFL), a federation of semi-independent craft associations.[29] Samuel Gompers headed the AFL, and it was made up of mostly skilled workers. Its objectives were limited and focused on achieving higher wages and shorter work days for its members—referred to as "bread and butter" issues.[30]

Gilded Age industrialists like AWC's Ayer and Wood operated without much government interference. Wood, like many industrial leaders, believed unions were not needed. He probably shared in the beliefs of George F. Baer, president of the Reading Railway Company, that labor's best interest would not be served by the union agitators but by "the Christian men whom God, in his infinite wisdom, had given control of property interests. . . ."[31]

In 1910, the population in Lawrence rose to approximately 86,000 from 63,000 a decade earlier. By 1912, the transformation of Lawrence into an immigrant city was complete. Of all the city's inhabitants, 74,000 or 86 percent were born abroad or had foreign-born parents. Despite Nathan Appleton's earlier vision of a model factory and town with good working and living conditions, and corporations being socially responsible, Lawrence was reminiscent of the worst features of 18th-century industrial England. Historian Ardis Cameron (1993) draws a grim picture of conditions in January 1912:

> . . . readers of Charles Dickens would have found Lawrence's dull streets and cluttered alleys, its back canals and purple ill-smelling river, its vast piles of soot covered brick buildings, its flimsy, damp, privies whose waste

---

[28] Melvin T. Copland, *The Cotton Manufacturing Industry of the United States* (Cambridge: Harvard University Press, 1917), 125.

[29] Cole, *Immigrant City*.

[30] Julie Greene, *Pure and Simple Politics: The American Federation of Labor and Political Activism, 1881–1917* (New York: Cambridge University Press, 1998).

[31] Edward G. Roddy, *Mansions, and Mergers: The Life of William M. Wood* (North Andover, MA: Merrimack Valley Textile Museum, 1982), 72.

oozed down open sewers and meandered through the city's shaded backyards a familiar landscape.[32]

"SHORT PAY, ALL OUT": DASHED EXPECTATIONS AND THE 1912 STRIKE

The Progressive Movement had emerged in the 1890s and 1900s in reaction to the economic inequities during the Gilded Age and the creation of the industrial economy. It was made up of an eclectic mix of muckraking journalists, urban reformers, socialists, and union activists who emerged to oppose the excesses of big business and to seek redress for many economic and social inequities. Their success with the Massachusetts legislature in shortening the number of hours women and children could work was the fuse that would set off the strike. When Progressive forces in Massachusetts were successful in shortening the work day prior to 1912, mill owners had accepted the changing regulations without cutting piece work rates, but they did not do so this time and further they did not inform the workers that their pay would be reduced accordingly.[33]

On Thursday, January 11th, the strike erupted when paychecks were opened, and there were shouts of "Short pay! All out!" Polish women in the Everett Mills were the first to shut down their looms. Bruce Watson in *Bread & Roses* says the strike began "like a spark of electricity."[34] This spontaneous labor action provided the mass of Lawrence workers their first opportunity to address their grievances. Prior to January 1912, no labor organization had succeeded in unifying the multiple nationalities working in the Lawrence mills. According to John McPherson, "The strike might have collapsed in a few days from lack of support and effective leadership, had Joseph Ettor . . ." of the International Workers of the World (IWW) not arrived as the strike began to help organize it.[35]

The IWW was a syndicalist labor organization. Syndicalism called for the overthrow of the wage system and for workers to come together into "one big union," creating a new industrial commonwealth. Their one big union would be divided into a series of departments corresponding to different industries.[36] They were the first U.S. labor organization to try to recruit both unskilled and

---

[32] Cameron, *Radicals of the Worst Sort,* 97.

[33] Mary Blewett, "Textile Workers in American Northeast and South: Shifting Landscapes of Class, Culture, Race, and Protest." International Institute of Social History. http://social history.org/en/research (accessed November 12, 2011).

[34] Bruce Watson, *Bread & Roses: Mills, Migrants, and the Struggle for the American Dream* (New York: Viking, 2005).

[35] John B. McPherson, *The Lawrence Strike of 1912* (Boston: The Rockwell and Churchill Press, 1912).

[36] Mel van Elteren, "Worker's Control and the Struggles Against 'Wage Slavery' in the Gilded Age and After," *The Journal of American Culture*, 26, no. 2, 2003, 188-203.

immigrant workers. Led by William "Big Bill" Haywood, the IWW believed that general strikes, boycotts, and even sabotage were essential to achieve their objectives. The IWW often appealed to social groups caught up in the rapid transition from pre-industrial to industrial society, largely first-generation immigrants from either southern or eastern Europe. Many workers, especially from southern Italy, had already developed transnational syndicalist politics.

Propaganda against the strike by government, industrial, and religious leaders had blamed outside agitators for the trouble. The city's establishment leadership failed to understand or refused to acknowledge that strikers now rejected their leadership, blaming them for the economic exploitation they suffered.[37] The city's desperate workers accepted the IWW's leadership, worked through their ethnic differences, and gained better wages and living conditions.

While it was a daunting task, a central strike committee structure was developed that overcame the strikers' ethnic isolation with representation from the 24 ethnic groups that spoke 22 different languages. O'Sullivan reported the strike committee "developed leadership among the workers of the most surprising caliber and personality." The committee established a relief system that assured no one starved during the strike.[38] According to labor historian Melvyn Dubofsky, a chronicler of the history of the IWW, soup kitchens were set up for single men and food or "store orders" were provided for families.[39] Funds for this effort came in from around the country, including support from regular trade unions, industrial unions, socialistic organizations, and private sources. Overall, the system worked "remarkably efficiently." [40]

This strike was also the first major labor protest where women workers provided significant leadership. Women led daily picket lines and effectively used their community-based networks to build support for the work stoppage.[41] The networks also helped different ethnic groups work through differences and built trust and kept the mills from operating. Cameron says observers blamed the strikers' militancy not on the IWW, but "on unruly and undisciplined female workers."[42] Reports had the district attorney saying that while one police officer could handle 10 men it took 10 officers to handle one woman.

Mill owners had successfully influenced much of the media coverage of the early parts of the strike and pressured the governor, the legislature, and the other city officials to crack down on the strikers. Robert Biggert, who has studied the

[37] Melvyn Dubofsky, "The Origins of Western Working Class Radicalism, 1890–1905," *Labor History*, 7, no. 2, 1966, 131.
[38] Mary K. O'Sullivan, "The Labor War at Lawrence." *Survey*, April 6, 1912.
[39] Dubofsky, "The Origins of Western Working Class Radicalism," 131.
[40] Ibid.
[41] Ardis Cameron, "Bread and roses revisited: Women's culture and working-class activism in the Lawrence strike of 1912." *Women, Work, and Protest; A Century of Women's Labor History*, ed. Ruth Milkman (Boston, 1985) (1985): 42-61.
[42] Ibid., 44.

tactics employed by the IWW in this and other strikes, concludes that repression by the city and state government officials and others helped to defeat the mill owners' cause. He cites four specific episodes. First was an attempt to portray strikers as anarchists that backfired. The owners of the AWC hired a local undertaker to plant dynamite in several locations. The IWW obtained evidence that newspaper articles about the dynamite being found had been printed before the dynamite was actually "discovered."[43]

The second was the death of John Ramey, an 18-year-old worker, who died from bayonet wounds to his back, and the third was the death of Annie LoPizzo, a bystander at a strike parade, which resulted in the arrest of the first strike organizers, Ettor and Arturo Giovannitti and the quick succession of strike leadership by Haywood and Elizabeth Gurley Flynn and the negative publicity generated by the event itself reflecting badly on the authorities.[44]

The fourth was an incident involving the children of the strikers. Children of the strikers were sent to live with sympathetic families in other cities so that the strikers would not be forced back into the factories because of hungry children, a tactic used successfully in Europe. On February 24, a group of mothers accompanied their children to the railroad station. Police brutally clubbed women and children alike and then threw them into patrol wagons.[45]

The ugly scene of February 24 was reported across the nation. The reports caused outrage and triggered an emotional Congressional investigation. Congressman Victor Berger, a Wisconsin Socialist, prevailed upon the House Committee on Rules for a hearing on mill conditions, which was scheduled to start on March 2. On March 1, after a day-long meeting with local and state officials, AWC's Wood agreed to a five percent raise for all workers. He did so because of pressure from other mill owners, the oncoming peak season, and fear of negative publicity coming out of the Congressional hearing, which might eliminate their tariff protections. The strike committee refused. In mid-March, after nine weeks, an agreement was finally reached between the workers and owners and the strike ended.

CONCLUSION

The 1912 labor action in Lawrence was a new kind of strike. It was the first time such large numbers of unskilled and unorganized foreign-born workers had successfully come together to obtain their demands. This historical strike was the most successful strike to take place in the U.S. textile industry. Workers

---

[43] Robert Biggert, "Why Are Strikes Successful? An Event Structure Analysis of the IWW's Bread and Roses Strike" (paper presented at the annual meeting of American Sociological Association, San Francisco, CA. 2004).
[44] Ibid.
[45] Ibid.

could no longer endure their conditions, and the strike began spontaneously and without recognized leadership.[46] While the IWW stepped in and provided able leadership for the strike, they failed to consolidate any organizing gains after helping to win it. Also, the vast majority of workers did not ascribe to the IWW's philosophy of revolutionary syndicalism and were not seeking to abolish the capitalist system, or to develop a common working class consciousness. In fact, this social upheaval was not a rejection of the American Dream by the workers, but a desire to be included in it.

The economic, political, and social leadership had failed the workers. They were acting on the belief that the accumulation of wealth was beneficial to society, and the men of wealth to whom God had given control served the best interests of society. Appleton's vision of a paternalistic management that paid good wages to prevent the development of a property-less underclass had long been abandoned. The textile firms in Lawrence were "soulless organizations."

By 1912, textile managers viewed labor as a mere commodity to be acquired at the lowest possible price. They believed their responsibility was to maximize stockholders' returns. In this case, as Baker points out, the stockholders for the most part were the Boston aristocracy, whose "wealth was based upon the profits of the mills of New England." Baker, while acknowledging this aristocracy's good works, including the education of black children in the south and missions to Hawaii, concludes: " . . . about conditions in the dark alleys of Lawrence, where their own money comes from—apparently they know very little, nor do they want to know."[47] The drive for dividends had clearly overtaken any sense of piety and efforts to prevent exploitative capitalism.

---

[46] Mary K. O'Sullivan, "The Labor War at Lawrence." *Survey*, April 6, 1912.
[47] Ray Baker, "The Revolutionary Strike." *The American Magazine,* May 1912, 27.

CHAPTER 8

Voices of Labor Militancy in Lawrence, 1912–1931

Ethan Snow

The 1912 Bread and Roses Strike took place in Lawrence, Massachusetts. Strikes of similar scale and duration occurred there in 1919 and 1931. These strikes, despite their sensational stories, are mostly forgotten. To bring these strikes to the fore, the oral histories of three individuals involved in the 1912, 1919, and 1931 strikes are examined to gain a richer understanding of the city's ongoing labor struggles and its legacy of labor militancy.

VOICES OF LABOR MILITANCY

Despite the blissful ignorance of mill owners and most city officials, all was not well in Lawrence in 1912. The city, boiling over with discontent brought on by squalid living conditions and oppressive workplace conditions, was soon caught up in one of the largest immigrant-led work stoppages in U.S. history. The strike, prompted in part by a state law that reduced the legal work week for women and children from 56 to 54 hours and resulted in a wage cut, affected nearly the entire city of 84,000. The humming industrial utopia of founder Abbott Lawrence's dreams became a city under the national spotlight as the strike's events, scandalous and sensational, were reported by scores of newspapers and magazines.

For the first time in the state's history, the militia was called upon to police civil unrest. Two strikers were killed in two days, one by the bayonet of a militiaman and one in a melee between strikers and police. The latter death set in motion a dramatic trial in which two popular strike leaders and a third man were acquitted of murder. Shortly after the strike deaths, dynamite was found at three popular strike meeting places. It was later revealed that men linked with mill owners had planted the dynamite to discredit the strike. Moving picket lines were used as a strike tactic for the first time in the United States.[1] Parents sent their children to sympathetic families in New York, New Hampshire, Vermont and other states to help lighten their burden and to focus national attention on the conditions in Lawrence. Strikers gained a great deal of public sympathy when the police arrested, beat, and jailed mothers and their children when they attempted to leave on Philadelphia-bound trains. The incident prompted an investigation by the U.S. Congress, which saw 13 Lawrence children testify, including one young girl who was scalped when her hair got caught in a loom. Eventually mill owners were forced by national publicity to negotiate with the strikers. Representing 50 nationalities and speaking 27 different languages, the strikers won their demands, marking a decisive victory for the fledgling U.S. labor movement.[2]

Just seven years later, another strike of similar scale and duration rocked Lawrence. 1919 was a big year for radical labor militancy across the country. In Massachusetts, there was a massive Boston police strike, a successful telephone workers' strike, a strike involving more than 5,000 New England fishermen looking for improved job security and wages, and a Boston trolley car operators' strike.[3] Added to the numerous strikes that swept the nation were riots, bombings, and direct confrontations with capital from a confident labor movement bolstered by the fiery passion of Eugene Debs, the recent success of the Russian Bolshevik revolution, and the period of relative labor power during World War I.

The textile industry experienced turbulence after the armistice ending the war led to the U.S. government's cancellation of its orders for textiles. The federal contracts provided steady work and increased wages for many in the industry. Upon the disappearance of these contracts, workers' wages were slashed and jobs were lost. In line with a national movement for the eight-hour day, Lawrence workers soon demanded a shortened work week from 54 hours to 48 hours with no reduction in pay to bolster employment. The eight-hour movement in Lawrence was organized by the traditionally conservative and skilled American Federation of Labor-affiliated United Textile Workers and the Central Labor Union "vowing to simply leave their looms after eight hours of work" ("Vote for 8-Hour Workday," *New York Times*, January 26, 1919). When the mill owners agreed to the eight-hour day but also announced a parallel cut in pay, the AFL's "old immigrant" workers celebrated a victory while Lawrence's 30,000-plus unskilled

---

[1] Chitty, A. B. and Priscilla Murolo. *From the Folks Who Brought You the Weekend: A Short Illustrated History of Labor in the United States*. New York: The New Press, 2001.

[2] Watson, Bruce. *Bread & Roses: Mills, Migrants, and the Struggle for the American Dream*. New York: Penguin Books, 2005.

[3] Russell, Francis. *A City in Terror: Calvin Coolidge and the 1919 Boston Police Strike*. Boston: Beacon Press, 1975.

and unorganized "new immigrant" workers struck realizing that the cut in pay meant a loss of nearly 11 percent of their wages. They were led by a General Strike Committee consisting of representatives from each of Lawrence's ethnic groups and headed by three radical Protestant ministers. While the decision to strike drew sympathy from workers in many textile cities across the region and country, none elsewhere actually went so far as to strike.[4] Lawrence was again the bellwether for American labor militancy.

For the second time in city history, officials could not handle the striking workers and called in supplemental police from neighboring communities. Unlike the 1912 strike, police regularly intimidated and beat strikers and refused to issue permits for public assemblies. Workers were forced to hold strike meetings hemmed in by the authorities on a cramped privately owned lot described as a "dump heap."[5] Police beat and arrested strikers on trumped-up charges, which often were supported by the district judge. Two strike leaders were kidnapped by masked men, beaten, had their lives threatened should they return to Lawrence, and dumped in remote areas of Andover. The Lawrence authorities brutally repressed the strike to avoid a repeat of 1912.

Despite the violent oppression of the authorities, sympathetic organizations and prominent radicals throughout the region generously supported the strike. With an influx of relief funds, strikers were able to set up cooperatives, soup kitchens, a strikers' "red cross," and even a strikers' guard to police their own. Strikers used many tactics that harkened back to 1912, including the evacuation of striking children to sympathetic families.[6] (Goldberg, 1989). With such a high level of organization and massive relief efforts, the strikers were able to outlast the mills. Community pressure and mounting orders for the spring season's new textiles finally brought mill owners to the bargaining table. After 15 brutal weeks, Lawrence's mills agreed to a 15 percent wage increase and the 48-hour work week ("Three Months of Labor Turmoil in Lawrence, Mass," *New York Times*, May 25, 1919). Lawrence workers had seemingly won again.

The late 1920s brought economic panic and depression to the United States. By this time, no longer geographically tied down by the need for water power, the textile industry was moving south, where cheap, unorganized labor was plentiful. Lawrence's workers felt the full impact of this production shift. In response, the radical National Textile Workers Union (N.T.W.), which opposed

---

[4] Arnold, Dexter, *"A Row of Bricks: Worker Activism in the Merrimack Valley Textile Industry, 1912-1922 (Massachusetts, New Hampshire)."* Dissertation, University of Wisconsin-Madison. Ann Arbor: Proquest/UMI, 1985. (Publication No. 8501566).

[5] Federal Council of the Churches of Christ in America. "Report on the Strike in the Textile Mills of Lawrence, Massachusetts: February 3–June 4, 1919." New York: Federal Council of Churches, 1920.

[6] Goldberg, David, *A Tale of Three Cities: Labor Organization and Protest in Paterson, Passaic, and Lawrence, 1916-1921.* Piscataway: Rutgers University Press, 1989.

the mills' sudden and widespread use of efficiency experts and a "stretch out" system where two men worked nine machines, organized a brief strike in February. It ended with no demands met and the N.T.W. significantly weakened by raids from authorities.

A second 1931 strike began on October 4 in response to the announcement that mill wages would be slashed by 10 percent effective October 13. At the time, workers were in three separate unions: the weakened Communist Party-affiliated National Textile Workers Union, its less radical splinter the American Textile Workers Union, and the American Federation of Labor-affiliated United Textile Workers. As October 13 approached, it became clear that mill owners would stand firm for the wage reduction; spontaneous walk-outs occurred at the Wood and Ayer mills. Eventually, more than 23,000 workers from 11 different mills walked off the job[7] and the three unions moved to organize the spontaneous walk-out.

The UTW and ATW secured permits to hold joint meetings on the common. The more radical NTW neglected the permit process and held a large gathering where a police confrontation led to their leader, Edith Berkman, being arrested. Lawrence once more brought in auxiliary police from neighboring towns to deal with escalating striker-police confrontations. Arrests were made and many strikers, held on immigration charges, were threatened with deportation. With no clear strike leaders due to fears of deportation and factional fighting between the unions, mill owners began moving machinery out of certain Lawrence mills. For the first time, they openly threatened to move out of Lawrence ("Unions to Retaliate if Work Shipped Out," *Boston Globe*, Oct. 28, 1931). A Lawrence citizen's committee attempted to end the strike by conferring with Massachusetts Governor John Ely. Ely's eventual visit to Lawrence and address before thousands of striking workers convinced many to return to work in the hopes that a raise in pay would follow; it never did.[8] After six weeks, and in the face of double digit unemployment across the Merrimack Valley, the strikers' resolve was broken ("11,500 Resume Work in Lawrence Mills," *New York Times,* Nov. 10, 1931). Workers began slowly funneling back into the mills that would take them. Many jobs were lost and some mills never opened again. A small contingent of radical hold-outs remained on the picket lines for several weeks until their numbers dwindled to nothing.

Radicals, communists, and Bolsheviks were forever blamed for the removal of the textile industry from Lawrence. Strikes after 1931 occurred though they were extremely small and none attempted to bring back the "one big union" tactics of the 1912–1931 strike period. It wasn't until 1937 that a strong union structure was created in the mills where mechanisms for disputes were resolved through labor-management arbitration and grievance procedures.

---

[7]Blakely, Sam. "The Lawrence Strike," *Labor Age*. Vol. 20, no. 12. (December 1931).
[8]Ibid., 7.

CONCLUSION

To many, the 1912 strike is known as the "Bread and Roses" strike, a romantic descriptive which perfectly encapsulates the aims of the brave immigrant strikers. Its events are immortalized in song, poetry, annual festivals, and monuments. It is analyzed and romanticized throughout scholarly works and popular memory as a phenomenal singular moment in history, a remarkable early victory for the American labor movement. Though to others, the "Bread and Roses" strike is much more. "Bread and Roses" describes an innovative tradition in labor militancy merely born in 1912. The traditions of "one big unionism," strength through ethnic diversity, and the important role of women and children were all pioneered in 1912 and used, built upon, and popularized by Lawrencians far beyond 1912. In order for it to be recognized, we must take the meaning of "Bread and Roses" beyond the books, poems, and songs and listen to the actual words of those who lived through this period. The 1912 strike can then be recognized as a more meaningful part of a larger history, a slow, steady march, not simply a singular event. By insisting that "Bread and Roses" be rooted in the stories and lives of the real people who struggled during this period of Lawrence's history, we can better understand the strike and its significance today. Uncovering the words and lives of ordinary people undoubtedly reveals richer stories about this remarkable time and helps us to establish a greater understanding of the true legacy of the Lawrence strikes and their importance to the city. Lawrence and its people deserve no less.

ORAL HISTORIES

The following are excerpts taken from oral histories of three people involved in one or more of the three strikes. The oral histories were conducted in the late 1980s as part of a University of Massachusetts Lowell history project that recorded the stories of Massachusetts factory workers. They provide an invaluable glimpse of life during this time period. Footnotes are provided to give chronological and contextual clarification. The original transcripts are housed at the Lawrence History Center.

1912

Julia Dublin Garbelnick *was born in London, England, in 1899, part of a family of Lithuanian Jews on their way to America. Her father was a well-known tailor who owned his own shop in Lawrence. Julia was starting her first year of high school in 1912 and thus was not directly involved in the strike's activities. Her oral history is a great example of how the strike affected many more than the 20,000 to 25,000 textile workers employed in the mills. Nonetheless, the success of* *the strike and its international importance became a point of pride for Julia, a proud Lawrencian, even after she moved out of the city. During the resurgence of interest in the strike, Julia was at the forefront telling her story to any who would listen. She was vehemently opposed to calling it the "Bread and Roses" Strike. She was a popular pianist during the silent film era and later worked in a doctor's office as a receptionist. She also was very involved in the area's Jewish community. She passed away in 1997 at the age of 97.*

(J signifies Julia Dublin Garbelnick and YE signifies the interviewer, Yilderay Erdener)

J: Well I was already . . . in the eighth grade when this happened. So I was, I was 13 years old. But I was always interested in what went on in the country, and what went on in the world. And I used to read a lot and I used to like to listen. And uh, so when this came up . . . I happened to be going to the synagogue and they were there for a rally. And I got interested. I was spellbound. I mean I was; I never realized what was going on. Oh yes, I knew they had the strike then. My aunts probably weren't working then because the whole city was striking. And so I used to attend those meetings. And uh . . .

Y: Which synagogue was this?

J: I don't remember the name of it, but it was, there were two. One was on one side, one on the other. And there's even racism in your own religion. The Jews that came from Lithuania were on this side, and the Jews who came from Russia, or Poland, or anything was on the other side. My father, they felt they were in a better class, you know what I mean? . . . It was Concord Street. . . . It was, going up Concord Street from Essex Street, it was on the left-hand side. And then across the street was the other synagogue.

Y: And you noticed that strikers were getting together there in that synagogue?

J: Yeah, the strikers were there. And there was, you know, a lot of the people. And there was a young man, he died about three years ago, I think. He was brilliant and he was handsome. He was a young man. And he was, he was fighting for them to, you know, to go on strike and get more money. Because families were living two and three families in one, in one tenement. They used to call them tenements in those days, not apartments.

Y: Can you recognize the young man if I show you a picture?

J: I don't know whether I would or not . . . He was very young. I don't think he was more than, well if I was 13 he must have been 19 or 20. . . . He was a handsome boy. No, I don't think I could recognize him. His name was Joseph Ettor. He was a handsome young boy. (Julia is shown a photo of Joseph Ettor) That's him? Well of course he's a grown man now here. 19, on January 13, 1912? Oh he was much younger looking than that. It says 1912, but he, this couldn't have been

1912, because he was a thin young boy. . . . I recognize it, because I've seen it, and I saw it in the paper a few years ago when he died.[9] I wanted to get in touch with his house, but I never did. I wanted to tell them that I knew the man when he was a young boy. . . . He was organizing it, and he was so dedicated. And his whole heart and soul was in it. It was amazing you know, to see a young fellow so interested and so dedicated. And I wish I had kept the article. They wrote a big article when he died. I had no one to be interested. My family are not interested in that. But he did, and he got them all out. He got them all, finally got them all out on strike. And that strike went on for nine weeks.

Y: What language did he speak?

J: English . . . Well evidently he could speak Italian, he was an Italian boy. Yeah . . . All the kids over there were talking English. We were all talking English. In fact, my mother was the only one that used to talk to us in Yiddish, in Yiddish, and we'd answer her in English. And that's how she got to learn how to talk English. . . . Yeah, see . . . We all talked English.

Y: Yeah. So your father was not directly connected with the mills?

J: Oh no, no, not at all. He had a tailor shop. . . . He was a tailor, yeah. He used to make, sew, make clothes for the priest, some of the high school teachers. There were men there. And a lot of his customers were from uh, Breen's Undertaking parlor.[10] He had a nice following. Yes, he did.

Y: So, in other words, this strike did not affect him as much as the . . . ?

J: Oh yes, it did. . . . When you're not bringing in any money, and you're hungry, you don't have clothes made. And my father was a tailor. If it wasn't for the priest and the school teachers, and Breen's customers there, I don't know how he would have gotten by. In fact, it was very very rough at that time, very rough. It was a bad period. In fact, my father had bought the house just two years ago. And one day during the strike, he didn't come home. His mortgage was due and he didn't have any money. And, but he did, he used to come home at night, at six o'clock every night. And this night he didn't come home until 9:30. And I was sitting there shivering. I thought my father committed suicide. I was terrified. You had no idea what fear went on in that terrible strike. And my brothers, my brothers were working in bowling alleys, so they earned a little money. And I was too young to work.

[9] It is likely that Julia is remembering a composite of Angelo Rocco and Joseph Ettor, both prominent IWW organizers.

[10] This is the same Breen convicted of planting dynamite in strike meeting locations to discredit the strikers. The Breen family remains a prominent Lawrence family, still operating their funeral home.

I don't think I went down to see the mobs. You know, I was a little girl, I wouldn't have gone there. . . . But this was, this was a very very tragic, unfortunate period. And but I feel this way. They came out of it not earning too much money. They got a very little, I don't think they got more than a dollar raise. You know, in those days a dollar was a lot of money. But I feel that the amount, that Lawrence, and Lawrence to me is my city, I don't care if I was born in England. England doesn't mean anything to me. The United States is my country. And I feel that Lawrence should get the recognition of, there was a lot of strikes before 1912, but Lawrence was the one that formed a union. And that is history. And I feel that Lawrence should get the recognition of being the first city in the United States to form a workers' union. And they should get the credit of it, and it should be written down in history. Not Bread and Roses.

J: Oh, and there was no steamed heat in those days either, you know. Nothing. No . . . It was, well I didn't know the suffering like that, because I was [unclear] with my little people and all that. But I know now that the suffering must have been absolutely impossible, horrible, horrible. Not only that, they didn't have money for food. Do you know my father was a tailor and he owned two houses. One in the back, it was a one family house, and two, and the one that we lived in was a two-family house. Downstairs his sister, and my aunt and uncle lived there with two children. And in back was a sick woman and she had five children. I think she was a widow. And she took sick. She was not well. So, and my mother before the strike used to always send her in food. But after the strike they still do that. Because, so somebody said to me—I think Kathy Flynn—"How did your father do that without money?" I says, "Because my father was a manipulator." My father would run up a grocery bill, he'd run up a butcher bill, he'd run up a um, um, um, what else? What else is there? Groceries and meat. Yeah, and things like that. And he ended up, and instead of paying them, he'd make them clothes. They'd pay them, you know, this is the way that he paid them back. This is the way that he bought a piano for me too. I think the man, the man had, took about seven years for that man to get enough clothes to have the piano paid for. When he needed a suit of clothes, my father made it and took it off the bill. This is how he manipulated. You know, you have to use, you have to use, well you had to use something in order to be able to manage. And don't forget my father had six children and we all had very healthy appetites. But thank god we were never hungry and we were never cold. . . . Because my father would . . . charge it up. And when they needed, he would make it for them and take it off the bill. That's why.

Y: And you were talking about the mortgage and your father comes home . . . ?

J: Yeah, this is, this is wonderful. It really was a miracle. When I saw my father come in, it was 9:30, because I was watching the clock. And when he walked in, I saw he was alive. I thought I was in heaven, you know? And I said,

"Pa, what happened? Why are you so late?" And he said, he says, well, he said, "I have good news." And I said, "What is it?" He said, "Do you remember there was a customer I had, he was a Colonel in the army?" And I said, "Yeah." He said, "Well, he came in. And I was telling him how bad things are, and the strike, and I couldn't. . . ." And he used to have been one of his customers. "And I couldn't meet the mortgage, and I couldn't do this, and I was afraid I was going to lose the house and I didn't know what I was going to do. So he turned around and he said—my father's name was Sam—"Sam, don't worry, I'm going to loan you that money and don't worry about it. You can pay me whenever you have it." And he paid him the money for the mortgage. Yeah.

Y: And how did the strike affect your brothers, sisters?

J: Oh, they were all younger than me. They were children. I told you two of my brothers worked in the bowling alley at night. They worked in the bowling alley until one and two o'clock in the morning so that they could make enough money so that my mother could buy material to have me, have a dress for graduation . . . as I said, my father, food we always had and things, things that had to be, you know, we had to live on, we always had, because my father would pay it up by making them clothes.

Y: Yeah. Yeah, and we were talking about 16 children sent to Washington. And I got I got a picture of those children here.

J: Now I know that the only one that I really knew . . . I know that Pearl Shinberg went. Yeah. Not Mrs., her name was, she was young, she was only a young girl . . . Pearl Shinberg . . . Her brother turned out to be a very fine doctor here in Haverhill. And her other brother was one of the biggest lawyers in Haverhill. But the lawyer is gone, he's dead. The other one who is married to my cousin, so that made me related to them. His wife died and he moved to Florida. So they're not here. And I was going to call, somebody asked me if I, that Kathy Flynn asked me if I would give, see if I could contact . . . I did. I called up. She still has a niece living here in Haverhill. And I called her up. And she says, "Julie, you're too late. She died a few months ago." So they're all gone now.

Y: So she was one of the 16 children [who]went to Washington?

J: Yes, yeah. Washington, yeah . . . I remember what she looked like. But she was very thin. They were all like skeletons when they went . . . I saw them at the synagogue. They all got together there, before they went. They all gathered down there. And they, the one that was directing them, you know, taking charge, he mentioned it and he talked to them. And he said, you know, well they were sending this group to Washington so Washington will see how under-nourished they were.

Y: Yeah. People talk about children are sent, were sent to New York, Philadelphia. Did you hear about that? And 119 kids sent to New York in February. . .

J: Well, no matter. They couldn't, they probably couldn't stand the heat[11] and there was no food. That I don't remember . . . I didn't read newspapers. Listen, yes I did a lot of reading then, but I don't know if we got newspapers in those days. I don't know.

Y: And they say that they were all suffering from (J: malnutrition) malnutrition then. But you do not have such problems, right?

J: Oh, no, no, no, no. We were never hungry.

Y: And what about, did you hear that a girl was killed in that strike?

J: . . . I don't remember that. . . . No, no. I don't remember that.

Y: A young woman, Amy Lopesa, or Lopeza, or P I Z Z A, I was . . .

J: There's no pizza in those days.

Y: No, her last name was LoPizzo.

J: No, I wouldn't remember those people.

Y: I don't know if you said that, but I read in the newspaper, you said that the name "Bread and Roses" is a "stab in my heart."

J: It is.

Y: Why?

J: Because that was such a horrible period of existence in those days. They were cold. You see the pictures. They were cold; they were hungry. They had no money. And to me calling it "Bread and Roses" is glamorizing tragedy. I think it's an insult. I think it's stupid. And I who have lived through it and seen it all, and I didn't suffer the way they suffered. Because thank God you know, we had, we weren't hungry and we weren't cold. But to call that strike "Bread and Roses"! It's an insult to humanity! . . . I would simply give it the historical name of the first, the first. . . . I don't know how I would put it, but I would say that it was the 1912 strike, Lawrence Strike, which gave the country the first union. It could be put in a different manner, because I'm not very smart at that.

But I, that's what, it doesn't need a glamorous title. There was nothing glamorous about the hardships and the heartaches, and the suffering that went on in that time. You don't glamorize it with a word of "Bread and Roses." And I want to see that eliminated. And I do want Lawrence to get the credit. I love Lawrence as if I was born there. I don't know what it is like now, but in my day

---

[11] It's not clear what she means by this. I can only assume she meant to say cold, referring to the severe cold of the winter of 1912.

it was a wonderful city to live in.[12] It was really wonderful. And the people didn't have a lot of money, but we appreciated everything that we had.

. . . Lawrence should be given the recognition and the honor of saying that she was the first city in the United States to have a union. So that when they had a strike again, people didn't go hungry. They were taken care of by the union. I mean didn't they agree with me? Didn't people agree with me? Do you like the name of "Bread and Roses"?

Background voice: Oh I believe they wanted bread and they wanted the roses, just like the factory owners had. They had bread and they had roses.

J: Who had roses?

Background voice: The owners of the factory.

J: Oh, but how can they compare themselves to them? They were millionaires!

Y: But that's what they wanted. They wanted bread and they wanted the roses.

J: Oh no. I read the article. They said, they were watching the parade. After it was over, the woman turned around and said, "Oh, now we can have bread and roses." Well, you can't eat roses . . . Uh, do you think that name is going to last? I want to accomplish that thing in my life. I want that name eradicated. I'm taking it very deeply because I saw the suffering. I saw what they lived through. I saw how everyone was suffering. And it was, and I remember, that was the year I graduated high school. I didn't even know whether I was going to have a white dress to wear for the graduation. If my little brothers didn't go work in the bowling alley, they wouldn't, my mother was saving all of her money for food, not for clothes. They went to work; they were youngsters. If I was 13, my brother was 15, and the other one I think was, my brother was 11, and the other one was, was uh, going on 10. They went to work and worked till one or two in the morning.

1919

Jack Dilavore *was born in Pietraperzia, Sicily, in 1905. He was 14 years old and beginning his first year of work in the mills in 1919. He lived through the 1912 strike, witnessing his father and uncle badly beaten by police. He worked at the Arlington Mills for 25 years and later took jobs at Raytheon and AT&T. He was an active musician as a member of many area bands, the musician's union, and the Arlington Mills band. A loyal family man who quietly and consistently went about his work, he like so many others made up the heart and soul of a working class city like Lawrence. Though his memories of the strike of 1919 are less detailed and comprehensive, his short account yields helpful*

---

[12] Julia was living in Haverhill at the time this oral history was conducted.

comparisons and appropriately positions the 1919 strike in the greater canon of Lawrence labor activism.

YE: So, there were many strikes after 1912.

JD: [The] 1919 strike was almost, not quite as bad as the 1912. But the 1919 strike it affected my family because a brother and sister of mine were sent to Roxbury. There were many children that were sent out, to help the families so they would have less children to take care. My family was affected in that way. There was a brother and a sister that was sent to Roxbury and it alleviated my family quite a bit. . . . Anyone sympathetic toward the strike would take in children and they fed them and clothed them and gave them a place to live and that went on for the entire length of the strike.

YE: People don't, I did not realize that they did it in 1919. They talk about 1912 sending children to other places.

JD: Yeah, the same thing happened in 1919. That's when my family was affected by it. More so than in the 1912. Course we had a larger family by then.

YE: And you were older also to realize some of the things . . .

JD: That were happening, sure . . . I was working in the Wood Mill at that time.

YE: And do you know why the strike? Obviously, it was again with the payment, some disagreement?

JD: Shorter hours . . . Shorter hours and trying to maintain the same weekly pay. Trying to have 44 hours pay for 40 hours work.[13]

YE: Did you succeed, do you remember?

JD: Yes. It was an area-wide strike. The whole city was involved.

YE: Well, that was an important turning point.

JD: Oh, yes. In the 1912 strike, they went from . . . 54 to 48.[14] . . . Then later on it gradually got down to 44 and then we went to the 40.

YE: Do you have other memories from 1919? It seems to be that everyone is talking about 1912, but they ignore other strikes in Lawrence.

JD: Well, it was in comparison with 19, it wasn't as brutal on the part of the police as the 1912 strike. They didn't have to call in the militia; but, it was quite

---

[13] The 1919 strike went from 54 to 48 hours.

[14] The 1912 strike was prompted when the work week went from 56 hours to 54 hours.

bad. I don't remember of any deaths in the city. Really, the 1912 strike seems to be more vivid in my mind than the 1919, of just how the police reacted.[15]

YE: How did they start this strike? I mean, did they come in and say "We are on strike?" Were there leaders who started the strike?

JD: Yes, there were leaders. They tried to get back some of the leaders that we had had in the 1912 strike, and they were successful in a few instances. I believe that was when Sacco and Vanzetti came to Lawrence.[16] Later on they were accused of being Socialists and they were jailed for implication with murder of somebody. Which somehow, the trial was rigged and they were found guilty. But later on they were found to have been innocent but they were already put to death. I believe they were put to death?

YE: So 1919, and then there was 1922 also? A strike in 1922.[17] Three years later.

JD: I'm not clear on those dates. . . . Whether it was 1919 or 1923 that we get the 40 hours.

1931

Anne Burlak Timpson was born in May 1911 in Slatington, Pennsylvania, to Ukrainian immigrant parents. Though she had the dream of becoming a teacher, she was forced to drop out of school to work in the local silk mills to help support her family. The conditions she faced in the mills brought her to join and become very involved with the Communist Party. She was fired from mill jobs for her

---

[15] This seems to be true of a lot of people. Correspondents in several magazines and periodicals mention their shock upon arriving in the city to find a relatively peaceful and normal situation. A correspondent from the *Forward Supplement* asked a woman on Essex Street. where the strike could be found to which she replied: "I have no idea—possibly over where the mills are, I don't know anything about it!" Even Julia Dublin Garbelnick in a recorded radio interview done in 1988 is surprised to learn that there was a strike in 1919, the year she was married. This was probably due to the ebb and flow of strike events where sometimes there was action and other times there was not.

[16] The Lawrence authorities were very careful to look out for the arrival of the leaders of the 1912 strike. Strikers were successful in sneaking Carlo Tresca into the city and other notable radicals visited the city to make speeches and urge the strikers onward. There is no evidence that shows Sacco and Vanzetti made a visit to Lawrence during the strike. Though as the center for radical labor unionism in the Northeast, it is more than likely that Lawrence was visited more than once by the Sacco and Vanzetti Defense Committee during the years of their famous trial. This could be what Dilavore is remembering. This remembrance is a testament to Lawrence's position as a center for radical and leftist militancy.

[17] A strike did occur in 1922 beginning at the end of March and lasting through to early fall. The strike started when mills announced a proposed 20 percent wage cut. Due to the depressed nature of the industry, the strike was met much more favorably by the community and for the first time was led by the conservative unions of the AFL. The strike ended when mills agreed to shelve the proposed wage cut.

Communist Party affiliation and attempts at organizing her fellow workers. She was soon hired by the National Textile Workers Union as an organizer and sent to New England. She was called to Lawrence in 1931 to replace Lawrence NTW organizer Edith Berkman who had been arrested and detained by federal authorities. After the strike, she continued organizing in New England's mill towns and even ran for public office twice on the Communist Party ticket. She remained a passionate member of the Communist Party until her death in 2002 at the age of 91. Her oral history offers an incredible look into the world of leftist organizing in the early 20th century.

(I refers to the interviewer and N refers to the interviewee, Anne Burlak Timpson)

I. When you were notified that you were needed in Lawrence in 1931, you didn't come alone, did you?

N. Well, nobody came with me. We had people here. Edith Berkman was a member of our union and she was assigned to work in the Lawrence-Lowell area. And, we had another organizer in the New Bedford-Fall River area. And then we had an organizer who took care of Taunton, for instance. Well, we had an organizer there. . . . If there was, they preferred a textile worker. I was preferred in many areas because I was a textile worker. And when I talked about looms and when I talked about conditions of work and what were some of the unreasonable things they wanted weavers to do . . .

Actually, we used to always say when we were making most of the money was when we had to work the least. Because when the looms were running, all we did was to patrol them and look to see if everything was in order. The looms, at that time already, were supposed to be mechanical so that if any of the threads broke—you didn't refer to them as threads anyway—whenever they broke, they would be tangling up. If you know anything about knitting sweaters, for instance, or knitting shawls, which is a very simple thing. You do the same thing over and over again until you make your whole shawl. You would watch to see that none of the threads broke because as soon as they broke, they would create an imperfection because they would get tangled with other threads and pretty soon it would be from a small tangle into a larger and larger area. And, you couldn't correct it unless you stopped the machine and you pulled out the threads that they went across and took out, ripped, is what we referred to, your ripped thing that was tangled up. And only when you came to the good material did you stop and you started all over again. And, that's when you had to know how to join the good part of the material so that when you started working the machine, it would not leave a bad section or a flaw. Because that would mean that that piece of material would have a flaw in it and would have to be sold as a second. And, then you don't get paid as much.

I. One of the questions that I wanted you to qualify for me is that actually the two strikes of 1931 were not won . . .

N. Well, it was in the same mills but because they didn't do what they wanted in the February strike, they came out on strike. And, that was also because not all the mills were involved in the February strike. I was not involved in the February strike. We had an organizer. I came to replace Edith Berkman.

I. The February strike, as I understood it, had to do with a method of work rather than wages. Anyhow in the second strike, the owners wanted to make a 10 percent reduction in pay and then they offered a five percent reduction. . . . I haven't been able to figure out when the workers finally went back to work. Do you know if they accepted the ten percent or the five percent reduction?

N. They were given the 5 percent.[18] You see, that was one of the reasons why we formed a new union because the AFL (American Federation of Labor) had a policy of going in to the management and negotiating with them. And they would make compromises without consulting the workers. And the workers were very dissatisfied. That's why the second strike actually took place because they got a cut in wages. They said that they could not correct the situation between the South and the North. They were paying less wages in the South because they were competing and the South was always used as a reason why the New England mills couldn't keep the difference. Now, what they didn't tell workers was that very often the same people were on the board of directors in the Northern mills as were on the board of directors in the South.

I. Did the Depression have anything to do with any of these decisions, because we're right in the middle of the depression years now?

N. Yes. Well, the North used to say, "We can't compete with the South." And, at the same time, if you did some research you would find that many of the mills in the South, which were owned by Congressmen and governors, in other words, the politicians, it was very easy to establish among the workers that they were not going to get fair conditions of work by dealing with the employers here because they say they cannot compete with the South. But, actually the employers in the South were the same people that were the employers in the North.

I. And the other thing that I absolutely have to have cleared up. I had always understood that Edith Berkman was the "Red Flame" and then I read a newspaper article that referred to you as the "Red Flame."

N. Well, the term was first used against Edith. I was not in the picture at all. I was in Rhode Island at the time. It was our union and she was our organizer, but it was used against her for only a matter of a couple of months. And then one of

---

[18] Most workers went back to work accepting an average 10 percent pay cut.

the headlines in the Lawrence paper, in fact, said, "One red flame jailed. Another rises in her place." That was one of the . . . that's when I came into the story. And then, of course, ever since then, Edith was not referred to. She was in jail. She was in the hands of the authorities. It was a federal arrest. She was not deported. But there is such a law as voluntary departure. She was not because we put on a big campaign to keep her from being deported and she's Portuguese.[19] She was going to be deported to Portugal. And Portugal was a fascist country at that time. And we fought against her being deported to Portugal because it would have meant that she would be put in a concentration camp or perhaps executed.

I. Was she a Communist?

N. Yes and so am I.[20]

I. Yes you are; I think I understood that. That would be another thing I would be curious about in terms of . . . It appeared that there was always friction in Lawrence between Communist organizers when they came. It didn't seem to exist at other times.

N. The AFL leadership were as vicious in attacking our organizers, both verbally and sometimes physically, as the employers. The AFL issued circulars in which they would say, "Join an American Union. These are foreigners." Edith was one of the people that they were referring to because she came from Poland. In New Bedford, they didn't have that problem because most of the organizers were native to the state. In our union, they preferred to have people who worked at the mill and who were known by the workers and so forth and so on. Whereas, the AFL as well as the employers, would refer to us as being foreigners even though people like myself were American-born and came out of the industry. Many of the organizers were from the industries and the union approached them to become organizers.

I. The anti-Communist feeling that prevailed in some areas at some times, was that an advantage or a disadvantage to you as an organizer because obviously you wanted to help the worker? But, if you were a Democrat or a Republican, would it have been less difficult for you?

N. Well, the Republicans and Democrats tried to avoid being involved in battles because as far as the employers were concerned, they didn't want any union. But they took advantage of this schism between the unions, because one of the things they wanted was unity among the workers. But unity for their advantage. And, we constantly tried to educate the workers that the employers are going to use

---

[19] Edith Berkman was not Portuguese, she was Polish. Timpson is remembering another woman strike organizer from the 1931 strike who was deported.

[20] Timpson was a proud Communist until her death in 2002. In 1932, she ran for Mayor of Pawtucket, Rhode Island, on the Communist ticket but failed.

any tactic that will break the unions. There used to be antagonism between the French-Canadians and the Italians. The Italians were referred to as the more aggressive people. The French-Canadians were criticized by other workers because they said they were the ones that cooperated with the employers. But, all of these things: men against women, older workers against young workers, Native Americans well, Native Americans are only the Indians, so . . . you know, the English-speaking.

A lot of the textile workers either originally came here from England or Wales or Scotland because that's where the textile mills were. There were some textile mills in Poland and some of the other industrial cities. So, you had the English-speaking workers that were favored and they used to use that in the propaganda of the newspapers, you know, against the workers from the other European countries that were Socialists. They used interchangeable Russian or Ukrainian or all the Slavs, for instance. In New Bedford, most of the workers were Portuguese. In Lawrence, most of them were Italians.

I. Did Elizabeth Gurley Flynn take part in the 1931 strike?

N. She did not. She may have come here to speak once or twice, but she didn't come in that strike. She was involved in the 1912 strike and there was another strike in 1919. She may have come here to speak at that time, too. I didn't meet Elizabeth Gurley Flynn until the '30s. She became a member of the Communist Party in 1935 or 1936 . . . she was an internationally known labor leader.

CHAPTER 9

Striking Women: Massachusetts Mill Workers in the Wake of Bread and Roses, 1912–1913

Anne F. Mattina and Domenique Ciavattone

The 1912 strike of workers in the woolen mills of Lawrence, Massachusetts, proved to be a watershed moment in American history. As landless immigrants with no status or political influence, the Lawrence strikers faced daunting barriers as they mobilized to protest pay cuts and overall working conditions in the bitter cold of a New England winter. Their stunning victory in the face of an overwhelmingly violent response to their efforts by mill owners, local, and state governments, clergy, police, militia, and Harvard undergraduates is legendary. Though the strike itself lasted only 63 days, it looms large in the history of American labor reform for several reasons, including its outcome as an enormous victory for the organizers affiliated with the Industrial Workers of the World (IWW). A presence in Lawrence for five years, IWW national organizers visited the city helping with work slowdowns and wildcat walk-outs in late 1911 and provided all-encompassing support during the strike itself.[1] The "One Big Union's" inclusive message bound together the polyglot of ethnic groups working in the city's woolen industry.

In addition to the IWW, the Italian Socialist Federation (ISF) played a significant role in the strike's success. The ISF's members were among the first workers out of the mills and provided local leadership and strategies to the larger strike force. Most were syndicalists with strong ties to radical labor organizations

---

[1] Melvyn Dubofsky, *We Shall be All: A History of the Industrial Workers of the World* (Chicago, 1969), 234.

throughout Italy and other European countries.[2] Female networks in Lawrence's ethnic neighborhoods added considerable strength to the strike force. Workers, wives, and mothers forged strong alliances with neighbors in their tenement blocks out of necessity born of poverty. The strength of these networks contributed to the solidarity essential to sustaining the strike of 1912.[3]

Important to this study is the recognition that union membership and strike activity by women were not socially accepted among the larger American culture. Picketing and parading were completely at odds with notions of feminine propriety. Though many immigrant women were not bound by such cultural constraints in their homelands,[4] mainstream American reaction to women's labor activism was one of disdain and horror. Traditional craft-based labor unions also ignored women workers, dismissing them as not worthy of representation. Not so for the Wobblies who encouraged women's participation and activism from their founding.

Together, these three elements—the IWW, ethnic organizations, and women's activism—proved a formidable combination in the fight for higher pay and better working conditions in Lawrence. In the strike's aftermath, mill workers throughout New England took to the streets in hopes of achieving similar outcomes. Dozens of strikes occurred from March 1912 to August 1913 in Massachusetts alone and while each had distinct local characteristics, they shared many of the hallmarks of the Lawrence strike. This essay explores the influence of the Lawrence strike on those subsequent strikes with a special focus on women's roles. In what follows, we provide a synopsis of Lawrence, highlighting key female figures and the strategic roles they played. Next, we turn our attention to consideration of several representative Massachusetts strikes during the subsequent 15 months with an emphasis on the roles women played. As will be demonstrated, the Bread and Roses Strike of 1912 had implications for workers beyond Lawrence's boundaries.

LAWRENCE, 1912

The Bread and Roses strike had its roots in the protective legislation enacted by the state, reducing the hours of labor for women and children from 56 per week to 54, causing a de facto reduction in wages. Effective January 1912, the first pay day brought "short pay" to workers. On January 11, Polish women

---

[2] Michael Miller Topp, "The Transnationalism of the Italian-American Left: The Lawrence Strike of 1912 and the Italian Chamber of Labor of New York City," *Journal of American Ethnic History,* 17 (Fall, 1997), 39-63.

[3] Ardis Cameron, *Radicals of the Worst Sort: Laboring Women in Lawrence, Massachusetts, 1860–1912* (Urbana, 1993), 33.

[4] See, for instance, Jennifer Guglielmo, *Living the Revolution: Italian Women's Resistance and Radicalism in New York City 1880–1945* (Chapel Hill, 2010).

walked off the job shouting for their co-workers to join them. By the end of the next week 10,000 workers had done so and by the end of the strike 20,000 to 25,000 were out.

In 1912, the tenements, streets, and mills of Lawrence teemed with immigrants from a multitude of countries. Conventional wisdom held that the strike was doomed to fail precisely because of the ethnic make-up of the force. IWW organizers however, preached an inclusive message, one that traditional labor unions had eschewed. "Do not let them divide you by sex, color, creed or nationality for as you stand today you are invincible," Big Bill Haywood implored them.[5] For the next several months, this message resonated through Lawrence's streets and meeting halls. The workers organized quickly, forming an official strike committee of 12 individuals, including one woman, Annie Welzenbach, a skilled mender (see Figure 7, p. 117). Welzenbach, 24 years old in 1912, is credited with bringing the English-speaking workers into the strike, another important ingredient to victory.[6] A general committee composed of 56 members responsible for the different ethnic groups involved also was established.[7] These individual ethnic units were charged with taking care of their own, providing soup kitchens, medical assistance, and clothing for their compatriots. The ISF in conjunction with the IWW raised funds for the strikers nationally and internationally.[8]

Workers met nightly in halls to listen to IWW speakers. Elizabeth Gurley Flynn, the most prominent female organizer, spoke directly to the plight of the women strikers, "The conditions are very bad here. The mill operatives are not paid what they are worth to the corporations. Just think of the mothers who work daily in the mills and then have their children kept at another house. It is unbearable when you think about it."[9] Gurley Flynn was a constant presence in Lawrence, enormously popular among the workers. Recognizing the constraints faced by female strikers, she began holding women-only meetings, explaining, "The women wanted to picket. They were strikers as well as wives and were valiant fighters."[10] Such meetings contributed to the women's empowerment.

Early on, the IWW warned against violence as a strategy. Despite their reputation as anarchists bent on destroying property and lives, violence had no place in official Wobbly ideology. Mass picketing began immediately as workers left the mills. City officials called for the state militia's help to contain the large

---

[5] Mary Marcy, "The Battle for Bread in Lawrence," *The International Socialist Review*, 12 (March, 1912) 538.

[6] Linda Sternberg, *Women Workers and the 1912 Textile Strike in Lawrence, Massachusetts,* unpublished manuscript, Lawrence Public Library.

[7] Cameron, *Radicals*, 126.

[8] Dubofsky, *We Shall Be All,* 250.

[9] "Woman organizer," *Boston Daily Globe* 1/21/1912, 3.

[10] Elizabeth Gurley Flynn, *The Rebel Girl, An Autobiography: My First Life, 1906–1926* (New York: 1955) 132-133.

numbers of strikers flooding the streets. Security was supplemented by the Pinkerton agency and Harvard undergraduates joined the force as reinforcements and strike breakers.

It is significant to this study that females dominated the Lawrence work force[11] (see Figure 8, p.118 and 11, p. 119). These women forged strong alliances with neighbors regardless of ethnic background. They shared food and child-care, laundry and papers necessary for gaining their children employment. The strength of these networks also contributed to the solidarity essential to sustaining the strike of 1912.[12] For the next several weeks, strikers took to the streets to both picket and keep strike breakers from entering the mills. In response, mill owners had police turn water hoses on them. Some effort was made by the state board of conciliation and arbitration to get the two sides talking, but the mill owners adamantly refused to meet with the general strike committee. They insisted on meeting only with representatives from recognized unions employed in their own mills. The strike committee was equally steadfast in its demand to be recognized as a legitimate bargaining unit.[13]

January 29 proved a watershed day for the strike. After hearing reports of the arrival of a trolley car filled with out-of-town strike-breakers, workers swarmed the scene. Newspaper reports and city officials blamed strikers for the ensuing riot as "scabs" were dragged from the cars. Pinkertons, disguised as workers, mixed in the crowd and beat the strikers back while generating fear and hostility among the general populace.[14] Among those arrested for rioting that morning were Margot Sonia and Serafina Peradelia. Later that day, worker Anna LoPizzo was shot and killed during a rally, most likely by police. Her death set in motion one of the key contributing factors to sustained labor unrest throughout Massachusetts in the ensuing months, the arrest and imprisonment of Joseph Ettor and Arturo Giovannitti.

Despite the fact that neither was in Lawrence on that day, national IWW organizers Ettor and Giovannitti were charged with being accessories to LoPizzo's murder. Authorities argued that their earlier presence in the city had incited the mob leading to the events of January 29. A day later during a demonstration, a young Syrian striker, John Ramey, was struck with a bayonet and killed. Quickly, the city issued orders banning strike parades and public meetings simultaneously, ceding responsibility for public safety to the state militia.

It is at this juncture that existing communication networks of women became essential to the life of the strike. The women of Lawrence seized the neighborhoods. "In the absence of formal gathering places, operatives grew increasingly

---

[11] Cameron, *Radicals*, 33.
[12] Cameron, *Radicals*.
[13] Chas. B. Neill, *Report on Strike of Textile Workers in Lawrence Mass. in 1912* (Washington, DC, 1912) 42.
[14] William Cahn, *Lawrence 1912: The Bread and Roses Strike* (New York, 1980) 150.

dependent on women's unauthorized networks to get out the news, gather information, coordinate activities, and sustain unity."[15] Organizer Pearl McGill met with women outdoors to help plan morning vigils for the purpose of ensuring solidarity on the picket lines. McGill, a button-worker from Muscatine, Iowa, had come east as an organizer for the Women's Trade Union League.[16] Working in Boston, she was drawn to Lawrence at the start of the strike, quickly became enamored of the IWW, and soon worked exclusively for the Wobblies.

One strategy the Lawrence women came up with was the moving picket line. The idea was to form a massive constantly moving human chain by linking arms, providing both unity and protection from arrest.[17] The strategy was so successful that it was replicated in numerous strikes across the Commonwealth in the months that followed (see Figure 8, p. 117). "Scab mugging," another tactic favored by the women, included following strike-breakers right to the gates of the factories, all the while hectoring and bringing down the wrath of strike-sympathetic passersby. Domacilla Lafskoski, an elderly woman, ended up being arrested while shoveling snow off her sidewalk in late February. Police said she was yelling "scab" at passersby, whacking her shovel while she hurled the epithet.[18] Four young Polish women were also arrested that morning for blocking the mill gates.

Through it all, the IWW, the ISF and other ethnic societies provided organizational support and resources to the strikers, acting in partnership with local leaders. Money was allotted to each family for food, coal, and wood. Women were in charge of cooking at the 11 soup kitchens organized around ethnicity.[19] The relief committee held meetings and raised money nationally and internationally for the Lawrence strikers. Pearl McGill traveled to workers' conventions throughout Massachusetts to garner financial and moral support.

Support for the strike extended beyond the working class. When local strike leader Annie Welzenbach and her sisters, Emma and Lillian Steindl, were arrested on charges of intimidation, the Progressive Women's Club of Lawrence issued a public condemnation of the police. Police, to avoid the possibility of a backlash from the strike force, removed the sisters from their homes at midnight. The club women compared these actions to those of Russian authorities and demanded that an "end be put to such injustices." Later, they hosted a protest meeting at the Colonial Theater with Wellesley College professor Vida Scudder as the keynote speaker.[20]

Violence continued through the month of February. The militia had to be called to the vicinity of the Arlington mills to break up thousands of picketing

---

[15] Cameron, *Radicals*, 140.
[16] "Applauds Foss; Appointment of Mrs. Evans," *Boston Daily Globe*, June 14, 1911, 16.
[17] Sternberg, *Women Workers*, 59.
[18] "To Send None Away," *Boston Daily Globe,* February 28, 1912, 2.
[19] Sternberg, *Women Workers,* 64.
[20] "Women are Awakening," *The Industrial Worker*, July 25, 1912, 5.

Polish women. They were contained by bayonets and charging police.[21] Striker Josephine Lis, Polish delegate to the IWW strike committee and occasional courtroom interpreter during Wobbly trials in Lawrence, was found guilty of molesting a soldier. She flatly refused to pay the $10 fine levied against her, choosing instead to be jailed. Eventually both the judge and her attorney convinced her to appeal the case and she was released on bond. "We can handle the men all right," prosecutor Douglas Campbell declared, "but it takes 10 men to handle one woman."[22]

Perhaps the most publicly creative action associated with the strike was the decision to send the children of the strikers out of Lawrence. The strategy, common among Italian and other European labor activists, was based on the premise that workers might be compelled to return to the mills before the strike was settled if they were worried about their hungry offspring. On February 10, 1912, Margaret Sanger, working on behalf of the IWW, accompanied a group of children on their "exodus" to New York City. By and large, response to the event and news coverage was favorable, save in the city of Lawrence. Mill owners and the mayor were furious at the action. City officials called for the National Guard, and threatened workers with jail if they tried to send any more children out of the city. Defiant strikers sent two dozen more children to Barre, Vermont, where Italian granite workers at the Socialist Labor Party Hall greeted them. The Lawrence police chief and city officials publicly vowed that not one more child would leave the city.

On February 24, the strikers returned to the train station with more children. They were met with brutal opposition as police seized children, tossing them into trucks. Parents surrounded the vehicles carrying the children and a 20-minute battle with the militia ensued. The children were sent out of the city to the poor farm.[23] Frantic mothers and fathers stormed City Hall only to be beaten back by police. Clashes occurred throughout the day "so demonstrative were they that 33, 27 of them women, were arrested."[24] Eventually, the children were returned to their parents who sent them on to Philadelphia. Accompanied by Anna Sachs, Anna Fulden, and Mary Sholik, the children were greeted as "*militi della medesima lotta*" (soldiers of the same struggle).[25]

The public was outraged by the violence, and nationally labor activists and social reformers called for an immediate investigation. A Congressional hearing was slated for March 6 and Sanger accompanied young workers to Washington DC. Spectators, including First Lady Nellie Taft, heard compelling first-hand testimony about conditions in the Lawrence mills. Carmella Teoli described losing

---

[21] "Bayonets Disperse Women," *The New York Times*, February 22, 1912, 1.
[22] "Judge Mahoney Laments," *Solidarity*, March 2, 1912, 5.
[23] "Police Clubs Keep Lawrence Waifs," *The New York Times*, February 25, 1912, 2.
[24] Ibid.
[25] I Bimbi di Lawrence a Filadelfia, *Il Proletario*, March 15, 1912, 2.

part of her scalp when her hair got caught in a machine.[26] Josephine Lis testified about being charged for a dipper of water during the work day. Lawrence officials attempted to counteract the vivid testimony, as workers were not the only witnesses called to Congress. One police officer complained of coming upon women armed with broomsticks and a baseball bat. He denied any violence on the part of the police or militia.[27] Under mounting public pressure and unable to break the strike force, the mill owners sought talks with the strike committee. The unified forced proved formidable and the mill owners capitulated to the workers' demands. Triumphant workers returned to the mills at the end of March.

The story of Lawrence workers' solidarity and activism did not end there, however. Ettor and Giovannitti remained in a Salem jail along with Joseph Caruso, awaiting trial. National IWW organizers stayed in Massachusetts raising funds for their defense and bringing the message of the Lawrence victory to workers in mills and factories. Pearl McGill presided over a mass meeting of 1,000 in Boston's Tremont Temple in August.[28] In September, thousands of Lawrence workers descended upon Boston parading through the streets demanding justice for the imprisoned organizers. McGill led 8,000 workers onto the Boston Common where they joined another 9,000 gathered to hear Big Bill Haywood's demand for the prisoners' release. The publicity generated by the workers' victory and Ettor's and Giovannitti's imprisonment sparked momentum as labor unrest spread throughout the Commonwealth.

BARRE, MASSACHUSETTS

Fast on the heels of the Lawrence strike, approximately 500 employees at the Barre Wool Combing Company walked off the job "and with shouts rushed into the street."[29] By the end of a week, the strike was estimated to be about 1,000: 700 from the Barre Wool Combing Company and an additional 300 recruits from the Norway Worsted Mill. Italian immigrants dominated the Barre strike force. There was no question as to where they got their motivation, at least in mill superintendent R. G. Thompson's perspective. "They are acting like a crazy lot of sheep running about the streets and waving flags, and I feel that they have become crazed by reading about the Lawrence strike."[30]

Wobbly organizer Samuel Fassel traveled to the small Central Massachusetts town to aid the strikers. Fassel wrote up their demands, basing them on those of the Lawrence strike. The demands included an increase in pay along with a

---

[26] Carmella Teoli Testifies About the 1912 Lawrence Textile Strike, *History Matters*, http://historymatters.gmu.edu/d/61/.
[27] "Police Say Women Led Lawrence Mob," *The New York Times*, March 2, 1912, 6.
[28] "Wants Crusade Like Wendell Phillips," *Boston Daily Globe*, August 21, 1912, 11.
[29] "Quit Work, Hurry Out," *The Worcester Telegram*, March 12, 1912, 10.
[30] "Quit Suddenly at South Barre," *Boston Daily Globe*, March 12, 1912, 12.

54-hour work week. Strike parades began immediately. Local officers attempted to deflect the mass picketing in front of the mill by turning fire hoses onto the crowd.[31] Riots broke out when Sheriff Emory A. Bacon ordered rifles, shotguns, and 100 armed guards to prepare for any violence among the strikers. "Specials," police officers from nearby towns, arrived to ensure order and sharpshooters armed with rifles took up position in the top floors of the mills.[32] Headlines in *Il Proletario*, the ISF paper shouted, "The Insurrection of the Hungry in Mass" and *"Come a Lawrence!"* (As in Lawrence).[33] The bloody conflicts included beatings by both police and strikers. Mill owners refused to recognize the IWW demanding instead to negotiate with John Golden, leader of the United Textile Workers (UTU).[34] The UTU represented only a small fraction of the workers and, as such, no negotiations took place.

Women played a significant role in the strike, picketing and parading daily. As they had in Lawrence, IWW organizers met with the women separately in outdoor locations.[35] On March 16, strikers set out to stop three freight cars filled with wool from leaving the mill yard. A group of women acting as decoys headed toward the tracks as the cars were being coupled. They were allowed to advance by unsuspecting guards who quickly realized their error. In the melee that followed, large numbers of men broke through the lines and rushed the trains, hurling stones at the cars as they set out of the yard. Women rushed from nearby homes wielding broomsticks and axes attempting to stop the train. Both Boston and New York newspapers reported the women's tactics as being similar to those used in Lawrence.[36] Another reported that the women fought "as hard as men."[37] Shots fired above the crowd by police sent the strikers into a frenzy and many were left wounded. The experience hardened the workers' resolve and they held fast to their demands. Railroad workers refused to transport any more goods from the mills.

The owners could not hold out any longer and right before noon on March 21, the strikers' demands were met. The employers set a work week of 54 hours, an overtime rate of 1¼ pay, an increase of five percent for piecework, and no discrimination against the workers involved in the strike. Organizer Nelson told a local paper, "We claim this is one of the greatest victories we ever had."[38] The total amount spent on the victory by the IWW was $50.

---

[31] Ibid.

[32] "Rifles and Shot Guns are Rushed to Barre by Automobile Load," *The Evening Gazette*, March 18, 1912, 1; "Negotiations Off at Barre," *Boston Daily Globe*, March 18, 1912, 16.

[33] *Il Proletario*, March 22, 1912, 1.

[34] *Annual Report of the Board of Conciliation and Arbitration* (Boston, 1913) 45.

[35] "Rifles and Shot Guns are Rushed to Barre by the Automobile Load," *The Evening Gazette*, March 18, 1912, 14.

[36] "Women Lead in Riot at Barre," *Boston Daily Globe*, March 17, 1912, 1.

[37] "Wild Riots at Barre," *The Evening Gazette*, March 16, 1912, 1.

[38] "Mill Gates Will Open," *The Evening Gazette*, March 22, 1912, 1.

CLINTON

On the day the Barre workers settled, a strike broke out in nearby Clinton at the Lancaster Gingham Mills; 1,300 weavers demanded a ten percent wage increase.[39] Pearl McGill was among the IWW organizers dispatched from Lawrence to lend her organizational skill.[40] Elizabeth Gurley Flynn spoke at a rally on March 28 describing "the objects and methods of the IWW and urged the strikers here to remain firm."[41]

The Clinton work force, comprised primarily of Poles and Greeks, proved up to the challenge. Workers at Clinton Wire Cloth joined the strike in early April.[42] Owners agreed to some of the workers' demands and it appeared that the strike was settled. However, local organizer Dennis Callahan was fired for his activism and the workers returned to the picket lines in solidarity demanding that Callahan be re-hired. Parades, meetings, and scab mugging became part of the daily routine. Mary Welsh and Rose Heinold were among those arrested for assaulting female strike-breakers.[43] Bavarian immigrant Heinhold and her husband were both active Wobblies and held strike meetings on their property. Strikers took to the streets and broke windows of the houses where workers had broken ranks and returned to work. It was also reported that the word "scab" was painted across the front doors.[44]

On June 2, a riot broke out in the center of town. The fracas began when several Greek strikers attempted to stop strike-breakers from entering the factory. A nearby police officer used his night stick to prevent the strikers from barring the scabs. Stones were thrown as more of the strikers gathered. Clinton police called for help from surrounding towns and 40 specials armed with clubs and guns arrived. Attempting to avoid being beaten, strikers ran into a Catholic church yard, throwing stones at their pursuers. Police opened fire into the church yard and seven strikers, four women and three men, were shot.[45] Though the events generated some news coverage, little effort was made on behalf of the Clinton workers by the national IWW or the state board of arbitration and conciliation. The mills continued to operate with about a quarter of the normal work force.

There were additional reports of police officers tripping young Greek girls as they picketed, and beating them as they lay on the ground. The Greek Consul arrived from Boston in an effort to stop the persecution of Greek strikers to little

---

[39] "Gingham Mills Shut Down," *The New York Times,* March 23, 1912, 7.
[40] "No Move to Open Mills," *Boston Daily Globe,* March 26, 1912, 5.
[41] "Men and Boys," *Boston Daily Globe,* March 29, 1912, 10.
[42] "Wire Cloth Strike Ends," *Boston Daily Globe,* April 16, 1912, 15.
[43] "Pulled Woman's Hair," *Boston Daily Globe*, May 31, 1912, 6.
[44] "Trying to Close Plant," *Boston Daily Globe*, May 17, 1912, 13.
[45] "Clinton Strike Rioters Quelled," *Boston Daily Globe,* June 4, 1912, 8.

effect.[46] The strike dragged on without resolution until June 26 when workers voted to return to the mills, no victory in hand. Throughout the spring and summer, strikes broke out in Lowell, Newton, Waltham, Chicopee, Webster, West Warren, New Bedford, and North Adams. (A strike was avoided in Fall River as mill owners voluntarily raised wages ten percent). Replicating the actions of Barre, local officials in each of these communities sounded a general alarm as workers took to the streets. Police officers from neighboring towns would rush to the affected area and violence and multiple arrests resulted. Women were active in all phases of these strikes: picketing, scab mugging, and running soup kitchens.

As noted above, large rallies protesting the continued imprisonment of Ettor and Giovannitti took place throughout the summer and fall. A defense committee was formed in Lawrence with Elizabeth Gurley Flynn at the helm, and Josephine Lis also serving. Pearl McGill and Gurley Flynn barnstormed around the state raising funds and generating support. Lawrence workers staged several one-day strikes in protest and held massive parades demanding the prisoners' release. Similar protests occurred throughout the United States and Europe, especially in Italy.[47] The Trial of Ettor, Giovannitti, and Joseph Caruso took place in October and November and all three were acquitted, thus providing workers with additional incentive to continue their quest for better pay and working conditions.

In January 1913, workers in the silk mills of Paterson, New Jersey, walked off the job in protest over increased responsibility with no accompanying increase in pay. The national IWW sent Gurley Flynn and other organizers to the scene. Though there were similarities between Paterson and Lawrence (including the deaths of two strikers), a smaller strike in Massachusetts during the spring of 1913 bears nearly all of the hallmarks of Bread and Roses.

HOPEDALE/MILFORD, MARCH 1913–JULY 1913

Hopedale, a small central Massachusetts town, was founded as a utopian community by reformers influenced by Transcendentalism. Among the original settlers, the Draper family dominated the town by the turn of the 20th century. The company was a leading American manufacturer of power looms and employed at its height several thousand workers. As the single largest employer in Hopedale, the owners of Draper manufacturing held sway over life in the small town as well as its larger neighbor, Milford. In 1913, Eben Draper, former governor of Massachusetts, ran the company. Though earlier generations of Drapers had comported themselves as paternalistic guardians of their employees, Gov. Draper, as he was known, was less sympathetic to the working class.

---

[46] "Consul Visits Clinton," *Boston Daily Globe*, June 6, 1912, 5.
[47] Many of these efforts were replicated 15 years later on behalf of Sacco and Vanzetti.

The strike of 1913 mirrored that of Lawrence, albeit on a smaller scale. Immigrant workers fed up with low wages and long hours, demanded redress and when they were denied took to the streets. Italian workers' circles, along with other ethnic societies and the IWW, organized and supported workers throughout the strike. The strike was marred by violence, including the murder of one worker and the wounding of many more. Strikers were denied access to public spaces and frequently jailed while attempting to picket. Workers' children were exiled to Providence and Woonsocket, Rhode Island, in a manner identical to that of Lawrence.

What distinguishes this strike from Lawrence's is the lack of female workers in the main strike force. During the time period under study here, Draper employed fewer than a dozen women. However, large numbers of women did participate in this strike by picketing and scab-mugging. Still more walked off their own jobs in sympathy, causing havoc on the streets. One woman in particular was essential to the strike's organization. Palmira Merolini served as translator and secretary to the strike committee as well as chaperone for the exiled children. Merolini's contributions will be discussed further below. Another distinction between this strike and Lawrence's is the fact that most of the strike activities did not occur in the same town where the manufacturing plant was located. Though Draper provided some housing in Hopedale, most employees with families lived in neighboring Milford, which was the location of strike rallies and parades.

In 1913, Milford had a large immigrant population dominated by Italians. In addition to those working at Draper, many others worked in the granite quarries of the town. The majority of these immigrants were from southern Italy and the largest number hailed from the area of Foggia. The Italians clustered in the Plains district and worshiped at Sacred Heart church. Like their compatriots in Lawrence, the Italians of Milford found support in ethnic societies, including civic, musical, and religious groups.

Worker circles supported the ideals of the IWW and raised funds for Lawrence strikers as well as Ettor's and Giovannitti's defense throughout 1912. "There were two radical circles in Milford, an IWW group on East Main St. and an anarchist group on Plains Street. Each had about 25 members, all Italians," recalled former resident Ralph Piesco.[48] An active participant in these radical circles was Ferdinando Sacco (a.k.a. Nicola) whose execution was a *cause célèbre* for anarchists all over the world.

Controversy erupted in Milford during March of 1913 when it became known that Draper employees had invited IWW speakers to address workers. Officials denied necessary permits for this meeting to take place at the town hall. Instead, workers met at Oliveri Hall and the meeting was conducted entirely in Italian. A few days later, another meeting was held at Charles River Hall with addresses

---

[48] Paul Averich, *Anarchist Voices* (Princeton, 1995), 96.

being delivered in English, Italian, and Armenian. On March 31, workers voted to strike. The workers immediately appealed to the IWW for help in organizing the strike force. Draper executives responded by sending out an alarm to nearby police departments and dozens of neighboring towns sent officers to protect the company. Unfortunately for the workers, the IWW was embroiled in a large-scale silk workers strike in Paterson, New Jersey. Joseph Coldwell, a local photographer sympathetic to IWW, emerged as strike leader. Both Ettor and Giovannitti visited during the strike and Gurley Flynn addressed workers in late June.

Workers' demands included a shop committee, a nine-hour day, abolition of the piece-work system, pay increases, restoration of their jobs, and impartial treatment when the strike was resolved. "One of the principal causes of the workers' discontent was the attitude of the supervisors," Danker asserts, and further, that these workers were "uniting in protest with immigrant workers across the nation who were demanding not just a decent living, but decent treatment as well."[49] From the outset of the strike, Eben Draper adamantly refused to negotiate with the strikers because of their connection to the IWW.

The strikers adapted similar tactics to those used in Lawrence: parading through the streets of Milford and Hopedale, singing and haranguing strikebreakers as they made their way through town on electric streetcars. On April 1, nearly 1,000 people turned out to march after a meeting at Driving Park Hall. "The parade was sensational and a great surprise to the residents of Milford and Hopedale, who generally doubted so many would be out."[50] A strike committee formed with representatives from the Italian, American, Armenian, and Polish communities. As in Lawrence, it was common for children and their mothers to march at the head of the line in the daily parades. Many of the marchers wore small red flags with the words, "Don't scab in Hopedale," on them.[51] Italian and Armenian bands accompanied the crowds to the Draper factory. The town of Hopedale, however, responded quickly by invoking a by-law, which prohibited parading without a license. After that, marchers were stopped by special police at the border between the two towns and ordered to turn around.

Eben Draper had little trouble connecting the Hopedale strike to Lawrence. In a letter addressed to local papers and later published in his company's newsletter, he briefly described the IWW influence and tactics in Lawrence. Draper wrote, "Soon after the end of the strike in Lawrence, men who had been affiliated with that movement began to come to Milford, where there was a large settlement of Italians, and began to preach the doctrines of the IWW. . . ."[52] Evidently he was

---

[49] Anita Danker, "The Hopedale Strike of 1913: The Unmaking of an Industrial Utopia," in Doug Reynolds and Katheryn Viens, editors, *New England's Disharmony: The Consequences of the Industrial Revolution* (Rhode Island Labor History Society, 1993, 74-91), 84.
[50] "Demonstration by Strikers," *Boston Daily Globe*, April 1, 1913, 1.
[51] "Citizenship Not the Issue," *Boston Daily Globe*, April 5, 1913, 3.
[52] "We Ask A Careful Consideration," *Cotton Chats Draper Company* (Hopedale, 1913).

not aware of the existence of socialist and anarchist workers' circles in Milford before 1912.

There was violence early on as an unidentified person shot at a streetcar entering the neighboring town of Hopkinton.[53] A Draper executive on his way home from work was hit in the leg and Milford officials called for help from surrounding police departments. The specials arrived from communities all over central and eastern Massachusetts and were housed in the Draper offices and were "accorded all manner of luxury," according to a newspaper report.[54] Strike-breakers also were recruited and housed in Hopedale under the watchful eye of police and Draper Company officials.

During the month of April, employees at two Milford firms, Greene Brothers and Lapworth Manufacturing, were persuaded to walk off their jobs in sympathy by Coldwell. All were young women, the majority of Italian descent. They joined the parade of several hundred Draper strikers through town and did not present any demands of their own employers until several days later. Greene Bros. and Lapworth employees asked for the abolition of the practice of "learners" working for the first three weeks on the job without pay, improvements in sanitary conditions, and raises. They picketed daily and used physical force to keep strike-breakers from crossing their lines. Seven police officers were assigned to keep the area secure but "through a reluctance to use extreme force on women, a small riot took place and a large squad of reserves had to be rushed to the scene before order was restored.... About 150 girls were involved in the fight."[55] The companies began bringing non-striking employees in to work by truck.

Though Palmira Merolini was identified in a news report as the leader of the women's strike, she did not work at either company. Merolini, born in Italy in 1888, immigrated with her parents to Milford around 1892. In 1913, she lived with her widowed mother in the Plains section of Milford and was active in the workers' struggle. Literate in both English and Italian, she served as secretary to the Draper strike committee and accompanied that group during a visit to Boston where they met with state officials attempting to mediate the strike. Merolini spoke at mass meetings and served as translator for visiting speakers. Merolini also chaperoned the strikers' children when they were sent to Woonsocket and Providence.[56] Jennie Calitri Paglia remembered her as "the lady in red" and as a

---

[53] "Shoot at Street Car," *Boston Daily Globe*, April 11, 1913, 1.
[54] "Demands Rejected by Draper Company," *Boston Daily Globe*, April 4, 1913, 1.
[55] Strike scrapbook *Milford Gazette*, April 25, 1913, Hopedale Public Library.
[56] Merolini married Antonio Boni, a chef, around 1915 and together they ran a restaurant in the North End of Boston. In another connection to the Sacco and Vanzetti case, Nicola Sacco's alibi was that he was at Boni's restaurant when the murder he was charged with was committed. Palmira worked with the defense lawyers for Sacco, translating letters and propaganda to and from Italy.

"firebrand." Paglia was among the children Merolini led in parade through the streets of Milford during the strike.[57]

The end of April saw increased violence as special officers shot and killed Emidio Bacchiocchi. The incident occurred in the woods between Milford and Hopedale. The *Boston Daily Globe* reported two versions of events. The first was provided by a Hopedale official who claimed that a small group of pickets, Bacchiocchi among them, threw stones at strike-breakers on their way to the Draper factory. To protect the workers, special police fired shots in the air over the heads of the attackers. "Some of the strikers must have been armed and have shot at the Hopedale specials, is the Hopedale contention, even if the dead man was unarmed." Coldwell presented the strikers' version, denying that any of the pickets were armed, contending that the specials had leapt out from behind a shed and opened fire as the men ran away.[58] That afternoon, Coldwell was arrested for violating the law against unlicensed parading in Hopedale and inciting a riot in Milford. He was released on bail several hours later.

Thousands of people lined the streets of Milford as Bacchiocchi's body was brought to Sacred Heart church for the funeral Mass. Afterwards, the body was placed in a hearse drawn by four white horses to be taken to the cemetery for burial. Immediately following the hearse was the slain striker's four-year-old son, carrying a sign in Italian reading "This is the son of the assassinated one." More than 800 men representing various Italian societies from the region came next. Behind them were two small girls dressed all in white representing angels of peace and mortality leading 700 women and girls. The remaining onlookers fell in behind the adult Italian band with the line stretching a mile through the streets. The crowd was estimated at 5,000.[59] No charges were brought against the specials. In response, three Milford police officers, all of Italian descent, turned in their badges and resigned from the force.[60] Bacchiocchi's murder hardened the resolve on both sides of the Draper strike.

Arturo Giovannitti arrived several days after the funeral and attempted to lead a group of 400 strikers and their children to Hopedale. State Police and Boston specials blocked the group at the town line. Giovannitti, along with Caleb Howard and Coldwell, were allowed to pass through the police lines but were immediately arrested upon crossing into Hopedale. Giovannitti's case was heard first thing the next morning and he was found guilty of participating in a parade and fined ten dollars.[61]

---

[57] Avrich, *Anarchist Voices*, 97.

[58] "Strike Tragedy Probed," *Boston Daily Globe,* April 25, 1913, 5.

[59] "Escort Fully a Mile Long," *Boston Daily Globe*, April 25, 1913, 5.

[60] "Inquest Held Today on Death of Bacchiocchi," *The Milford Daily News*, April 30, 1913, 3.

[61] "Giovannitti, Coldwell and Howard Jailed at Hopedale This Morning," *The Milford Daily News*, May 31, 1913, 1.

On May 3, word reached Milford that Big Bill Haywood and Joseph Ettor were on their way to take charge of the strike. Though Haywood never showed up, Ettor did, and addressed a mass meeting during a thunderstorm. He denounced the police for failing to make any arrests in the Bacchiocchi death declaring, "It was not the IWW that killed Bacchiocchi but the Hopedale officers." He urged them to remain unified as "a sure way to win the fight."[62] The state board of arbitration also arrived in Milford at this juncture hoping to begin mediation. Strikers were not in inclined to meet with Draper management but there was little hope of that occurring regardless. Eben Draper left town that day to spend two weeks at Hot Springs, Virginia.[63]

Milford women took to the streets to demonstrate solidarity and dissuade strike-breakers from travelling into Hopedale. Maria Recchia, a 40-year-old mother of six, was arrested for picking up a stone to throw at one such worker. Two police officers grabbed her arm before it was actually thrown and hauled her before a judge. There was a great outcry in the community when it was learned that Recchia was forbidden from having her two-week-old nursing infant in jail. The situation was rectified and neighbors brought the baby to Recchia in her cell.[64]

Groups of women, armed with brooms and sticks, gathered at the streetcar barn to stop strike-breakers coming in from nearby towns. Perhaps recognizing the futility of such action, they escalated their efforts by jumping onto the cars themselves, and refused to pay any fare. They rode into Hopedale "hooting" the entire way and were immediately returned to Milford on the next car.[65] Several days later male strikers prevented a streetcar from going through town. After stopping the car, they demanded that all passengers get off. After determining who among the crowd were Draper strike-breakers, the men let everyone else back on and sent the scabs on their way on foot.[66]

In what seems like an unnecessary act, a circular addressed to the women of the Plains district appeared late in May. Written in Italian and addressed to "Our Wives and Sisters," it read, "Why do you remain in bed or why do you not follow us in battle? Imitate your sisters in Paterson who follow their husbands and brothers in the hard battling. So do you tomorrow, Saturday morning at 6 am in Lincoln Square with your children. Wives, our companions in pain and misery, follow us," and was signed "A Group of Husbands." About 50 women and girls gathered on Main Street the next morning to jeer strike-breakers on

---

[62] "Ettor Talks in Thunderstorm," *Boston Daily Globe*, May 7, 1913, 13.
[63] Ibid.
[64] "Patrol Picketing Still On; Woman is Arrested," *The Milford Daily News*, April 24, 1913, 1.
[65] "Children to be Sent from Town," *Boston Daily Globe*, May 25, 1913, 14.
[66] "Strikers Stop Car, Push Passengers Off, and Hold Back Draper Workers," *The Milford Daily News,* May 23, 1913, 1.

their way to the Draper plant with some jumping onto the cars and riding them into Hopedale.[67]

Consiglia Bernadino was arrested for throwing a rock at a streetcar and found guilty. She was sentenced to three months in the county workhouse. She appealed and was let go on a $500 bond.[68] Adrianna Sanchioni, Ersal Monti, and Elizabeth Sabatucci were arrested for disturbing the peace. Arresting officers testified that the trio was shouting "scab" and waving their arms as streetcars left for Hopedale. The judge in the case "arraigned the women severely for their action railing, spitting, and brawling, instead of staying at home where they belong." According to a report, "the prisoners laughed as they were sentenced and openly declared they would pay no fine."[69]

The town of Milford was at its breaking point. Selectman debated taking off early and late streetcars. Merchants in town attempted to negotiate a settlement, to no avail. Eben Draper remained committed to his original position of refusing to negotiate. A committee, including Bacchiocchi's widow and Palmira Merolini, traveled to the State House in an attempt to get the current governor involved. They were not successful. Several by-laws were unearthed in Milford prohibiting disorder and "illegal occupancy of sidewalks" and public pressure was exerted to enforce them. The acting clerk of courts circulated a petition to secure the appointments of 25 to 35 more police officers.[70] Still, the strike dragged on. Several days later, the cancellation of the workman's morning streetcar was announced.[71]

Despite being offered what was presented as an increase in wages, the Greene Brothers strikers refused to return to work. Theresa Ferrante and Angie Sanclemente, representing their co-workers, met with management and went over the figures offered, demonstrating how no raise was actually on the table. In addition to demanding more money, the committee also asked for better stock to work on and more considerate treatment.[72]

As the strike entered its third month, the situation worsened for the strikers. The Draper factory had no trouble filling their spots and even built housing for the strike-breakers. Eben Draper remained committed to his original position not to negotiate. More children were sent away and many strikers also moved on to

---

[67] "Several Heads Smashed in Wildest Strike Riot," *The Milford Daily News*, May 24, 1913, 1.

[68] "Circulate Petition for More Police for Milford. Children Went Sunday," *The Milford Daily News*, May 26, 1913, 1.

[69] "Ex-Governor Draper Says IWW Conducts Strike to Aid in Socialist Propaganda," *The Milford Daily News*, May 27, 1913, 1.

[70] "Circulate Petition for More Police for Milford: Children Went Sunday," *The Milford Daily News*, May 26, 1913, 1.

[71] "Strike Picket Stone Worker on Way to Shop; Officers Search Another for Weapon in Vain," *The Milford Daily News*, May 29, 1913, 1.

[72] Ibid.

find other employment. Though buoyed by a visit from Gurley Flynn in late June, it was too late to have much effect on the outcome. By early July, the Draper strike was over and workers were forced to reapply for their positions. In addition to not winning any concessions from the company, they were assessed $1.00 a week by the IWW local to help pay off strike debts.

CONCLUSION

As we celebrate the centennial of Bread and Roses, it is important not to envision it as a singular event but rather as a part of a much larger pattern of American labor activism during the early 20th century. The Lawrence victory resulted from the synergy of complementary forces, including a labor organization committed to egalitarian principles, local ethnic societies with national and international ties, and a strike force of fiercely determined workers.

Lawrence's immigrant women took to the streets with their grievances, unconstrained by American ideals of feminine propriety. They were fighters refusing to back down, putting themselves and their families at risk, as they stood defiant in the face of their employers. Sending their children away was an astonishing act of bravery given the potential consequences. Their activism evoked a repressive and often violent response from the police and militia, which in turn generated much publicity from an incredulous press. After the settlement, noteworthy in itself, the imprisonment of Ettor and Giovannitti kept the Lawrence story alive in labor halls across the Commonwealth for months. Workers in nearby communities seized the opportunity to demand wage increases and better conditions. People with no access to power through standard channels realized that they could improve their lives through creative public protest. Despite linguistic and cultural differences, there was solidarity to be found in their status as workers.

The IWW, unlike mainstream unions, recognized the value of women on the picket line and encouraged their participation. From Greek women in Barre rushing the trains to Italian women in Milford assailing streetcars and scabs, the Massachusetts mill workers adopted the fierce stance of their Lawrence sisters. Just as whole families found work in the mills and factories, so too did they attempt to find justice on the streets. Wives, daughters, mothers, and sisters picketed and paraded, cooked and sang, were beaten, arrested, and shot alongside their male counterparts giving lie to the claim that they were not worthy of union representation. Though their names are not as recognizable as such leaders as Flynn or activist Sanger, the Massachusetts mill women contributed in no small way to American labor reform.

CHAPTER 10

The Triangle Fire Centennial Commemoration

Adrienne Sosin and Joel Sosinsky

On March 25, 1911, less than one year before the famous 1912 Bread and Roses textile workers' strike in Lawrence, Massachusetts, began, 146 garment workers died and more than 70 workers were injured in the Triangle shirtwaist factory fire in New York City. Since March 25, 1961, the 50th anniversary of the Triangle fire, the International Ladies Garment Workers Union (ILGWU) and its successors, along with the New York City Fire Department (FDNY), have held an annual joint memorial ceremony at the site of the Triangle fire at the former Asch Building, now the Brown Building of Science, owned by New York University (NYU). On March 25 each year, dignitaries and the public solemnly place flowers and wreaths below the three plaques on the corner of the building at Washington Place and Greene Street. The ILGWU, which represented most of the workers who died in the fire, placed the first plaque there in 1961. The second plaque, placed in 1991, cites the building in the National Register of Historic Places, and the New York City Landmarks Preservation Commission placed the third plaque in 2003. March 25, 2011 marked the centennial of the Triangle factory fire.

At the Bread and Roses academic symposium, a panel composed of members of the Remember the Triangle Fire Coalition (RTFC) provided their perspectives and recollections of organizing, planning, and executing the Triangle fire's centennial commemoration events to offer information about the processes in organizing the Triangle commemoration as instructive to others planning similar labor history memorial events.[1] Panelists shared web site images and photographs of the centennial and spoke about their individual perceptions and experiences working with the coalition in preparing for the events marking the Triangle fire centennial. The session began with a historical description of the Triangle fire, because even those who know about the Triangle fire tragedy often are not cognizant of information about the event itself, its aftermath, its role as a forerunner to the Bread and Roses strike commemoration, its lasting impact, and how references to the Triangle fire continue to influence today's global labor movement, particularly in the garment industry and in other contexts as well.

HISTORY OF THE TRIANGLE SHIRTWAIST FACTORY FIRE

As described during the Bread and Roses symposium session, the story of the Triangle fire has relevance to understanding the situation labor finds itself in today. During the early part of the 20th century, as the industrial era morphed in the United States from an agrarian to a commercial society, there was a companion revolution in fashion. Most clothing before the Civil War had been hand-tailored; the invention of the sewing machine in 1846 and the necessity for military uniforms for Civil War soldiers caused a revolution in clothing production: creation of patterns made to standardized sizes, thus creating a "ready-to-wear" industry in men's clothing.[2] Women's clothing fashions also changed after the Civil War; corsets were abandoned by the upper classes in favor of clothing that, while modest, required less assistance in dressing. Charles Dana Gibson's popular illustrations in *Life* and other magazines frequently depicted stylish Gibson Girls wearing shirtwaists, light or white cotton or linen blouses often trimmed in lace, called "the sartorial symbol of American womanhood," by Leon Stein, whose research and publication of *The Triangle Fire* (1962) at its 50th anniversary has helped keep the memory of the fire alive.[3] Shirtwaists and skirt combinations were practical and utilitarian because they could be washed separately, making them very desirable for frugal working women as well as suitable fashion for active upper class women.

By the end of the 19th century, New York City had become a major center of garment manufacturing. By 1900, most mass garment production had moved

---

[1]Moderated by Rose Imperato, panelists included public historian Sheryl Woodruff, playwright, actor, and performance artist LuLu LoLo, American history professor Daniel Levinson-Wilk, and teacher educator Adrienne Andi Sosin. RTFC members Joel Sosinsky, Sherry Kane, Artie Rothschild, and Michael Sosin joined in the session.

[2]Yeshiva University Museum, *A Perfect Fit: The Garment Industry and American Jewry* (New York, 2005), 15.

[3]Leon Stein, *The Triangle Fire* (1962; Ithaca, New York, 2011), 12.

from small tenement sweatshops into modern skyscraper loft factory buildings such as the Asch Building in Greenwich Village, where in 1902 the Triangle Waist Company located on the ninth floor, expanding onto the eighth and tenth floors by 1909.[4] Higher ceilings in the new factory buildings allowed for greater concentration of workers, and there was no law in New York then requiring factory buildings to install fire sprinklers or for building owners to conduct fire drills.

Workers were treated with blatant disregard for their lives and well-being. Triangle's owners, Jewish immigrants themselves who had become contractors and then launched their business as partners, Max Blanck and Isaac Harris were dubbed "the Shirtwaist Kings" based on their rise to fortune in manufacturing and selling blouses.[5] In the competitive environment of the garment industry, the owners' driving force was to meet buyers' demand and increase productivity. An inside contracting system provided distance between the owners and the cutters, sewing machine operators and finishers who actually manufactured the clothing.[6] Despite their own working class backgrounds, the owners of the Triangle Waist Company led the garment manufacturer's association in successfully fighting unionization in 1909–1910,[7] and they continued to lead a fight against new fire regulations, which were called for by the city and fire chief. Instead of investing in automatic sprinklers and losing work time for fire drills, the system by which insurance brokers were compensated based on premiums paid encouraged manufacturers to purchase huge amounts of fire insurance.[8]

More than 600 Triangle Waist Company employees were still at work at 4:40 p.m. on Saturday, March 25, 1911, even though all the other businesses in the building already were closed. Blanck and Harris adamantly refused to sign the ILGWU contracts ending strikes in 1909 and 1910 which, among other concessions, reduced working hours to half a day on Saturdays.[9] As the work day was ending, an accidental fire of paper patterns and fabric scraps began on the eighth floor, which quickly spread upwards. Most of the workers on the eighth floor were able to escape by elevator, and a telephone call alerted the owners, salesmen, and workers on the tenth floor who escaped over the rooftop.

---

[4] David Von Drehle, *Triangle: The Fire That Changed America*, (New York, 2003), 46-47.

[5] Von Drehle, *Triangle: The Fire That Changed America*, 37.

[6] Stein, *The Triangle Fire*, 161.

[7] Von Drehle, *Triangle: The Fire That Changed America*, 63.

[8] Leon Stein provides a detailed description of how insurance brokerage commissions were calculated, supporting the continuance of dangerous practices. Subsequent to the fire 36 of the 37 insurance companies from which its insurance brokers had purchased fire insurance coverage indemnified Triangle's owners. Additionally, three years after the fire, a civil action was settled by an insurance company paying $75 each to 23 victims' families who brought suit against the owner of the Asch Building. (169-176).

[9] Philip Dray, *There is Power in a Union: The Epic Story of Labor in America*, (New York, 2010), 269.

But by the time the sewing machine operators on the ninth floor recognized there was a fire, one of the two stairwells was aflame and the other stairwell door was locked, a regular practice to discourage contact with union organizers and prevent employees from stealing, taking breaks, or leaving early.[10]

The New York City fire department rushed to the scene of the fire, but even its tallest fire ladders only reached the sixth floor. More than 50 workers, mostly young Jewish and Italian immigrant girls, flung themselves from the ninth-floor windows to their deaths. Some fell from the narrow interior fire escape when it collapsed; some were crushed when they jumped into the elevator shaft; and the rest died from the smoke and flames. In fewer than 20 minutes, 146 employees were dead and more than 70 were injured. A huge crowd made up of friends and relatives from the nearby Lower East Side and Little Italy gathered on the street and witnessed the grisly scene.

Factory fires were not uncommon in 1911, nor were industrial accidents and deaths from inadequate safety protections rare. In this case the scale of death, the ages of the victims, that most were immigrant girls recently on strike, and available riveting eyewitness accounts from the spectators gathered at the scene made the Triangle fire an event demanding banner headlines in the New York metropolitan area and in newspapers across the United States and in other countries. Similar to the practice followed by the *New York Times* after the terrorist attack on the World Trade Center on September 11, 2001, newspapers published accounts of the fire and personal descriptions alongside photos of the victims.

As the facts of the fire became known, especially that the Triangle's owners had resisted the union's demands for safer working conditions, newspaper editorials began to demand justice for those killed and safer working conditions for the living. The conservative *New York Times* editorial of March 26, 1911, called the fire a "calamity" that ". . . compels horror and pity rather than condemnation of any person or any system,"[11] and the following day's editorial stated, "A mass meeting, with eloquent speechmaking, will neither undo the wrong that has been done, nor point out a way to punish the persons who may be guilty of causing it through negligence or mismanagement, or to prevent a similar occurrence in the future. . . . No new laws are needed. Enforcement of existing laws is imperative."[12] In contrast, *The Jewish Daily Forward* used the full length of its front page on March 29, 1911, to print a Yiddish language dirge by poet Morris Rosenfeld, whom Leon Stein called "the poet laureate of the slum and sweatshop,"[13] which stirred the mounting anger already seething in

---

[10] Dray, *There is Power in a Union,* 270.

[11] The *New York Times* archive, Editorial, March 26, 1911, http://query.nytimes.com/mem/archive-free/pdf?res=9B03E0D61331E233A25755C2A9659C946096D6CF.

[12] The *New York Times* archive, Editorial, March 27, 1911, http://query.nytimes.com/mem/archive-free/pdf?res=9F02E6DA143EE033A25754C2A9659C946096D6CF.

[13] Stein, *The Triangle Fire*, 145.

the strongly socialist Jewish community. *Il Progresso* published articles and drawings that incited anger in the Italian community, and the socialist organ *The Call* published front-page cartoons and line drawings accompanying articles that directly blamed the owners for the tragedy and tied the Triangle fire to the excesses of capitalism.

As the Red Cross collected donations for victims' families, public protest meetings were held. On April 2, 1911, the Women's Trade Union League (WTUL) convened a memorial meeting at the Metropolitan Opera House attended by 3,500 people.[14] ILGWU historian Leon Stein described a scene in which the city's wealthy sat in the orchestra, "the men in high hats and plush-trimmed overcoats, the women trailing furs and feathers,"[15] and mourning garment workers sat in the balcony. In a call for class consciousness, WTUL organizer Rose Schneiderman condemned the upper and middle classes for countenancing business practices that harmed workers, ending with the words, ". . . it is up to the working people to save themselves. And the only way they can save themselves is by a strong working-class movement."[16]

When the WTUL and the manager of the ILGWU shirtwaist makers Local 25 petitioned the city charities commissioner to bury the bodies of the seven unidentified and unclaimed victims, they were refused, allegedly in fear of hysteria that a public funeral would create, and the mayor announced the city's intention to bury the unclaimed bodies in a city-owned plot on April 5. In response, the WTUL and ILGWU committee had handbills written in English, Yiddish, and Italian distributed, publicizing their intention to hold a silent funeral procession on that same day. More than 400,000 people (one tenth of the entire New York City population at that time) walked in or witnessed the "Trade Parade" that took place during a downpour. Now famous contemporaneous photographs held by the Library of Congress show marchers carrying black banners announcing, "We Mourn Our Loss," with horses draped in black netting pulling a hearse that held a symbolically empty coffin and unionists and victims' relatives marching alongside. The processions flowed through the streets toward Washington Square, but were diverted by wary police from directly passing the Asch Building, site of the fire.[17]

Eloquent demands for justice and for better working conditions came not only from the unions, but from middle-class citizens who were waking up to realize the inhumanity of the sweatshops. Following the Metropolitan Opera House meeting, a Committee on Safety assembled, and, with support from the WTUL and the National Consumers League, the labor unions, Jewish and Italian clergy and ethnic organizations, and individuals from all social classes, clamored

---

[14] Dray, *There is Power in a Union,* 272.
[15] Stein, *The Triangle Fire,* 141.
[16] Stein, *The Triangle Fire,* 145.
[17] Stein, *The Triangle Fire.* 152.

for stronger safety laws. On June 30, 1911, with cooperation from Tammany Hall boss "Silent Charlie" Murphy, who foresaw the voting power of his aggrieved immigrant constituents, Governor John Alden Dix signed the law that established and allocated funds to a Factory Investigating Commission (FIC), led by New York State Senator Robert F. Wagner Sr. and New York State Assemblyman Alfred E. Smith. WTUL leader Mary Dreier became one of the four commissioners appointed to the FIC. Frances Perkins, who personally witnessed the Triangle fire, and Dr. George Price from the Joint Board of Sanitary Control, provided leadership. Rose Schneiderman, who also witnessed the fire, and Clara Lemlich, the labor activist credited with having called for the 1909 uprising and who lost friends in the fire, joined as field investigators. The FIC's charter granted it vast power, including the power to subpoena witnesses and documents, to elect its own members, and to change its rules, which allowed it to expand its scope. It visited factories and mills across New York State and held public hearings that gathered testimony from more than 200 witnesses regarding industrial safety, sanitation, and diseases that resulted from hazardous processes.[18]

Between 1911 and 1914, the FIC suggested and the New York State Legislature passed 36 laws, which strengthened and expanded the state Department of Labor, providing for more frequent inspections and tough citations for factories that failed compliance.[19] New York's factory safety laws mandated automatic sprinklers, doors that opened outward, fire inspections and drills, addressed rubbish and industrial waste removal procedures, improved restrictions on child labor, and adopted innovations from Europe, such as Worker's Compensation Insurance, which had been struck down earlier. The New York State laws were broadly copied, and were followed years later by New Deal federal labor legislation, including the Fair Labor Standards Act of 1938 and the National Labor Relations Act of 1935, both passed into law during Frances Perkins' tenure as Secretary of Labor in the Franklin Roosevelt administration. Even the Occupational Safety and Health Act of 1970 referenced the Triangle Shirtwaist Factory fire as a reason for its enactment.[20]

As a result of the coroner's inquest immediately after the fire, Blanck and Harris were charged with manslaughter. Even though their trial began more than a year later in December 1912, sentiment was still strong among the victims' relatives and ethnic communities that the Triangle owners deserved punishment. However, in cross-examinations by defense attorney Max Steuer, the immigrant seamstress witnesses were made to seem as if the district attorney had rehearsed

---

[18] Von Drehle, *Triangle: The Fire That Changed America*, 213-215.

[19] Stein, *The Triangle Fire*, 208.

[20] UCLA Institute for Research on Labor and Employment, "OSHA at 40: Looking Back, Looking Ahead" *Research & Policy Brief*, (no. 8, April, 2011), 3. http://www.irle.ucla.edu/publications/documents/ResearchBrief8.pdf.

their testimony, and Blanck and Harris were acquitted when the judge's instructions strictly required that the prosecution prove that the owners knew that the stairway door was locked on the day of the fire. The verdict was met with outrage from the victims' relatives and from the general public.

Clearly the Triangle fire directly resulted in many of the safety protections now universally expected: physical ones like requiring working fire exits, automatic sprinklers, extinguishers, drills and appointed fire wardens, and instituting sanitary workplace hazard protections. There were less visible effects of the progressive labor laws that began to make sweatshops more humane. Triangle is credited with inspiring and providing a model for the New Deal's progressive legislation comprising the basic "social safety net" U.S. citizens take for granted today.

Regretfully, much of the progress that followed in response to the Triangle tragedy has been dissipated bit by bit over time. Since 1947 the National Labor Relations Act of 1935, known as the "Worker's Law," and the National Labor Relations Board, the administrative apparatus designed to protect workers' rights to organize and bargain collectively, have been weakened through amendment and court rulings that have had the effect of diminishing union power and allowing flagrant union-busting.[21] It is in this present day environment that the Remember the Triangle Fire Coalition was founded to advocate for a centennial remembrance and memorial, and for activism on behalf of working people.

At the 50th Anniversary Memorial Meeting of the Triangle Fire on March 25, 1961, the ILGWU, New York University, and the New York City Fire Department produced an anniversary commemoration that became an historic event, attended by Frances Perkins, Eleanor Roosevelt, and Rose Schneiderman, with 14 of the remaining survivors of the Triangle fire. Documented by Leon Stein, the event brought together the survivors to meet each other again, who, "50 years earlier, almost to the hour, had lain bleeding and battered at the bottom of the elevator shaft down which each had leaped from the open ninth-floor elevator door."[22]

In recent years, since it took over representing the members of ILGWU Local 23-25 in New York City, Workers United has coordinated with the New York City Central Labor Council and the New York City Fire Department to produce the public ceremony that commemorates the anniversary of the Triangle fire. The FDNY officers stand in formation and a fire officer tolls a bell as a student or a relative reads each victim's name aloud. The ritual ends as firefighters raise a modern fire truck's ladder only to the height of the sixth floor to show the inadequacy of the fire fighting equipment of 1911. In preparation for the annual commemoration ceremony, with support and logistics coordination

---

[21] Ellen Dannin, *Taking Back the Workers' Law: How to Fight the Assault on Labor Rights,* (Ithaca, New York, 2006).

[22] Stein, *The Triangle Fire*, 220.

provided by the Amalgamated Life Insurance Company and Amalgamated Bank (each founded by the Amalgamated Clothing Workers Union, also a predecessor of Workers United), union staff arranges permits, staging, and sound equipment, creates a program and invites speakers and dignitaries to sit on the platform.

As a large crowd was expected to commemorate the Triangle fire centennial, the unions and Central Labor Council were aware that there would be additional preparations necessary. They anticipated needing a Jumbotron to broadcast the ceremony to those assembled in the street below the Brown Building. Speakers included Secretary of Labor Hilda Solis and New York City Mayor Michael Bloomberg, as well as the New York State Congressional delegation and union officials. Representatives from the Bangladesh Center for Worker Solidarity shared their current struggles against the same industrial ethos that caused the Triangle fire.

By 2009 the Remember the Triangle Fire Coalition (RTFC) had become an integral part of the annual commemoration ceremonies. The RTFC's involvement resulted in invitations to family members of the Triangle fire victims to be seated on the dais, and the speakers at the centennial included the RTFC's family representative, Suzanne Pred Bass, who spoke about her two great aunts, one who died in the fire, and one who survived it.

THE REMEMBER THE TRIANGLE FIRE COALITION

A potent way of remembering and honoring the victims of the Triangle fire has been repeated each March 25 since 2004 when Ruth Sergel, the founder of the Remember the Triangle Fire Coalition,[23] recruited volunteers to write in chalk a name and the date of the Triangle fire as the cause of death on the sidewalk in front of the street address where each victim of the Triangle fire lived in 1911. While the sidewalk chalk is ephemeral, photos posted on her web site, called "The Chalk Project," document each chalked memorial. Since 2004, chalk volunteers have grown to include descendants of Triangle family members, residents in buildings where victims lived, historians, unionists and teachers.

Ruth's organizing "Chalk" moved her to organize a coalition to fully and properly commemorate the Triangle fire's losses as well as memorialize the positive changes that followed. Her vision for the RTFC was one in which its, ". . . role was not to direct but to create a platform that supported people in doing what they knew best. We hashed out a simple focus—to build a network of support for the centennial and the establishment of a permanent memorial."[24]

Through a sophisticated application of a WordPress blog, the RTFC established a domain, http://rememberthetrianglefire.org. The web site offers a menu of web

---

[23] Ruth Sergel, "Remember the Triangle Fire Coalition," *New York University Journal of Legislation and Public Policy*, 14 (no. 3, 2011), 611-623.
[24] Sergel, "Remember the Triangle Fire Coalition," 618.

pages that display the coalition's mission statement and a brief historical statement, the list of participating organizations, the memorial project, and the "Names Map," an interactive map of New York City's environs that individually pinpoints each victim's home address showing its distance from the site of the Triangle fire, and lists the age, likely country of origin, and final resting place of each victim, which can be filtered to a range of victims' ages. The menu also links to the interactive calendar of events held by coalition members and sponsors, which during the centennial month of March 2011 was filled with multiple event listings each day. The pages for Resources and Education provide a list of recommendations to Triangle-related music, poetry, adult literature and non-fiction accounts, plays and dramatic works, historical books and articles in print, artistic endeavors, young adult literature, lesson plans and curriculum links, and student work.

The RTFC home page is programmed to accept contributions, displaying with acknowledgment the names of the organizations that provide financial donations in coordination with City Lore as the Coalition's 501(c)(3) fiscal sponsor. In this way the RTFC web site provides interested organizations an easy way to join the coalition online. A minimal $20 administrative fee was always waived upon request. Ruth Sergel, who until after the centennial almost single-handedly managed the RTFC web site, sent a welcome message to every registrant as positive reinforcement via e-mail upon joining. By the time the centennial took place, more than 200 individuals and organizations had joined the coalition. Since the centennial, as it pursues its missions of memorialization and education, the RTFC maintains its web site along with its complementary Facebook page and a Twitter account, and the Constant Contact database for email blasts.

Many grant applications were submitted to fund the coalition's activities. The coalition gratefully accepted financial support from the 21st Century ILGWU Heritage Fund and the Margot Gayle Fund of the Metropolitan Chapter of the Victorian Society in America, in support of creation of the Triangle Fire Open Archive. A grant from the New York Council for the Humanities was used in support of the Open Museum. Funding is now being sought for the Triangle Memorial project and the RTFC's ongoing educational activities.

The RTFC forged alliances with many organizations interested in participating in the centennial. Important and lasting connections were forged with Workers United, the successor union to ILGWU Local 25, and the New York City Central Labor Council. Early on, the coalition established an alliance with the American Society of Safety Engineers (ASSE), an organization that credits its foundation to the Triangle fire. At the centennial, the ASSE published a booklet devoted to safety lessons of the Triangle fire, and it has continued to partner with the RTFC in preparation for erecting a permanent Triangle memorial. In 2008, the Education and Labor Collaborative (ELC) began its collaboration with the coalition. The ELC sponsored an institute on Teaching Triangle and cosponsored the centennial event in Cooper Union's Great Hall. The coalition also reached out to the Triangle Shirtwaist Factory Fire Memorial Association of workers compensation attorneys which hosts an annual fundraising dinner to memorialize the fire and its impact in changing New York State labor laws, in which proceeds are used for scholarships for children of parents injured in workplace accidents.

As it became known that a coalition to remember the Triangle fire was in formation, the members of victims' families began to come forward. Michael Hirsch, a researcher and associate producer of the Home Box Office documentary, *Triangle: Remembering the Fire*,[25] identified many family members of both victims and survivors who associated with the coalition, including the Maltese family, who lost their grandmother and two aunts in the fire.

During his long tenure as a New York State senator, Serphin Maltese made sure that the state legislature issued a yearly proclamation to remember the Triangle fire, and the Maltese family has been stalwart in devotion to the memory of the victims. They now moderate a Facebook group, the Triangle Fire Memorial Association, Inc., as an informal extension of the earlier Triangle Fire Survivors Group, which holds an annual memorial event at Christ the King High School in Queens and at Calvary Cemetery, where many of the Catholic fire victims were interred.

A special relationship began between the RTFC and Cornell University's School of Industrial and Labor Relations' (ILR) Catherwood Library, which contains the archives of the ILGWU and the Amalgamated Clothing Workers Union. ILR's library staff has maintained a dedicated online resource about the Triangle fire that contains primary and secondary source materials from those union archives to support students and researchers.[26] ILR updated the web site for the centennial, including the names of the previously unidentified victims. Cornell ILR is now accepting and cataloguing the RTFC's own archives.

Prior to the centennial, the RTFC organized participation in monthly public meetings and special events. A public launch of the coalition's effort to mark the centennial took place at Judson Memorial Church on March 25, 2009. After the launch, the monthly meetings grew larger, and the RTFC leadership decided to formalize their process by creating by-laws and a committee structure. City Lore, acting as 501(c) (3) fiscal sponsor, scrupulously maintained finances and the coalition's treasurer supplied a public report at each monthly meeting.

The RTFC's preparation for the centennial was somewhat like running a clearinghouse that matched people with projects and venues. In one instance, the coalition's intercession with contacts at the Judson Memorial Church provided

---

[25] Home Box Office, *Triangle: Remembering the Fire*, https://www.hbo.com/documentaries/triangle-remembering-the-fire/.

[26] Cornell University School of Industrial and Labor Relations, Catherwood Library, Kheel Center, http://www.ilr.cornell.edu/Trianglefire/.

the venue for the theatrical production of the oratorio composed by Liz Swados, *From the Fire*.[27] In another, RTFC organizer LuLu LoLo took responsibility for hosting gatherings at which participants cut and glued fabric in the shape of blouses to hangers, and labeled sashes with each Triangle fire victim's name and age. Opening the commemoration in 2011, the RTFC staged a memorial procession in which more than 1,000 people marched carrying 146 poles lofting symbolic shirtwaist kites from Union Square down Broadway to the Brown (Asch) Building. These shirtwaists continue to be brought to the annual commemoration and to demonstrations to signal RTFC participation.

The RTFC also made an important contribution in setting up and providing photos for the Jumbotron, and Ruth Sergel's personal work video streaming on the Jumbotron and on the Internet was key in making the ceremony visible to people on the street and around the world. In yet another method of involving people across distances, the RTFC instigated "Bells", an interactive social media event, where at precisely 4:45 p.m. on March 25, 2011, again on March 25, 2012, and from now on as a growing tradition, people ring all kinds of bells at the Brown Building and in cities and towns across the United States to commemorate those lost in the Triangle fire. Bell ringing is reported via Facebook, Twitter, and email, and the geographical source for each bell is marked on a second interactive map within the RTFC web site, exhibiting the extent of geographical distance among people who feel it important to mark the tragedy in a symbolic way.

On the evening of the centennial, Cooper Union donated its Great Hall to host an evening of speeches and musical tributes to the Triangle fire's victims. Along with the Education and Labor Collaborative, the RTFC held a program in which performers and unionists from across the United States and from Bangladesh delivered messages of solidarity. *Di Fayer Korbunes*, a forgotten contemporaneous popular song about the Triangle fire, which was rediscovered in the Library of Congress, had its debut performance by the band, Metropolitan Klezmer, and an audio recording of the song is part of the *Activist New York* exhibition at the Museum of the City of New York.

Publication of books and poems, art exhibits, school projects, films, TV and radio interviews, and scholarly conferences were timed to coincide with the Triangle centennial. The Labor and Working Class Studies Association, the City University of New York, and the Fashion Institution of Technology, State University of New York, each held Triangle-themed scholarly conferences during the centennial week. Just as at the Bread and Roses Centennial academic symposium from which this chapter evolved, these meetings afforded opportunities for scholars and activists to share interpretations and new findings related to the events surrounding the Triangle fire and its legacy.

---

[27] *From The Fire*, created by Elizabeth Swados, Cecilia Rubino, Paula Finn, and Bonnie Roche-Bronfman, http://www.trianglefromthefire.com.

NYU's Grey Art Gallery, located on the same block as the Brown (Asch) Building, held an exhibition devoted to the Triangle fire and premiered the Home Box Office documentary, *Triangle: Remembering the Fire*. The New York State Fashion Institute of Technology hosted talks and art exhibitions, including *Art/Memory/Place*. The New York City Tenement Museum hosted a mini-performance of the *Waistmaker's Opera* and readings by historians and authors of fictional accounts of the Triangle fire. The museum at the Eldridge Street synagogue held a centennial memorial procession and ceremony, and talks, exhibits, and art shows were held at private galleries. *The Triangle Fire*,[28] a documentary with re-enactment, was shown on PBS's *American Experience*, and the American Society of Safety Engineers produced the film, *A Century of Safety*.

Original live theater productions that debuted during the centennial included: *From the Fire*, an oratorio and dramatic performance composed by Elizabeth Swados and colleagues; *Birds on Fire* by Barbara Kahn; *Fabric, Flames, and Fervor: Girls of the Triangle*, the Looking for Lilith Theatre Company's originally-devised performance piece; *The Waistmaker's Opera*, a student-acted musical performance; and *Triangle, A Puppet Play with Live Music for the 100th Anniversary of the Triangle Shirtwaist Factory Fire* by Brad Kemp. In addition, *The Triangle Factory Fire Project* by Christopher Piehler and Scott Alan Evans was performed in Rochester, New York, and in New York City.

The occasion of the Triangle centennial prompted Cornell University Press to issue a centennial edition of Leon Stein's 1962 *The Triangle Fire* with a new foreword written by Michael Hirsch, the researcher who identified the six previously unidentified victims. This new information prompted a dedication ceremony at the monument erected by the Red Cross in 1912 at the Cemetery of the Evergreens for a new footstone inscribed with the six names. Other books published to coincide with the Triangle fire centennial included *The New York City Triangle Factory Fire*, an Arcadia Publishers *Images of America* book of vintage photographs, and Albert Marrin's young adult book, *Flesh & Blood So Cheap: The Triangle Fire and its Legacy*.[29] A more complete list of the publications and performance events related to the centennial appears on the RTFC's web site.

As the RTFC gathered participating organizations, Facebook friends and Twitter followers online, Ruth Sergel began to receive emails and posts that contained references to Triangle fire-related materials in private collections. In response, the RTFC contracted with Buscada, a creative technology company, to create programming for an online "Open Archive," a themed and searchable

---

[28] *The Triangle Fire*, PBS American Experience, Jamila Wignot, producer and director, http://www.pbs.org.wgbh/americanexperience/films/triangle/player/.

[29] Albert Marrin, *Flesh & Blood So Cheap: The Triangle Fire and its Legacy* (New York, 2011).

catalog of materials submitted by the public that would become part of the Triangle fire history. In addition to providing a web-based option to upload photos and documents, the Buscada team[30] came to RTFC meetings and held open dates at venues like the Brooklyn Historical Society to which people could bring in objects and have these accessioned into the Open Archive collection. More than 200 donated photographs and photos of objects, including family photos, records from Our Lady of Pompeii, the church which lost 18 members in the fire, and oral histories by union members connected to the ILGWU, including those who participated in the 1982 Chinatown garment strike, became an additional online resource available through the RTFC web site.[31]

Buscada recently expanded its involvement to develop the Triangle Fire Open Museum, in which physical objects seen in the Open Archive are installed at different locations around New York City with a published guide to locating each of the items. The Open Museum was initially hosted at the New York City Tenement Museum, the Fashion Institute of Technology, the New York City Fire Museum, the offices of Workers United, the Museum of Chinese in America, and the Murphy Center, City University of New York. The Open Museum project is currently seeking funding for future exhibitions.

SOCIAL ACTIVISM

Throughout history, workers have struggled for workplace safety, the right to representation of their choice, decent wages, and to gain a better quality of life for themselves and their families. More than 100 years following the Triangle fire, the struggle for dignity at work continues at home in the United States as well as in places all over the world where global companies source their goods, especially in low-wage countries in Central America, Bangladesh, India, Pakistan, and China. In the belief that the solidarity that brought about social progress following the Triangle fire must again be brought to bear on behalf of workers around the world, the RTFC has forged alliances with international labor organizations, including the International Labor Rights Forum (ILRF), United Students Against Sweatshops (USAS), and Occupy Wall Street (OWS). Kalpona Akter and Babul Akhter, founders of the Bangladeshi Center for Worker Solidarity, traveled to attend the Triangle centennial and share their current struggle for workplace safety.

As militant union organizing and the struggles for women's suffrage that followed the Triangle fire were successful in changing lives and work places for the better, the RTFC actively supports and demonstrates on behalf of current struggles for labor and human rights. As recently as December 18, 2012, the

---

[30] *Triangle Fire Open Archive* by BUSCADA, http://buscada.com/project/triangle-fire-open-archive/.
[31] Sergel, "Remember the Triangle Fire Coalition," 621.

RTFC and OWS together organized an action at the Port of Newark against Wal-Mart's importation of goods made in the Tazreen factory in Bangladesh, where a November 24, 2012 fire similar in many ways to the Triangle fire killed more than 112 mostly female workers who were forced to jump from the windows or who were burned to death.

THE TRIANGLE FIRE MEMORIAL

Since the 2011 centennial commemoration, the RTFC's focus has shifted to attend to the second part of its original mission: to erect a public art memorial to the victims of the Triangle fire at the site of the fire. The memorial's intended design goals are to provide viewers with an inspiring educational experience, and to resonate with contemporary labor and social justice concerns as it memorializes the 146 workers who died in the Triangle fire. RTFC organizers envision the memorial as a "destination" piece of public art that will attract visitors to see the building, to learn about the Triangle fire, and to appreciate the activism that instituted policies to protect and benefit the vast majority of people who toil each day.

The mission of installing a permanent public art memorial at the fire's site has taken many volunteer hours and much negotiation within and outside the coalition. Enabling construction of a permanent memorial required that the RTFC incorporate as a New York State not-for-profit corporation as a first step toward obtaining 501(c)(3) status. This status allows donations it receives to be considered "charitable donations" under the U.S. Internal Revenue Code. Funds collected for the memorial will provide the costs for construction, installation, and maintenance of the memorial, and the RTFC's educational outreach with lessons that involve the memorial.

It has been a long and involved process to engage all of the communities interested in the Triangle fire, and to cope with the myriad problems and requirements that accompany trying to please many different constituencies. To accomplish the memorial project, the RTFC needed to form relationships with the New York City Landmarks Preservation Commission (NYCLPC), with local community groups and with NYU, the owners of the Brown (Asch) Building, to secure architectural specifications and permission to erect the memorial. These alliances took time and effort to establish. In December 2012, the RTFC and NYU reached an agreement that allowed a juried Triangle Fire Memorial Design Competition to begin.

This competition launched an open-call process to solicit designs that meet the architectural requirements and limitations set by NYU, the NYCLPC, and the coalition. The winning design will be installed on the exterior of the Brown Building. It has taken more than 100 years to get to the point where a memorial to the Triangle fire can be erected at its site as an important signifier to workers, women, immigrants, and social activists that their voices can make a difference.

The Bread & Roses Centennial Academic Symposium held in 2012 offered an opportunity for RTFC organizers to recount their experiences and share their thoughts about organizing for the Triangle fire centennial, the preparations for building the Triangle Fire Memorial, and current RTFC activities. It is hoped that this account will be considered informative and instructive, and that plans to memorialize workers and reinvigorate labor will enjoy similar successes as did the centennial commemorations of the Triangle fire and the Bread and Roses strike.

CHAPTER 11

The Cloth From Which We Are Cut: Using Music, Narration, and Images to Tell the Story of the 1911 Triangle Shirtwaist Fire

Vicki Gabriner and Linda Stern

Theater is a weapon, and it is the people who should wield it.
Augusto Boal, *Theatre of the Oppressed*, 1985

Song is a beautifier and a liberator.
40 Years Workmen's Circle, New York, 1940

How can key historical events be portrayed to have the greatest impact in the immediacy and power of live theater? It is a question of crucial importance if we as activists, teachers, researchers, students, and artists want to leave this as part of our legacy. We must find the burning speeches and courageous actions from the past, draw the connections to current issues, and inspire people to keep fighting the good fight.[1]

It was the driving motivation for *A Besere Velt* [ABV; Yiddish: A Better World], the Yiddish Community Chorus of the Boston Workmen's Circle (BWC), as we began work in 2010 on the show that would culminate in *The Cloth From Which We are Cut*, a commemoration of the 100th anniversary of the 1911

---

[1] Note on usage: We use the spelling "theater" except in those instances where the person, book, or group, spells it "theatre."

Triangle Shirtwaist Fire in which 146 very young immigrant garment workers, primarily Jewish and Italian women, died.[2]

The chorus was entering a two-year period during which we would commemorate the centennials of two of labor's most galvanizing events—the horrific 1911 Triangle fire, and less than a year later, the turbulent 1912 Great Lawrence Textile Strike (also known as the Bread and Roses Strike). Calling the Boston, Massachusetts area its home, the *ABV* chorus was geographically and politically positioned to resonate deeply with both events.

We dove in for two years of intense concentration—researching the historical record; discovering the roles played by individuals, unions, political figures, and factory owners; finding images to illustrate the events; watching documentaries; and selecting, arranging, and learning the music to tell this story. The resulting concert, performed in six locations in three states in 2011, employed narrative, images, and music effectively to tell the powerful story of this event. By so doing, chorus members placed themselves in the great historical stream of artists and activists who have created theater and music of social change as far back as ancient Greece.

WHAT IS "THEATER OF SOCIAL CHANGE"?

It goes by several names, including: "Theater of Social Protest," "Theater of (or, for) Social Change," "Theatre of the Oppressed," "Political Theater," "People's Theater." . . . Its over-arching purpose is to act and sing out against social and economic injustice and for those issues and individuals usually located at the bottom of society's food chain, and most often invisible in the land of art and culture.

> How the aesthetic and the political go together is certainly, in my view, fundamental. Because art reaches a part of the human sensibility that's very difficult to define but that's recognizable. What street theater and political theater should reach for is to make an irresistible aesthetic. We should make it so beautiful that people have to know it's true.[3]

It is often, but not always, connected to a particular social/political movement. In 1965, El Teatro Campesino grew out of the Chicano farmworkers' fight.[4] A year earlier, in 1964, SNCC (Student Nonviolent Coordinating Committee)

---

[2] Note on usage: The Triangle Waist Company was the official name of the factory about which we are writing. It is referred to in various ways, such as Triangle Shirtwaist Company and the Triangle. We have varied the usage according to the context.

[3] *Theater and Social Change: A special issue edited by Alisa Solomon.* North Carolina: Duke University Press, on behalf of the Yale School of Drama/Yale Repertory Theatre, Fall 2001, Volume 31, Number 3. "What Do We Want to Achieve? A conversation among Judith Malina, Hanon Reznikov, and Tameron Josbeck," 153-159.

[4] Karen Malpede Taylor. "El Teatro Campesino," in *People's Theatre in Amerika.* New York: Drama Book Specialists Publishers, 1972, 293-308.

members John O'Neal and Doris Derby, and actor/journalist Moses Gilbert at Tougaloo College in Mississippi, created the Free Southern Theater (FST) to be an extension and representation of the black civil rights movement. A racially integrated group, it refused to perform in front of segregated audiences. In their General Prospectus for the Establishment of a Free Southern Theater, the founders wrote:

> Through theater, we think to open a new area of protest . . . one that permits the growth of and self-knowledge of a Negro audience, one that supplements the present struggle for freedom. . . . We feel that the theater will add a necessary dimension to the current Civil Rights Movement through its unique value as a means of education . . . stimulate thought and a new awareness among Negroes in the deep South, . . . staging plays that reflect the struggles of the American Negro.[5]

It challenges the usual rules defining theater. It is performance where the barriers between audience and performer are minimized, the Fourth Wall (the metaphoric, invisible wall that separates the actor from the audience) is breached, and authority is shared, not simply vested in the actor.

> The *poetics of the oppressed* is essentially the poetics of liberation: the spectator no longer delegates power to the characters either to think or to act in his place. The spectator frees himself; he thinks and acts for himself! Theater is action![6]

It is designed to empower those who perform in it as well as those who are in the audience. It is a call to action. It inspires activism.

> The modern theatre mustn't be judged by its success in satisfying the audience's habits but by its success in transforming them. It needs to be questioned not about its degree of conformity with the 'eternal laws of the theatre' but about its ability to master the rules governing the great social processes of our age; not about whether it manages to interest the spectator in buying a ticket—i.e. in the theatre itself—but about whether it manages to interest him in the world.[7]

---

[5] Civil Rights Movement Veterans, http://www.crmvet.org/info/fsthome.htm, Free Southern Theater Founded (CRMVets), Free Southern Theater (From SNCC 50th Anniversary Conference) [PDF].

[6] Augusto Boal. *Theatre of the Oppressed.* New York: Theatre Communications Group, 1985, 122. Originally published in Spanish as *Teatro de Oprimido* in 1974, copyright © by Augusto Boal and in English by Urizen Books in 1979. Translation copyright © 1979 by Charles A. & Maria-Odilia Leal McBride.

[7] *Brecht on Theatre: The Development of an Aesthetic.* Edited & translated by John Willett. NY: Hill and Wang, A division of Farrar, Straus & Giroux, 1964, 161/Glossary.

If one were to start at the middle of the 19th century, and move through the modern period to the present, an impressive pantheon of individuals and groups come to mind when one thinks of the Theater of Social Change. There are individuals like Harriet Beecher Stowe, whose book and book-turned-play, *Uncle Tom's Cabin; or, Life Among the Lowly*, is credited with energizing the anti-slavery movement in the years before the Civil War; Bertolt Brecht, German poet, playwright, and theater director, author of *Mother Courage, The Caucasian Chalk Circle*, and *The Threepenny Opera*, a pivotal artist who influenced most aspects of 20th-century theater culture; Vaclav Havel, playwright, dissident, and later President of Czechoslovakia and the Czech Republic, author of *The Memorandum* and *The Increased Difficulty of Concentration*; Anna Deveare Smith, best known for her "documentary theatre" style in plays such as *Fires in the Mirror* and *Twilight: Los Angeles*, in which Smith, alone on stage, inhabits a multiplicity of diverse characters, all based on interviews with real individuals; Augusto Boal, Brazilian theater director, writer, politician, founder of Theatre of the Oppressed, who famously said: "Perhaps theater is not revolutionary in itself; but have no doubts, it is a rehearsal of revolution!"; Earl Robinson, singer/songwriter, composer of the cantata *Ballad for Americans*, made famous by the great baritone Paul Robeson, and *The House I Live In*, which became one of Frank Sinatra's signature songs.[8]

And there are groups such as the *Artef* ("Arbeter Teater Farband," [Yiddish: "Workers' Theater Union"]), founded as a radical alternative to mainstream Yiddish theater under the auspices of *Freiheit*, the Yiddish Communist daily; the Federal Theatre Project, a federal relief program of the Depression-era Work Projects Administration (WPA), well-known for its *Living Newspaper* productions, and musicals that it either produced or from which it drew inspiration, Marc Blitzstein's *The Cradle Will Rock* and the International Ladies Garment Workers Union's *Pins and Needles*; the Living Theatre, founded by Judith Malina and Julian Beck in 1947, one of the first companies to produce Brecht in the United States and to perform in non-traditional venues such as on the streets and in prisons; the Vermont-based Bread and Puppet Theater, known for its giant puppets and effigies, its performances incorporating elements

---

[8] For more information on individuals cited in this paragraph, the reader can refer to the following (in addition to other titles listed in this chapter's other endnotes): David Reynolds, *Mightier Than the Sword: Uncle Tom's Cabin and the Battle for America*. New York: W. W. Norton & Company, Inc., 2011; Meg Mumford, *Bertolt Brecht: Routledge Perfomance Practitioners, Routledge Modern & Contemporary Dramatists Series*. London and New York: Routledge, 2009; Vaclav Havel, *The Garden Party and Other Plays*. New York: Grove Press, 1993; Alisa Solomon, "Rethinking Power, Rethinking Theater: A conversation between Lani Guinier and Anna Deavere Smith," 31-45; Earl Robinson, *Ballad of an American: The Autobiography of Earl Robinson*, with Eric A. Gordon. Lanham, MD: The Scarecrow Press, 1998; Michael Denning, *The Cultural Front: The Laboring of American Culture in the Twentieth Century*, London and New York: Verso, 1997.

of dance, sculpture, music, and language, founded in 1963 by ongoing director Peter Schumann.[9]

It would be incorrect to assume, on the basis of the above list of well-known theater groups and performers that the Theater of Social Protest lives only in the domain of professionals. "Plays help make ideas palpable," writes Alisa Solomon, film critic and director of the Arts & Culture concentration in the master's program at Columbia's Journalism School. Sometimes called "guerrilla theater," "agitprop," or "street theater," this is a subset of social change theater that has been used effectively by political organizers, who are amateurs in terms of acting and often draw their performers from the local activist community.[10]

Robert Forrant, professor in the History Department at the University of Massachusetts Lowell, and chair of the Bread & Roses Centennial Steering Committee, reflects on the value of this kind of theater as compared to how he contemplates the acts of teaching and learning:

> The way I think about it when I teach is that people are reached in multiple ways. If you look at this as an educational endeavor, what you've done is to take all these pieces of information and reach out to an audience that might not get the facts of this important historical event in any other way. They're not going to read a heavy academic book or maybe not even a popular written version of the event.[11]

WORKMEN'S CIRCLE

In the *ABV* chorus, many members have been touched by the tradition of political theater and music, even if they don't know many details about it, and a majority have been involved in struggles for social justice, a combination of interests that track a direct line back to the nascent days of Workmen's Circle.

Tolle Graham, a founding member of the Yiddish Community Chorus, is an organizer, and environmental safety and health trainer with MassCOSH

---

[9] For more information on groups cited: Edna Nahshon, *Yiddish Proletarian Theatre: The Art and Politics of the Artef, 1925–1940,* Westport, CT: Greenwood Press, 1998; Susan Quinn, *Furious Improvisation: How the WPA and a Cast of Thousands Made High Art out of Desperate Times,* New York: Walker Publishing Company, Inc., 2008; Peter Schumann, *The Radicality of the Puppet Theater,* St. Johnsbury, VT: Troll Press, 1990.

[10] Alisa Solomon, "Introduction." The following definition of "agitprop" comes from Meg Mumford's book on Bertolt Brecht: "Agitprop is a type of political theater that uses bold rhetorical techniques to inform and mobilize its audience about urgent social issues. Its name derives from the Department of Agitation and Propaganda established in 1920 by the Soviet Communist Party. While agitprop theater has been used in different times and places, it was particularly prominent during the interwar years in Europe, where it was associated with Marxist politics.... Agitprop tends to instruct its audience about the way forward in a forceful and often reductive manner...."

[11] Phone conversation, Robert Forrant, Linda Stern, Vicki Gabriner, December 24, 2012.

(Massachusetts Coalition for Occupational Safety and Health). For the bulk of her working years, Tolle says, she has found that "Popular Education" methods, which use music, theater, poetry, and story-telling based on the writings and practice of Brazilian educator/writer Paulo Freire (1921–1997), "have been an incredibly valuable tool for engaging workers, unions, immigrants, women, and community in identifying and organizing for key issues that affect their working conditions and lives."[12]

Vicki Gabriner, a soprano in the *ABV* chorus, remembers creating political agitprop theater with some of the local African-Americans with whom she worked in the mid-'60s during her civil rights organizing days in Fayette County, west Tennessee. "Imagine yourself in a rural black church," she explained, "sitting in the midst of more than 100 black women and men, tired after a full day's labor, fanning themselves non-stop on a hot summer's night,

> their hand-held fans emblazoned with the name of the town's black-owned funeral home. Perhaps the church is surrounded outside by angry whites. Inside, the church is filled with powerful movement energy. The show is about to begin! A small group of people stand in front of the congregation/ audience: an African-American farmer/civil rights activist; a white male civil rights volunteer playing a white landowner, known colloquially as "Mr. Charley"; and two people dressed up like a cow. The farmer is complaining to "Mr. Charley" that the way they "share" the cow is not fair. "Why?" asks Mr. Charley. "It's perfectly fair! You own the front of the cow, so you have to feed her, and I own the back of the cow so I collect the milk." The audience howled, immediately understanding this caricatured picture of the economic inequality of the system under which they lived. It provided an opportunity to release tension by laughing about something that was profoundly unfair, affirm the bare truth of their lives, and thus prepare for another day in the struggle.[13]

Founded in 1900 by Jewish immigrant sweatshop workers in New York City, Workmen's Circle was a progressive, secular Jewish organization rooted in community and mutual aid, culture, the struggle for *a besere velt*, and the union movement.[14] It was called the "Red Cross of Labor" because of its key role in organizing unions and labor lyceums (organizing opportunities to learn about labor issues and give support to striking workers) in the major garment industries.

---

[12] Conversation with Tolle Graham, February 8, 2013. Paulo Freire, *Pedagogy of the Oppressed*; translated by Myra Bergman Ramos, London, New York: Penguin Books, 1996.

[13] Conversation with Vicki Gabriner, January 23, 2013.

[14] For information about the history and current activities of Workmen's Circle, the reader can refer to the following two websites—Boston Workmen's Circle at http://www.circleboston.org and National Workmen's Circle in NYC at http://circle.org—as well as the book, *The Friendly Society: A History of the Workmen's Circle*, by Judah Joseph Shapiro, New York: Media Judaica, 1970.

In the era before and after the Triangle Shirtwaist Fire, Workmen's Circle was one of the most prominent social/political/cultural organizations for and of working class Jews on New York's Lower East Side.

In Boston, today's Workmen's Circle Center for Jewish Culture and Social Justice is a multi-generational community, as well as an arts and culture center, where a secular Jewish identity is rooted in cultural heritage and the pursuit of a better world. BWC's activities include: *Shule* (Yiddish: school) on Sunday mornings for children from kindergarten through seventh grade; political and cultural activities for teens and young adults; adult education; Yiddish classes; and action committees on the Middle East, economic justice, and Jewish-Muslim relations. And, of course, the chorus, *A Besere Velt*.

For the last decade and a half, *A Besere Velt* has been singing its heart out, following in the century-old musical footsteps of so many Workmen's Circle chapters around the country. In the 100-plus years that Workmen's Circle has been in existence, choruses and cultural events have always been central—choruses were located in cities across the U.S. and at least one city in Canada. In a two-page spread of photographs of Workmen's Circle choruses, the WC Yearbook of 1940 describes "song" as "a beautifier and a liberator."[15]

When the newly-regenerated Boston Workmen's Circle decided in the 1990s that it wanted to re-create a fully-functioning choral group—a Yiddish chorus, in the tradition of Workmen's Circle and other left-wing Jewish immigrant organizations in the early years of the 20th century—Lisa Gallatin was recruited to lead the chorus (and also became the music teacher in the *shule*). She brought with her the valuable experience of two decades of union organizing, which had included creating and leading a union women's picket line singing group, *On the Line*. Only recently, Lisa commented that despite being a union organizer for 20-plus years, she knew little about the history of the radical Jewish labor movement until her introduction to Yiddish folk music in 1997 when she became the founding choral director of *A Besere Velt*.[16]

"I believe in the power of music," Lisa muses, "but I must confess that I am often subject to feeling that music isn't the 'real' work of social change movements. But," she adds, "when I remember the depths to which the *ABV* chorus moved audiences with the Triangle Fire show, as well as the transformative experience the show created for every chorus member, then," she said, "I can feel the power."

In the Yiddish folk repertoire the BWC activists began to explore, they found the sounds from the *shtetl*s, the Yiddish theater, the concentration camps and the ghettoes, the sweatshops and union meetings. Over the years, Lisa has created new choral arrangements, often by weaving traditional Yiddish folk songs

---

[15] National Executive Committee of the Workmen's Circle. *40 Years Workmen's Circle.* New York: 1940.

[16] Conversations with Lisa Gallatin, December 27, 2012 and February 12, 2013.

together with familiar civil rights and labor anthems. And while few people in the chorus knew Yiddish beyond a few common phrases, those who did helped to teach pronunciation and meanings and played a major role in helping bring the chorus up to speed.

Thus, it was logical that the Boston Workmen's Circle *ABV* chorus, with members aged ten to 80 years old and almost 100 strong, would be drawn to participate in the 2011 Centennial Commemoration of the Triangle Shirtwaist fire. The organizational and individual connections ran deep. Some of the deceased Triangle workers who died without money for a cemetery plot elsewhere, or were unidentified, were buried in the New York City Workmen's Circle Cemetery. As *ABV* chorus members approached working on the Triangle Fire Centennial, we knew that any one of our grandmothers (or grandfathers) might have been one of those 146 young victims who died in a fire that could have been prevented.

THE UPRISING OF THE 20,000, THE FIRE ITSELF, AND THE REFORMS THAT FOLLOWED

Five hundred garment factories in early 20th-century New York were located primarily on the Lower East Side. The ILGWU organized the recently arrived immigrant workers, most of them Jewish. These factories were housed in buildings eight to ten stories high, some even as high as 20 stories. This left workers vulnerable because quick egress in case of fire would be difficult; the horse-drawn fire engines had ladders that only reached to the sixth floor. Conditions in the shops included crowded work spaces, poor ventilation, long hours, low pay, and employment of young teenagers. Small fires were not uncommon.[17]

ILGWU, Local 25, organized a mass meeting at Cooper Union in November 1909 in response to the growing intolerable working conditions. Clara Lemlich (1886–1982), a young Jewish worker known for giving speeches on street corners, for which she had already been viciously beaten up, grew impatient with speech after cautious speech given by mostly male union leaders. She jumped up, saying, "I want to say a few words!" in Yiddish, her native tongue. "I have listened to all the speakers," she continued. "I have no further patience for talk, as I am one of those who feels and suffers from the things pictured. I move we go on a general strike."

Workers erupted in cheering. Moderator Benjamin Feigenbaum urged the workers to consider their decision to his question carefully. He asked, "Will you take the Jewish oath?" The audience responded by raising their right hands and affirming out loud together, "If I turn traitor to the cause I now pledge, may

---

[17] Information from David Von Drehle, *Triangle: The Fire That Changed America*, New York: Grove/Atlantic, Inc., 2003.

this hand wither from the arm I now raise." Called the "Uprising of the Twenty Thousand," 15,000 workers went on strike immediately, and another 5,000 joined in by the second day of the strike. Factory owners, spearheaded by Triangle bosses Max Blanck and Isaac Harris, created the Employers Mutual Protection Association. Streetwalkers, who were organized by management thugs, physically attacked picket lines. Members of the Women's Trade Union League (WTUL, an organization of progressive women, mainly middle and upper class, fighting for suffrage and women's rights), joined the strikers in walking the picket line, bailing arrested strikers out of jail, and in some cases getting arrested, too. It was an unprecedented coalition between women of differing class backgrounds.

Smaller shops caved in first, followed in early 1910 by the larger ones. Workers won higher wages, shorter hours, and were now allowed to belong to the union. The Triangle owners, however, continued to oppose the factory becoming a "closed shop"—which would have greatly strengthened the union's bargaining power because a worker would have had to be a union member to be hired or would have been required to join the union within a specified period of time.

On Saturday, March 25, 1911, a fire broke out at the Triangle Waist Company at closing time, 4:40 p.m. No one knows exactly what caused it, perhaps a match carelessly disposed of, but it spread quickly, igniting bins of scrap cotton, tissue paper patterns, dust, and machine oil. Workers trying to escape the inferno were faced with locked doors, doors that opened inward, narrow stairways, and a single flimsy fire escape positioned over a skylight. Fire buckets on the shop floor did little good and the nets that firemen carried were ineffective. There were heroic acts such as elevator operators keeping the elevators going until the cables warped. New York University law students in the building next door found ladders to lead workers and managers to safety. Huge crowds watched in horror. Frances Perkins (1880–1965), who was having tea nearby and heard the sirens of fire engines, joined the throngs of helpless observers. She would later become the first female Cabinet member when President Franklin D. Roosevelt (1882–1945) appointed her to the position of Secretary of Labor in 1933. She later stated that being witness to the fire impelled her to work her entire life for decent conditions of health and safety in the workplace.[18]

In a little more than half an hour, 146 workers were dead, some asphyxiated, some burned, some by jumping from the eighth, ninth, and tenth floors. Policemen who had been arresting strikers only a short time before now transported victims' bodies to a temporary morgue on a nearby pier. A huge outpouring of grief and anger followed the fire, and it became a turning point in the demand for reforms. A

---

[18] Linda Stern reports: "On a display bulletin board at the 8/4/11 Garden Party in Newcastle, Maine, to recognize Frances Perkins' monumental achievements, I saw a news clipping that quoted Perkins as having stated: '[The Triangle Fire] . . . was a never to be forgotten reminder of why I had to spend my life fighting conditions that could permit such a tragedy.' I wanted to remember the quote, so I copied it into a small notebook I carried with me."

few days after the fire, a funeral cortege carrying the coffins of the six unidentified workers made its way through the streets of New York, while 350,000 grieving citizens stood for hours in the pouring rain to show their respect and outrage.

The New York State Legislature appointed the Factory Investigating Committee whose purview was the entire state. Investigators included union activists such as Clara Lemlich, who had jump-started the 1909 strike, and Rose Schneiderman, a sewing trades worker and WTUL activist. Up-and-coming Democrats who had been elected to the New York State legislature the year before in 1910 were asked to serve on the committee: they included Alfred E. Smith, the 38-year-old majority leader of the Assembly and Robert F. Wagner, at age 33, the youngest Senate leader in state history. New state laws were passed in 1913. They included requiring automatic sprinklers in high-rise buildings, doors opening outward, regular fire drills, a limit to the numbers of workers in a shop, and better protections for women and children.

The trial of the owners revolved around technicalities, and some immigrant workers were not allowed to testify in their native language. In the end, the all-male jury, which included a number of business owners, was more sympathetic to the class interests of the owners than to the young female immigrant workers. Harris and Blanck were acquitted, to the outrage of the victims' families and the general public.

CREATING THE SHOW

How were we to dramatize and put music to these tragic events, connect them skillfully to present struggles, and motivate our audiences to activism? Vicki Gabriner volunteered to be the point person for the Triangle show. After conferring with Lisa Gallatin, Vicki sent out an email invitation to chorus members to join the Triangle Fire Centennial committee. "The Triangle Shirtwaist workers who died in the fire are part of our history, " she wrote. "As Jewish progressives, children of immigrants, and members of Workmen's Circle, their struggle resonates with so many issues with which we are still involved today." The message continued:

> We are going to create a show with narrative, music, and visuals, as we have done several times already, powerfully, to commemorate other historical events and issues. Do you want to be part of the script committee? Formulate the shape of the show? Research visuals? Original documents? Music? Read secondary historical descriptions & analyses of the event, its precursors & outcomes? Write narrative? Bring this story to life for the next generation? Honor our parents and grandparents by telling a piece of their collective history?

Fifteen people came to the first scheduled meeting. Although chorus members had been singing together for a varying number of years, we introduced ourselves at the start of this particular endeavor through the prism of what motivated us to want to help with the creation of the Triangle Fire show.

"My grandmother might have worked there."

"I worked as a union organizer, so the labor movement is very near and dear to me."

"It's part of our history and the kind of thing Workmen's Circle should be doing."

"I'm a librarian—I've done a lot of research in library archives with original sources, letters, including some family history that involved sweatshops."

"My grandparents were in the *shmate* (Yiddish: "rag" or "textile") business."

"I'm a high school teacher; I do a unit on labor history and I'm a shop steward in the teacher's union."

"I grew up in New York City and one of the first jobs I had was typing for the International Ladies Garment Workers Union one summer."

"My daughter went through the *shule,* and I remember when she was in fifth grade how her *shule* class worked on putting the themes of social justice and *tikkun olam (Hebrew/Yiddish:* repairing the world) into action by leading a demonstration against a contemporary sweatshop operation, which that year was the Gap Store."

Posting several large pieces of paper on the wall, we brainstormed on content and the connections of the Triangle's historical events to the present day, as well as theatrical and musical possibilities. As we look back on that initial brainstorming session, the connections to the final show are easily visible. Unions, for example, were brought to the forefront by the ongoing struggle in Wisconsin by municipal union members whose right to collective bargaining was being challenged by Governor Scott Walker. The Wisconsin strike grew in momentum just as we were putting finishing touches on the show. Linda Stern, a chorus member, remembers going to a militant support rally of numerous public employee unions at the Massachusetts State House in late February 2011 on a very cold winter day.

Health and safety in the workplace and the exporting of unsafe factory work to the developing world were also central. Of course, we could not know then that a fire in a Bangladeshi clothing factory that occurred in December 2011 *as we were writing the script,* would resonate painfully with what we were describing from 100 years ago—even the fact that trapped workers jumped to their deaths from the eighth, ninth, and tenth floors.[19]

We wanted to tell an important story through the vehicle of good music and a creative, well-executed show. We wanted to educate our contemporaries and the next generations about the history of our struggle for social justice. It was important that we make the connection to current issues like globalization and

---

[19] *New York Times*, "Bangladesh Factory Fire Kills at Least 201," December 14, 2010.

sweatshop labor in other countries. We also wanted to acknowledge the progress in labor legislation that resulted from the disaster, including the role of the unions and the transformation of Frances Perkins and others. Finally, we wanted to honor the people who died in the fire and send out a call to action to continue the fight for social justice. The back of the concert program for our first performance stated:

> But fighting for the right to organize for safe and healthy workplaces is as important today as it was in 1911. Currently, the Occupational Safety and Health Administration (OSHA)—the federal agency founded just 40 years ago to safeguard worker health and safety—is under attack. The Republican majority in the House just last month [February 2011] voted in favor of drastic cuts that would cripple enforcement. Even at today's funding levels, it would take 167 years to inspect every workplace and the cuts threaten to put workers' lives at risk. Commit yourself to an action today. Please call your Senator and visit www.masscosh.org for more information.[20]

We understood that if these performances were to strengthen our organization by reinforcing the bonds among our members and drawing in others to join, the show had to be engaging. The music had to be good. To this end, we explored various theatrical possibilities. Should the program portray events in chronological order? Would the "Living Newspaper" Theater of the '30s serve as a good theatrical model? Should we have actors planted in the audience? We decided that we would start by reading the most recent book about the Triangle Fire, David Von Drehle's *Triangle: The Fire That Changed America*. That way we'd all be "on the same page."

Some of us next read the detailed first-person accounts in Leon Stein's *Out of the Sweatshop: The Struggle for Industrial Democracy*, and found them especially informative. The group pored over the online website "Remembering the Triangle Factory Fire: 100 Years Later," created by the Kheel Center at Cornell's School of Industrial and Labor Relations. We networked with other librarians and related groups such as the Jewish Women's Archive.[21]

Lisa Gallatin began to select and arrange music in line with the needs of the show and the capabilities of the chorus. Though Lisa was the final arbiter of cultural and musical questions, she suggested that we work with a professionally trained director. Holly Newman, a Workmen's Circle member with a master's degree in Theater Education and years of experience directing theater, agreed to

---

[20] Program for *The Cloth From Which We Are Cut* performed by the *A Besere Velt* Yiddish Community Chorus of the Boston Workmen's Circle, March 6, 2011, Kheel Center for Labor Management Documentation & Archives, ILR School, Cornell University, Kheel Center Triangle Fire Centennial Commemoration Collection. *A Besere Velt,* http://www.ilrcornell.edu/trianglefire.

[21] Leon Stein, ed. *Out of the Sweatshop: The Struggle for Industrial Democracy,* New York: Quadrangle/New York Times Book Company, 1977; The Jewish Women's Archive website is at http://jwa.org.

come on board in that capacity. Holly had worked most recently with the Roxbury Repertory Theater at Roxbury Community College and with True Colors, the youth theater group of the Theater Offensive, whose mission is to "form and present the diverse realities of queer lives in art so bold it breaks through personal isolation and political orthodoxy to help build an honest, progressive community." Holly said that her progressive political activism in the Boston area over the last 40-plus years, as part of the Second Wave of the Women's Liberation movement, a tenant organizer with Boston's City Life/*Vida Urbana*, and in her capacity as the representative of the Massachusetts Nurses' Association at the New England Medical Center, piqued her interest in joining forces with us to help create and direct the Triangle Fire Centennial show.[22]

After several meetings of the larger group, a sub-set of six people volunteered to be on the script committee. We knew that although we would not be exactly replicating shows we had created in the past, which included the 100th anniversary of Workmen's Circle, the Warsaw Ghetto Uprising, and the Jewish immigrant experience, we would be following in some way the successful format we had used in other shows, some combination of narration, songs, and visuals. We decided that the narration would consist largely of quotes from individuals involved with the fire and the events surrounding it. In one meeting when the script committee found itself stuck as it tried to determine which quotations we would include, Holly suggested that we read aloud the passages we had earmarked as our favorites. We were profoundly moved by the simple act of reading words that had been written or spoken 100 years ago. It was a potent demonstration of the power of the word. We were all surprised by how helpful it was in moving us along in our script-writing journey. Smaller groups of two or three people took on the challenging task of actually writing the script. Seven plus versions were created until the final one emerged. Professional actors rather than chorus members were hired for the major speaking parts. The four actors selected, one man and three women, contributed to the professionalism and power of the show.

Committee members not directly involved with writing the script searched for the images we projected throughout the show. Images included immigrants arriving by ship to Ellis Island, newspaper headlines describing the 1909 Uprising of the 20,000, Rose Schneiderman at her sewing machine, Clara Lemlich, women shirtwaist makers being arrested, and the fire itself, union members in funeral procession holding signs reading "We Mourn Our Loss."

THE CONCERTS

As the lights dimmed, chorus members, dressed in black, the women in colored scarves, stood on the stage in several rows of choral risers. We had scrapped the chronological approach, and instead started in at the point of the spreading inferno.

---

[22] Conversation with Holly Newman, January 26, 2013.

The piano broke the opening silence and the chorus sang *S'falt a shney* (Snow is Falling), setting the mood with the plaintive musing of a garment worker who mourns the years of her youth lost in the clatter of so many sewing machines. A chorus member does a voiceover, as Kim Shaw, the chorus's American Sign Language interpreter, begins to silently, but actively, translate, gesturing expressively with her hands and face. Then the voices of the *A Besere Velt* chamber ensemble, positioned throughout the chorus, are heard shouting in rhythmic composition.

> *Girls, it's spreading fast. Which way do we go, which way? I can't get through, it's too crowded. Take the elevator; no, the stairs.*

The young garment workers, panicked, are trying to escape the rapidly spreading fire.

> *Girls, it's spreading fast. Which way do we go, which way? I can't get through, it's too crowded. Where's my sister? Jump. I'm burning. Jump.*

Rosa Blumenthal, a chorus member, pierced the air with her shrill and heartbreaking cry:

> "*Where's my sister?*"

The actors move onto and off the sides of the stage, delivering their lines—quoting from a newspaper report describing the procession for the six unidentified victims, another gives voice to Rose Schneiderman's rebuke to the wealthy women and men sitting in the Metropolitan Opera House at a public meeting about a week after the fire:

> We have tried you citizens; we are trying you now, and you have a couple of dollars for the sorrowing mothers, brothers, and sisters by way of a charity gift. But every time the workers come out in the only way they know to protest against conditions, which are unbearable, the strong hand of the law is allowed to press down heavily upon us. I can't talk fellowship to you who are gathered here. Too much blood has been spilled.

We sing *Bella Ciao* to make visible the young Italian immigrant workers. One of the actors describes the scene: "Today I observed many a Jewish girl with her arm around an Italian girl's neck, not able to speak, one to the other, but both understanding they are fighting the same fight for each other's interests."

> *Oh we are women, and we are marching, Bella Ciao, Bella Ciao, Bella Ciao, Ciao, Ciao!*

A note of hope is struck at the concert's penultimate moment:

> *But there was another fire, too.*
> *A fire worth remembering*
> *A fire that burned in our hearts, that warmed us*
> *That lit the way through a long cold winter*
> *In that hopeful flame that gave us courage*
> *That gave us each other*
> *In that fire that burned in our hearts*
> *In the fire that burns in your own*
> *You can read*
> *Our names.*[23]

The final song is *Ale Mentschen*, Beethoven's "Ode to Joy" sung in Yiddish and English, accompanied by a slide of a demonstration where people held signs proclaiming, "Wisconsin workers, we support you."

We performed six successful concerts at six locations in three states. It was the first time the chorus had performed a show multiple times. After all our rehearsing, we liked being able to bring our performance to several different audiences. Lisa spoke for a lot of chorus members when she articulated the desire to "take the show on the road for six months, performing for unions around the country. In these hard times," she explained, "they need it."[24] Our first show was held on the opening night of the 2011 Boston Jewish Music Festival (March 6, 2011). After that, we travelled to New York City where we were part of the city-wide commemoration activities organized by the Remember the Triangle Fire Coalition, which culminated over the Triangle Fire anniversary weekend of March 25-26, 2011. Performing in the Middle Collegiate Church on the Lower East Side, we were just a stone's throw from the Asch Building, where the fire occurred. In late spring, we traveled to Barre, Vermont, and in September 2011 we performed at the National Yiddish Book Center in Amherst, Massachusetts. Later in the fall, we performed at Simmons College in Boston, another opportunity for Boston-area people who had not been able to get tickets for the opening performance. Still later in the fall, we traveled to Andover, Massachusetts, where we performed as part of a kick-off and fundraiser for the Bread and Roses Strike Centennial Year.

Each performance had its own personality and special significance. Clara Lemlich Shavelson's daughter, 87-year-old Rita Margules, and her granddaughter, Jane Margules, attended our New York performance, and Adela Margules, another granddaughter, had attended the first Boston performance. To meet the daughter and grandchildren of Clara Lemlich was overwhelmingly moving for chorus members; we were, as they say in the vernacular, "blown

---

[23] Michael Hickey, Composer, and Ryan Gilliam, Direction and Libretto, *The Waistmaker's Opera,* created by Downtown Art. Premiered May 2010 in the streets of New York.

[24] Conversation with Lisa Gallatin, December 27, 2012.

away," when Adela wrote to us: "My family absolutely loved the performance. They thought it was the best and most moving part of the entire [NYC] commemoration." After the show in New York, another audience member wrote to us:

> What was especially moving, sitting in the front row as we were, were the faces and expressions of the chorus members as they were performing. Believe it or not, this added to the emotion for the audience as well. They reflected what we were feeling and did it while singing so beautifully. I could not stop crying so I do not know how anyone up front could perform while they were clearly so emotional about the material as well.

She hit the nail on the head. We in the chorus were deeply affected. One of the altos wrote: "It was such an honor to perform with all of you in NYC. There was a connectedness to our group that felt extremely powerful."

The show in Barre, Vermont, carried with it its own drama, demonstrating how the show functioned as a vehicle through which we linked up with progressive activists in places other than Boston. Barre also holds an interesting connection to the 1912 Bread and Roses Strike. It took two years to organize our concert in Barre, where we connected with the radical labor history of the granite-producing town where mostly Italian immigrant granite-miners took in 35 Italian children from Lawrence, as part of the Children's Exodus during the 1912 Bread and Roses strike. This remains a proud moment in Barre history.

We were scheduled to perform over the Memorial Day Weekend of 2011. On the day before the concert, a microburst broke loose over Barre, the biggest storm in decades, leaving in its wake washed-out roads, downed bridges, and houses sliding into the overflowing lakes and rivers. The basement of the Barre Socialist Labor Hall, where we were to perform, was under more than six feet of water. What to do? The remarkable organizers in Barre managed to change the venue to the Barre Opera House, where we performed on a stage where Helen Keller, author, lecturer, and social activist, probably best known for overcoming the obstacles of being blind and deaf, Socialist Party leader Eugene V. Debs, anarchist Emma Goldman, John Philip Sousa and his band, and silent film star Tom Mix with his horse had once performed.[25] Doing sound check during a thunderstorm, we wondered if the electricity would hold; it did. And the whole build-up to the concert contributed to a particularly intense program for performers and audience alike!

---

[25] With union consciousness at the center, the Socialist Labor Hall was built by Italian granite workers in Barre, Vermont, in 1900. They used it for lectures and meetings, a choral society and band, and Italian classes. It housed a bakery and a cooperative society for supplying groceries. The building, now a National Historic Landmark and owned by the Barre Historical Society and City of Barre, continues to be a center for community activities and progressive events. Karen Lane, "Old Labor Hall, Barre, Vermont: Preserving a Working-Class Icon." *Labor's Heritage: Quarterly of the George Meany Memorial Archives,* Silver Spring, MD: George Meany Center for Labor Studies, Spring/Summer 1999, 48-61.

ON TO BREAD AND ROSES

We now shifted gears and focused on The Great Lawrence Textile Strike of 1912, the Bread and Roses strike. The strike followed the Triangle fire by less than a year. A production depicting the Bread and Roses strike would be an event of a very different nature in subject and tone. Though it was a bitter strike in the dead of winter, the unity among immigrants from nearly 30 nations was instrumental in their victory. The strike committee was made up of union members from all the major language groups in Lawrence. Women in their informal networks provided a powerful means to communicate and act. While the events around the Triangle fire involved the Jewish community in a central way, the Lawrence strike included Jews as one ethnicity among many.

The Bread and Roses strike had elements of militant speeches, parades, collaborative decision-making, and music. Our show took on the rhythms of marches. From the beginning, we visualized the effectiveness of beating drums and found an outstanding drum trio, which provided both solos and the underlying beat of the show. The *Internationale* was sung in many different languages; it was the one song everyone in 1912 knew in their own language.

Judith Schwartz, an *ABV* soprano, agreed to be the point person for the Bread and Roses centennial commemoration. We were a group of about ten as we started reading Bruce Watson's *Bread & Roses: Mills, Migrants, and The Struggle for the American Dream*. We did research at the Lawrence History Center and used other resources to understand various aspects of the strike, such as the Children's Exodus and the involvement of the Industrial Workers of the World. We performed a triumphant and upbeat show at the Boston Teachers Union Hall in Dorchester in April 2012 and then again at the Bread & Roses Festival in Lawrence on Labor Day 2012. Audience members stood as we sang the *Internationale* in five languages (English, Yiddish, Italian, Russian, and French). The performance emphasized the unending nature of resistance and the fight for human dignity that continues today.[26]

SUMMARY

In the final analysis, the chorus was successful in dramatizing these two important century-old labor events and creating a bridge to current labor and worker issues. The Triangle Fire and the Bread and Roses Strike propelled the

---

[26] Bruce Watson, *Bread and Roses: Mills, Migrants, and the Struggle for the American Dream*, New York: Penguin, 2005; Lawrence Heritage State Park: www.mass.gov/dcr/parks/northeast/lwhp.htm; *The Internationale*: Originally written in French at the time of Paris Commune, *The Internationale* has been sung around the world by communists, socialists, and those fighting for their rights, in dozens of different languages. It begins "Arise ye prisoners of starvation, arise the wretched of the earth. . . ." Information about *The Internationale DVD* can be found online at http://www.akpress.org/internationaledvd.html.

issues of sweatshops, poor working conditions, the power of labor organizing, worker safety advances, and child labor to the forefront, and the chorus's shows reflected those themes. Using documents, eyewitness testimony, archival photographs, and music, we connected the past history of labor struggles and tragedies with present issues such as global sweatshops, anti-union campaigns in the United States, immigrant labor, and women's rights.

CHAPTER 12

Lessons Learned: A Comparison of the Textile and Apparel Industry of Early 19th-Century Lawrence and Lowell with China Today

Virginia M. Noon

In this chapter, the textile and apparel industry of early 19th-century Lawrence and Lowell will be compared with the industry in China today. A critical 30-year period in each region's industrial development will be considered, focusing on the motivations and challenges presented by rapid industrialization. By looking at workers' lives and work environment, a comparative perspective emerges.

Today, China is a dominant force in the global market in every manufactured product category from inexpensive consumer goods, to a wide range of textile and apparel, to electronics and automobiles and everything in between. Deng Xiaoping's policies of reform and opening established in 1978 were followed by rapid economic development. The coastal province of Zhejiang provides a glimpse into the high degree of product specialization and volume of production found in some regions of China. The town of Qiaotou has 380 factories and manufactures more than 70 percent of the buttons for clothes made in China. In Wuyi, one billion decks of playing cards per year are produced, providing cards for half of China's domestic market. Fifty miles away, the town of Yiwu makes one-quarter of the worlds drinking straws and, in another part of Zhejiang, Songxia produces 350 million umbrellas annually.[1] Much is made of the oversupply of Chinese products flooding the U.S. market as well as the working conditions of those producing the products. This chapter highlights those concerns and draws the parallels between China today and Lawrence and Lowell, Massachusetts, during the early industrial revolution.

---

[1] Peter Hessler, *Country Driving: A Journey Through China from Farm to Factory.* New York: HarperCollins, 2010, 85.

In the early days of the American industrial revolution, the New England textile industry emerged as a global leader. "The most recognizable of trademarks carried over the Pacific to Shanghai and Singapore were the symbols of American made textiles. For example, the image of a dragon imprinted on cloth signified that it was produced in the Pepperell Mill in Biddeford, Maine. An Indian head with three feathers told the world that the cloth was made in Nashua, New Hampshire. American merchant John Cushing wrote in 1830 that in China, "from the Emperor to the laborer," everyone wore clothing made of cotton produced in New England. Cushing correctly predicted that the American mills would dominate the Asian market. Two decades later, a British reporter in India wrote, "American cotton manufacturers are already clothing our own Indian army." The mills had commercial customers too, in Africa, Argentina, Brazil, Chile, Mexico, and Turkey. The looms of New England ran faster and faster to meet the demand. The mill women worked faster and harder to keep up. The mill owners made fortunes, even as social critics scorned them for exploiting their workers and abolitionists condemned them for using cotton picked by slaves."[2]

Working conditions found in the factories of Lowell and Lawrence in the early to mid-19th century through the turn of the 20th century were hauntingly similar to some of the poor working conditions in factories today in China and other developing nations. Each country's initial rapid industrial development resulted from careful planning by private industrialists in the United States and by the state-controlled central government in China. In both China and New England, quiet and picturesque rural communities were transformed into major industrial centers. In New England, innovation and technology never seen before were the catalysts for unprecedented growth at the dawn of America's industrial revolution.

In today's global economy, garment assembly is often the first industry to enter developing markets and is an important foreign currency earner and stimulator of economic growth and development. In China, textiles and apparel exports ranked second only to the mechanical and electronic sectors in 1995.[3] Massive labor supplies first from rural New England and then Europe to Lawrence and Lowell and from all regions across China to the Special Economic Zones (SEZs) fueled manufacturing in both countries. Workers were motivated by the opportunity to improve the quality of their lives and those of their families yet found very harsh living and working conditions. The struggle for a safe and fair work environment by factory workers in the United States was slow and hard and change emerged only after many injuries and deaths in the workplace, mobilization and unionization of workers, and eventually, government support and regulation. Workers in China and many other developing countries today face many of the same

---

[2] William Moran, *The Belles of New England: The Women of the Textile Mills and the Families Whose Wealth They Wove*. New York: St. Martin's Press, 2002, 15.

[3] Li & Feng Research Centre, "Apparel Production and Cluster Development in China," Li & Feng Research Centre, no. 10, Hong Kong, 2007.

challenges as those of the New England textile workers nearly 200 years ago. This chapter considers what lessons can be learned from the struggles of those who came before and how these lessons might assist in the development of both ethical and safe workplaces across today's global manufacturing supply chains.

MILLS ALONG THE MERRIMACK RIVER

Francis Cabot Lowell (1775–1817) was the man most responsible for the development of the textile manufacturing industry in New England. While spending time in England in the early 19th century, Lowell studied the British textile industry, the mightiest in the world. As a prominent Boston businessman, his many contacts arranged for him to see what few foreigners were allowed to see: the operations of the mills of Lancashire, Birmingham, Manchester, and Leeds. He marveled at the yarn-spinning machinery created by James Hargreaves, Richard Arkright, and Samuel Crompton. Most of all, Edmund Cartwright's power loom fascinated Lowell as it turned out finished cloth. Spellbound by the genius of British technology, Lowell also saw firsthand the horrors of the English factory system. Corporal punishment and child labor were common. Children and adults were taken against their will from the poorhouses and workers were recruited from the poverty-stricken masses on the streets. Men, women, and children labored in intolerable conditions. Lowell became determined to instill in his corporation a "sense of decency." By 1814, Lowell and Paul Moody developed a power loom partly based on what he had seen in England. The machine greatly reduced the amount of labor needed to produce finished cloth. Pooling resources with his brother-in-law, Patrick Jackson, and with the help of other investors, he established the Boston Manufacturing Company and built a mill in Waltham, Massachusetts. The first fully integrated textile mill, it produced cotton fabric from "bale (of raw cotton) to bolt (of finished fabric)."[4]

In 1817, at the age of 42, Francis Cabot Lowell died. He never saw his dream fulfilled and Nathan Appleton and Patrick Jackson, as principals of the Boston Associates, oversaw the growth of the mills. Because the site in Waltham did not provide enough water power to support the type of mill complex they hoped to build, a new location 28 miles northwest of Boston at the confluence of the Concord and Merrimack Rivers soon became the home to a mile of mills along the Merrimack River. The Pawtucket Falls provided a power source and the Pawtucket Canal, built earlier to skirt the falls, became the spine of a canal system that would power the new city of Lowell. Established in 1826, it is credited with being the first large-scale planned industrial community in the United States.[5]

---

[4]U.S. Department of the Interior, *Lowell: The Story of an Industrial City, Official National Park Handbook 140,* Washington: Division of Publications National Park Service, 1992, 32; Moran, *The Belles of New England,* 14, 48-50.

[5]Department of the Interior, *Lowell: Handbook 140,* 1992, 2, 42; Moran, *The Belles of New England,* 55.

With the Merrimack Manufacturing Company up and running, the Boston Associates expanded their operations. Gaining control of vast amounts of land and water rights, they completed the canal system in 1826 and built more than 5.5 miles of canals during the next 20 years. The Boston Associates controlled every aspect of establishing new mills. They sold the land, leased the water rights, put up the buildings, supplied the machines that were fabricated in their machine shops, and constructed whatever new roads and canals might be needed. The mills shared top managers and directors who maintained the power to set uniform wages, making it impossible for workers to shop around for better pay. Sharing "black lists" of workers who had been released from employment allowed management to control the work force.[6]

After the Merrimack Manufacturing Company came the Hamilton (1826), Appleton (1828), Lowell (1829), Middlesex (1831), Suffolk and Tremont (1832), Lawrence (1833), Boott (1836), and Massachusetts (1840) mills, filling up all of the power sites along the canals. By 1846, Lowell's mills turned out nearly one million yards of cloth per week and in 1850 there were ten large mill complexes employing more than 10,000 people. Until the Civil War, Lowell was the largest concentration of industry in America.[7] Following the Lowell model, "mill fever" broke out across New England. The Boston Associates extended their empire farther up the Merrimack River at the Amoskeag Falls, establishing the Amoskeag mill complex in Manchester and Nashua, New Hampshire. Ten miles north of Lowell, Amos and Abbott Lawrence bought up land in Methuen and Andover for their first mill. In 1845, the Essex Company hired Charles Storrow to design the city of Lawrence and within a few years there were 14 churches, 14 public schools, and 15,000 people. Modeled after Lowell, the river was dammed, canals were built to power the mills, and a boarding house system was set up for women workers. Despite Abbott Lawrence's hopes for the city and Storrow's urban plan, Lawrence was built hastily and with shoddy materials. While the development of Lowell had been "dignified, steady and orderly: the development of Lawrence was seen as crude, thoughtless, boom-or-bust." It would later become the scene of turmoil with a mill dam collapsing in 1847 killing 15 Irish immigrants. In 1860, the Pemberton Mill collapsed and burned, killing 65 women and 23 men, most of them Irish. An additional 275 workers were injured, many of them seriously. By the turn of the century, exploitation and labor unrest had become hallmarks of Lawrence.[8]

The first wave of mill girls came to Lowell from rural New England. They came to improve their lives and those of their families. Francis Cabot

---

[6]Moran, *The Belles of New England*, 56; Department of the Interior, *Lowell: The Story of an Industrial City*, 1992, 32-33.

[7]Department of the Interior, *Lowell: Handbook,* 1992, 39.

[8]Ibid., 61.

Lowell thought that women should work in the mills for only three years or so, then move on to further their education, marry, or find new careers. He did not want thousands of women to become economically dependent on the mills for all of their working lives.[9] The mill women were required to live in well-supervised boarding houses; their wages were set at two dollars above the cost of room and board. At the beginning, living conditions were relatively good. The boarding houses had six to seven bedrooms, three beds to a room, two women to a bed. There was a spacious dining room where generous servings of high-calorie meals were offered three times a day. Strict rules of protocol and decorum were observed and the doors were locked tight at 10 p.m. However, the boarding houses were crowded and poorly ventilated. Privies or outhouses located behind the boarding houses were used and some privies contaminated the wells that were the source of drinking water. Visits to the public bathhouse were infrequent. Common living experiences in the boarding houses provided a unique solidarity among the mill girls that aided the workers a bit later as they fought for their rights. [10]

Many of the young women spent evenings in "Self Improvement Circles" that they organized, discussing classical literature and reading aloud from their own writings. Some of the mill girls attended evening lectures by such notables as John Quincy Adams, Ralph Waldo Emerson, and Henry David Thoreau. They managed to form debating clubs, charitable associations, and missionary societies. They also shared information about new colleges and new seminaries opening for women and some would save their wages and eventually leave the mill to attend and begin to live independent lives. Many worked long enough to pay off the family farm, put their brothers through college or save for their own weddings. Francis Cabot Lowell envisioned the creation of a manufacturing enterprise that would bring about social change and not duplicate the abuses he had seen in England. The mill girls shared some things in common with the owners, including language, religious heritage, and direct links to the American Revolution. They were first-generation daughters of the American Revolution. For many observers, Lowell was the wonder of a nation.[11]

FACTORY RULES–ENVIRONMENTAL AND OCCUPATIONAL HAZARDS

It was said that you could feel and hear Lowell long before you arrived there. Except for meal breaks, the howl of the machinery never stopped during the 12- to sometimes 14-hour work day. Though women experienced a newfound freedom, they were ruled over by the dictates of the factory

---

[9] Moran, *The Belles of New England,* 15.
[10] Moran, *The Belles of New England,* 17-18.
[11] Moran, *The Belles of New England,* 14-18.

bell.[12] Workers inhaled the dust that cycloned around them. Windows were nailed shut to achieve the high humidity needed to keep threads from breaking and keep the machinery running. The humidity resulted in respiratory ailments, including tuberculosis and influenza. Cotton dust filled the work rooms "as snow falls in winter"; workers were covered in it from head to toe. Lung illnesses plagued the mills for many years and 70 percent of early mill workers died of respiratory diseases compared with four percent of farmers during the same period. Textile workers were among the first to be diagnosed with "brown lung" or byssinosis.[13]

The earliest attempt to regulate occupational disease by intervening in the production process came in Massachusetts in 1911 with the banning of the suck shuttle on weaving looms, thought to be a cause of tuberculosis (TB). Weavers had to mouth the loom's shuttle, constantly rethreading the shuttle by placing their mouth over the "eye" of the shuttle and sucking the filling thread through. Because more than one weaver often used the same shuttle and hundreds of shuttles were "kissed" each day, the process was thought to be a transmitter of infectious disease. Later it was determined that the suck shuttle did not cause TB. While many textile workers suffered from symptoms of cotton dust-related lung disease, no direct link was established between the suck shuttle and byssinosis.[14]

IN SUPPORT OF WORKERS: THE RULES OF THE GAME

In the 1830s, no regulations supported workers' general health and well-being. Though the original Boston Associates had pledged to deal honorably with their employees, as time passed, new managers placed no limits on how much work they expected and there was no serious interest in industrial safety. Profit maximization soon trumped all else. In 1834, the first "turn-out" in protest of wage reductions took place in Lowell. In October 1836, a second strike occurred when mill owners increased the amount deducted from wages for room and board; more than 2,000 women—one-third of the female work force—walked off the job. Strike leaders were dismissed from their jobs and black-listed from the city's mills. In the 1840s, led by Sarah Bagley, president of the Lowell Female Labor Reform Association (LFLRA), workers petitioned the state legislature for

---

[12] Department of the Interior, *Lowell: Handbook 140*, 1992, 50.

[13] Byssinosis is caused by the inhalation of cotton dust. As early as 1837, physicians testified to the dangerous conditions in cotton mills. Eventually the disease progresses to a point where the worker experiences severe respiratory problems. Symptoms remain with individuals even after they are no longer exposed to cotton dust. It was not until the mid 1970s that byssinosis was recognized as an occupational disease by the federal government. Charles Levenstein, Gregory F. DeLaurier, and Mary Lee Dunn. *The Cotton Dust Papers: Science, Politics, and Power in the Discovery of Byssinosis in the United States*. New York: Baywood, 2002, 1, 7.

[14] Levenstein, *Cotton Dust Papers*, 25-26.

a ten-hour work day for men and women. Despite signatures from 10,000 workers statewide, more than 4,000 of them from Lowell, Lowell's state representative sided with the corporations and opposed the petition, which failed.[15]

Yankee women eventually left the mills and the harsh conditions of employment, replaced by a work force of Irish immigrants fleeing their homeland during the Great Famine. After the Irish came the French-Canadians in the 1860s and 1870s and the Greek and Polish and other nationalities in the 1890s and early 1900s. Lowell became a city of immigrants with each ethnic group living together in their own neighborhoods.[16] While women had led the first job actions in Lowell, after the Civil War males led many of the protests. The initial focus was on the reduction of working hours and the removal of children from factories. It took nearly 100 years for a successful national union to emerge with the establishment of the Textile Workers Organizing Committee in 1925.

Lowell's mills expanded through the second half of the 19th century; however, it lost its dominant role to Fall River, Massachusetts. By 1890, Fall River's textile work force numbered 19,000 mill hands, compared with Lowell's 15,000. Technological innovation resulting in the general use of steam power combined with Lowell's inland location accounted for this shift out of its accustomed leading role. The coastal cities of Fall River and New Bedford were more accessible to shipping and sea-borne coal, the energy used to power steam engines.[17]

CHINA, TEXTILES, AND A NEW WORLD ORDER

Today China is the world's largest exporter of textiles and apparel, responsible for one- third of global market share. Textile and apparel manufacturers from around the world have set up shop there, eager to take advantage of its abundant supply of low-cost, skilled labor and the absence of industry regulations. Policy-wise, the government established Special Economic Zones (SEZ's) along China's coastal provinces, made infrastructure improvements, and eased domestic immigration. These moves supported rapid industrial development.[18]

SEZs have dramatically advanced economic reform and opened up China's economy to the world. Shenzhen, established in 1980 by Deng Xiaoping, is China's first SEZ. On China's southern coast, less than one hour from Hong Kong by train, Shenzhen is part of the government's carefully planned economic

---

[15] Moran, *The Belles of New England,* 22, 29, 69; Department of the Interior, *Lowell: Handbook 140,* 1992, 55-60.

[16] Ibid., 56, 66-68.

[17] Department of the Interior, *Lowell: Handbook 140,* 1992, 65.

[18] Li & Feng, "Apparel Production and Cluster Development in China."

strategy.[19] Investors interested in opening a firm in Shenzhen or any of China's other SEZs are offered "preferential policies" on such things as land acquisition, taxation, customs clearance, and the use of foreign currency. Along with foreign direct investment (FDI), Shenzhen has attracted young, skilled migrants from across the country. Between 1990 and 2005, Shenzhen's gross domestic product (GDP) has averaged 27 percent annual growth.[20]

Like Lowell, Shenzhen is a "type" of planned industrial community. While the Boston Associates, a private corporation, planned Lowell, Shenzhen is one of seven SEZs established by China's central government. From a small fishing village in Guangdong province, Shenzhen became an industrial and financial hub. Its rapid development—known as "Shenzhen speed"—demonstrates the importance of China's market-oriented reforms to industrialization and urbanization. However, this transformation came at significant cost to the health and welfare of peasants and mill workers. Poor air and water quality pose health hazards to city dwellers. Traditional family structures and values were altered as migrants left their families and traveled great distances to factory towns. And, millions of rural villagers have been forced from their homes and relocated to make way for industrial and commercial development. Over time, the rapid growth led to sharp increases in start-up and property costs and thousands of low-wage garment assembly jobs were priced out of the zone and apparel producers moved to other parts of Guangdong province.[21]

DONGGUAN CITY AND GUANGDONG PROVINCE

In 1978, the Hong Kong-based Taiping Handbag Factory opened the first foreign factory in Dongguan. The "processing factory" imported supplies and materials from Hong Kong for assembly and returned products to Hong Kong for global export. In the first year, the company made one million Hong Kong dollars ($128,000 USD), becoming a model for the thousands of factories that followed them there. Dongguan developed with no special plan and benefitted from its proximity to Shenzhen and Hong Kong. The first investors in Dongguan were Taiwanese and Hong Kong businesses that made clothing, toys, and shoes. Cheap land, an abundant labor supply, and weak regulations were made available and led to factories that were two- or three- story houses or makeshift buildings. In the 1990s, manufacturing shifted to electronics but the work remained quite labor intensive. In other words, while the products had gotten more sophisticated,

---

[19] Rachel L. Snyder, *Fugitive Denim: A Moving Story of People and Pants in the Borderless World of Global Trade* (New York: Norton, 1979), 252; Wanda Guo and Yueqiu Feng, "Special Economic Zones and Competitiveness: A Case Study of Shenzhen, the People's Republic of China," *Asian Development Bank*, (no. 2, 2007).

[20] Guo, "Special Economic Zones and Competitiveness."

[21] Snyder, *Fugitive Denim*, 252.

the work itself has not. Small- to medium-sized factories, along with factories the size of small cities, dot Dongguan. According to Chang:

> If you wear athletic shoes, chances are you have worn a pair that was made in the Yue Yuen factory in Dongguan. The Taiwanese-owned factory is the biggest manufacturer for Nike, Adidas, and Reebok, along with smaller brands like Puma and Asics, all of whom stopped making shoes years ago and farmed out production to factories that could do it more cheaply. Yue Yuen's secret is vertical integration: It controls every step of the manufacturing process—from initial design to making glues, soles, and molds and lasts to cutting, stitching, and assembling the finished products. One-third of the world's shoes are made in Guangdong Province and the Yue Yuen plant is the biggest of them all.[22]

Seventy thousand people, mostly under the age of 30, work at Dongguan's Yeu Yuen factory. Workers sleep in factory dorms, eat in factory cafeterias, and shop at factory commissaries. The factory runs a kindergarten for employees' children and maintains a hospital with 150 staff members. There is a movie theater, a performance troupe, volunteer activities, and English classes. It operates its own power plant and fire station. Yue Yuen offers some stability, providing an average salary of about $72 a month and relatively good living and working conditions. Like Lowell in the 1830s and 1840s, the work week is long, with hours capped at 11 per day and 60 for the week with Sundays off. There is some upward mobility; some managers and line supervisors are rural migrants who started out on the assembly line. The challenges faced by the factory to maintain profitability, provide a safe work environment, and offer fair wages for thousands of migrants are somewhat comparable to the challenges faced by New England's mill owners in the 1830s and 1840s. But, in China, the scale of the challenge and the fact that the industrial transformation is taking place within a rapidly changing global economy complicate the historical process.[23]

Like Lowell, much of China's initial labor supply came from the countryside. In 1984, a government directive allowed farmers to relocate; six years later 60 million migrants were on the move. In 2010, China's 130 million migrants worked in factories and restaurants, on construction sites, and as delivery workers, and house cleaners. It is fair to say that migrants power the assembly lines of China's export economy. They represent the largest movement of people in human history, some three times the number of people who traveled to the United States from Europe over the late 19th century and first two decades of the 20th century. Like the mill girls of New England, migrants left their homes to improve the quality of their lives and the lives of their families. Money sent home to families is currently the biggest source of wealth accumulation in rural China.

[22] Snyder, *Fugitive Denim*, 252.
[23] Ibid., 99.

With small plots of land easily managed by their parents and few opportunities in the rural towns, the choice to "go out" is understandable. Many such journeys end at the Guangzhou train station in southern China, where a common work search method is to visit a "talent market" where all types of jobs are posted.[24]

While some factories are state-owned, Chinese entrepreneurs privately hold many, and there are joint ventures with foreign investors and some factories that are entirely foreign-owned.[25] The minimum wage is set regionally and currently Shenzhen maintains the highest minimum wage, 1,500 Yuan, equal to $236 USD per month for a 40-hour work week. Dormitory conditions are similar to the 1830s boarding houses in Lowell. Buildings are usually a short distance from work and rooms are shared. A dormitory at the Yeu Yeun factory in Dongguan houses 2,000 female workers. Some spaces have toilets and running water in the rooms while others have facilities located at the ends of the halls. Meals provided by the factory are served in cafeterias or taken to the dormitories. Housing provided by the firm may or may not be deducted from a worker's wages.[26]

MULTINATIONAL COMPANIES AND REFORM

In the mid-1990s, labor abuses in factories under contract to Gap, Nike, and other large multi-national apparel companies were well documented. In 1995, Charles Kerrigan, from the National Labor Committee, organized a tour across the United States with two Central American teenage factory workers who worked for the Gap who were paid 12 cents an hour. The "modern" sweatshop story soon emerged and companies like the Gap responded by revamping their corporate guidelines. Producers guaranteed workers' rights in their global factories and some of them established independent monitoring by third-party auditors. Internal codes of social compliance required that suppliers to companies like Gap or Nike agreed to unannounced factory monitoring by third-party Vendor Compliance Auditors (VCOs). Such things as work hours, living conditions in the dormitories, safety records, the use of protective gear, and door size at exits were to be checked. While strides in corporate social responsibility were made, fires in Pakistan in October 2012, when 300 workers lost their lives in a recently certified factory and in Bangladesh one month later when 112 workers perished trying to escape through locked doors, make it clear that monitoring is not yet effective.[27]

---

[24] Chang, *Factory Girls*, 12, 17.

[25] Qingliang Gu, "The Development of the China Apparel Industry," A report presented jointly by China Textile University and Harvard Center of Textile and Apparel Research, 1999.

[26] "Shenzhen Has the Highest Minimum Wage," *China Daily*, Aug. 10, 2012 http://www.chinadaily.com.cn/bizchina/2012-08/10/content_15662517.htm; Chang, *Factory Girls,* 103.

[27] Snyder, *Fugitive Denim*, 253, 254, 257, 273; "The Challenges of CSR," *Women's Wear Daily*, Oct. 24, 2012, 1.

THE ROLE OF LABOR LAW AND TRADE UNIONS

Laws on the books in China since 1995 promise a five-day, 40-hour work week, $48 a week minimum wage, and guaranteed overtime pay. The laws are ignored more than they are followed, especially in small firms. It is illegal to hire workers under the age of 16, but under-age teenagers routinely borrow or present fake identity cards to employers and this behavior is seldom challenged. A 2008 law required employers to pay overtime, provide insurance, and give laid-off workers one month of severance pay for every year worked. The law also made it harder to lay off workers. Credit Suisse estimates that these laws add 15 to 20 percent to the cost of running a business. Laws designed to give workers a voice and channel their frustration through an arbitration system produced a backlog of cases. In 2008, the year factory shutdowns surged, 700,000 labor disputes went to arbitration, more than double the previous year. The publication of labor laws likely increased protests. China has not had a major fire as deadly as those in Pakistan and Bangladesh since 1994, but workplace accidents are quite common. According to the official labor statistics in China, workplace fatalities have declined but numbers remain higher than anywhere else. In 2010, nearly 90,000 people were killed and nearly 400,000 injured at work. Large factories in China are generally in compliance with codes of social responsibility but in Guangdong province and across the Pearl River Delta and other manufacturing centers many makeshift factories pop up in residential complexes and small buildings and are prone to the worst safety problems. Factory managers report that although there are more guidelines and stricter enforcement than five years ago, policing is more often done at the larger workshops with the smaller fly-by-night production facilities not being watched with the same scrutiny. The challenge for the responsible factory is to keep up with the high degree of auditing required by their multinational partners. While the requirement for social compliance auditing is similar among companies, presently there is no uniform system of inspection by multinationals and questions remain as to the accuracy of factory records.[28]

Though largely unreported in the Western press, strikes are frequent in China. Nearly every week, thousands of workers protest their working conditions. Strikes remain illegal and strike leaders can be imprisoned, and still they occur. In China, no independent trade unions exist. Under the current system, only the government-run union, the All-China Federation of Trade Unions, which has more than 170 million members, is permitted. The union has a wide presence in state-owned enterprises and has made a big push to establish branches in foreign companies. Its most notable victory was in unionizing Wal-Mart stores

---

[28] Snyder, *Fugitive Denim*, 275; Facts and Details, "Chinese Labor Rights: Laws, Unions, Unrest and Strikes," http://factsanddetails.com/china.php (accessed May 22, 2011).

in 2006. The Federation generally sides with industry and is rarely seen as an advocate for workers.[29]

In June 2010, Xintang, China's denim production capital, was rocked by several days of protests against the maltreatment of migrant workers. Two dozen people were arrested as thousands of laborers took to the streets protesting against general labor conditions and the broader social problems resulting from the wealth gap between locals and migrant workers. Social benefits for Chinese citizens are tied to the city of their birth by a household registration system that makes it difficult to get health care and education for their children when they move for work. In December 2012, the China Labor Bulletin (CLB) documented more than 100 labor disputes and strikes with the majority related to wage disputes when factories moved to cheaper parts of China or closed down.[30]

FROM THE MERRIMACK RIVER TO THE PEARL RIVER DELTA

The critical 30-year period in each region's development saw New England and China emerge as global leaders in the manufacture of textiles and apparel. The city of Lowell became the model for textile production throughout the greater Merrimack Valley and New England. By 1850, there were 1,000 mills along the rivers of New England and 100,000 mill workers producing a vast supply and selection of woven fabrics. The abundant supply together with the invention of the "sewing machine" by Elias Howe in 1846 resulted in the birth of the ready-to-wear industry.

Despite Cabot Lowell's hopes, New England's mills were treacherous places to work and the ready-to-wear industry was no better. Requiring only a table for cutting fabric and the sewing machine to assemble garments, many small factories and manufacturing workshops popped up throughout the urban centers, specifically in New York City. Workplaces with poor ventilation and little room to move with few and sometimes blocked or locked exits were common. The catastrophic fire at the Triangle Shirtwaist Factory in New York City on March 25, 1911, claimed 146 lives. Those who perished were young immigrant women and girls. The fire led to legislation requiring improved factory safety standards and helped spur the growth of the International Ladies' Garment Workers' Union, which fought for better working conditions for garment workers.[31]

---

[29] Snyder, *Fugitive Denim*, 252; Facts and Details, Chinese Labor Rights.

[30] "Rioting Slows in China Denim Capital," *Women's Wear Daily,* June 20, 2011, 2; "China Factory Safety In Spotlight After Fire," *Women's Wear Daily*, Dec. 6, 2012, 1.

[31] Moran, *The Belles of New England*, 169.

Garment assembly is often the first industry to enter developing markets. Requiring little technology and a large labor force, garment manufacturing takes advantage of cheap labor in the next "best place." Developing countries with generally unregulated and often difficult working conditions will survive for a time but eventually labor unrest paves the way for reform. Deadly fires on a catastrophic scale continue to occur in today's garment industry. Fires among Bangladesh's 5,000 factories have killed at least 1,071 workers and injured 3,127 in 279 incidents since 1990. Codes of conduct and social responsibility programs have not stopped the carnage.[32]

The shift of production from China to other developing countries is occurring. When assembly in Shenzhen became more expensive, factories moved to the boarders of the SEZs. Industry buyers and sellers within China fear for the future of the business there and report that profit margins have all but disappeared. The central government's policy is focused on high-end production and high-tech goods with little attention paid to lower-end manufacturing like basic clothing and textiles. With the rising costs for personnel and raw materials across China and pressure to keep costs low by buyers, factories are shutting down across the Pearl River Delta and other manufacturing zones. Factories moving to the poorer, less developed regions within the interior of China face the challenge of transporting finished goods from China's land-locked interior, negating any savings in overall production costs.[33]

In Lawrence and Lowell, no laws supported workers' rights. Massachusetts was the first state to regulate occupational disease in the industry in 1911 with the banning of the suck shuttle, thought to be responsible for the spread of tuberculosis. The dangers of exposure to cotton dust were first reported in 1837; however, it took 143 years for the federal government to recognize byssinosis, or "brown lung" as an occupational disease. Protest in support of a ten-hour work day began in 1840 but it was not until 1874, 34 years later, that the state enacted a ten-hour day for some workers. Social reformers and trade unions were the agents of change in the United States. In China, no independent trade unions exist and labor laws are not always enforced. Consumer outrage and product boycotts are important drivers for change, but the effectiveness of these programs remains uncertain. It took the United States a very long time to do "the right thing" in support of workers' rights, occupational health and safety, and environmental protections. China can learn from the successes and failures of the United States and other developed countries in areas of labor law, workplace safety, and pollution control. Giving workers a voice through independent free trade unions, along with the freedom to assemble and strike, is critical. An active system of regulation, inspection, and sanctions must be established to give teeth to what

---

[32] "Bangladesh Fires Stir Call for Action," *Women's Wear Daily*, Jan. 29, 2013, 1.

[33] "China's Sourcing Pains Other Nation's Gains," *Women's Wear Daily*, September 20, 2011, 1.

laws exist on the books. The role of the consumer in creating demand and influencing multi-national corporations to employ ethical business practices should not be understated. As apparel and textile manufacturing and other industries move to places with even fewer rights and regulations, it is important to consider the lessons learned.

CHAPTER 13

Bread and Roses: Why the Legend Lives On

Robert Ross

The Lawrence textile strike of 1912 has come to represent working class struggles for dignity and respect and a more expansive ambition for a full life—the "roses" part of the iconic duality. Recent research suggests that the slogan was not used during the strike and that the phrase (and the poem that carries it) has its origin in less revered events in Chicago. It is a constructed memory. That the legend continues to grip the imagination of workers and feminists and intellectuals is indicative of a deeper reality—that aspirations for dignity and respect loom large in a working class life.

THE STRIKE

On January 11, 1912, a group of Polish women textile workers in Lawrence, Massachusetts, discovered that their employer at the Everett Mill had reduced their total wages as a consequence of a Massachusetts law, which had cut the legal work week from 56 to 54 hours. The reduction was about $0.32. They walked out. The next day, January 12, workers in the Washington Mill of the American Woolen Company also found that their wages had been cut. Prepared for the events by weeks of discussion, they walked out, calling, "short pay, all out."

The strike that resulted was sometimes referred to as the strike for three loaves of bread.[1] When a Congressional Committee investigated the food budgets of two families (one Lithuanian, the other Portuguese), its members found the

---

[1] Bread & Roses Centennial Exhibit. 2012. "What Happened?" [Ethan Snow, Emily Levine, Robert Forrant] Node 3. Online at http://exhibit.breadandrosescentennial.org/node/3 Accessed April 3, 2012.

families spent between 15 and 24 cents a week on bread.[2] So 32 cents is about two weeks of bread for each of these families. Their walk-out began an iconic American strike.

> The strikers wanted not only decent pay, but a chance to enjoy the good things of life. They carried signs saying, "We want bread and roses too![3]

Thus states one of the 252,000 entries that Google reports using the phrase "bread and roses strike"; 174,000 of them link "bread and roses strike" with Lawrence; 98,000 join the phrase with Lawrence and women.[4] Although there is noticeable change over the last few years, many of these sites repeat the inspiring observation. The workers, these sites say, usually identifying the women, though afflicted with hunger and occupational diseases and hazards, nevertheless asserted their aspiration for what the poet James Oppenheim called "art and love and beauty" that their "drudging spirits" lacked. Some versions refer to the slogan on picket signs and some to banners.[5] The great troubadour Utah Phillips and the younger idol Ani DiFranco frame their performance of the eponymous song as picket signs.

The strike involved about 25,000 workers. The vast majority of the Lawrence textile workers were immigrants and about half were women and children. The Massachusetts law limiting hours was actually aimed at the hours of women and children; since these were half of the work force of the mills, the owners decided they could not operate for the extra two hours; they therefore complied with the law by giving all of the workers a reduced work week.

Working conditions and life in the mills and neighborhoods of Lawrence were grinding and miserable. Wages averaged below nine dollars a week and the budgets calculated by Congress required far more than this for a family.[6] Infant mortality was 172 per 1,000, higher than 28 of the 34 cities for which data were

---

[2] U.S. Congress. House of Representatives. Rules Committee. *Report on Strike of Textile Workers in Lawrence, Mass.* (62nd Congress, 2nd Session 1912) [not fully reproduced here] Table B. Excerpts available at: http://www.marxists.org/history/usa/unions/lawrence-strike/economics.htm.

[3] "'Bread and Roses' strike in Lawrence, Massachusetts." PeaceSojourner. March 30, 2012. http://peacesojourner.blogspot.com/2011/03/bread-and-roses-strike-in-lawrence.html. Last Accessed 12/26/2012.

[4] These data were generated on April 2, 2012. It will be different on any other date and time; and probably on any other computer—not only is the web itself dynamic and changing, but Google shapes the results of one's searches to previous searches from the same IP address.

[5] Joyce Kornbluh. 2012. "Bread and Roses: The 1912 Lawrence Textile Strike" Excerpt from *Rebel Voices: An IWW Anthology*, Charles H. Kerr Publishing, Chicago. Available online at http://flag.blackened.net/lpp/iww/kornbluh_bread_roses.html. Accessed February 6, 2014. Mass Moment. 2012 "Bread and Roses Strike Begins. January 12, 2012" Massachusetts Foundation for the Humanities. Available online at http://www.massmoments.org/moment.cfm?mid=16. Last accessed on December 26, 2012.

[6] U.S. Congress, 1912.

available in 1909. A local doctor, Elizabeth Shapleigh, wrote: "A considerable number of the boys and girls die within the first two or three years after beginning work. . . . [T]hirty-six out of every 100 of all the men and women who work in the mill die before or by the time they are 25.[7]

From January to March, the workers endured repression and hardship. Martial law and militias were arrayed against them, including the use of armed Harvard University students as part of a militia. When one of their number was shot to death in a demonstration (probably by a police officer), two of their leaders, Joseph Ettor, an IWW leader and editor, and Arturo Giovannitti, an Italian poet and Socialist, were charged with murder.

The strikers had to overcome numerous obstacles. The largely English-speaking male AFL union—the United Textile Workers—did not support the strike, averse to both its immigrant- and women-led nature. The radical IWW, however, had been anticipating the situation for months and sent talented organizers to assist the workers. The strikers were of a polyglot background, speaking dozens of languages and divided, potentially, by membership in different churches. The organizers devised an essentially multi-cultural approach to the problem of unity: they organized units by nationality and language, encouraging all to be included. Among the charming tales of the strike is that while all the language groups knew *The Internationale* they did not know each other's versions: so they sang to each other as they marched. In the end, they won wage and other concessions that would last for a few years, though they were not permanent. Textile workers up and down the East Coast similarly demanded and largely won wage advances.

The poem by the radical writer James Oppenheim is often cited as having been inspired by the Lawrence strike. It includes the lines:

> *"Our lives shall not be sweated, from birth until life closes; Hearts starve as well as bodies; Give us bread and give us roses."*

And,

> *"Small art and love and beauty their drudging spirits knew. Yes, it is bread we fight for—but we fight for roses, too!"*

And so, we have the making of a legend. Scorned and oppressed, disdained by white male craft unionists, immigrants and women won the day with a new form of organization—industrial unionism—that presaged the victories to be enjoyed later in the century. The sometimes tedious struggles for marginal economic advances was now to be framed in the more nearly accurate light of labor struggles

---

[7]This proposition was made in testimony to Congress; I know of no epidemiological work that supports such a high estimate of mortality. Suffice to say life was hard and the work was hazardous. (Joyce Kornbluh, 2012 [1988]).

as based on striving for dignity and respect. The "roses" may represent the time to appreciate art, but it may also be the time to simply "be," to live one's own life without forever toiling at the whim of another.

More than this: later, in the 1960s, when social history was making a revival with a perspective "from below"[8] and labor history was experiencing a rebirth,[9] the Bread and Roses story became part of a narrative of inclusion of women and of minority racial and ethnic groups. It came to symbolize more than labor's struggles but the whole story of female and ethnic inclusion.

DIGNITY AND DEGRADATION: NOW AND THEN

The twinning of struggles for material decency and for dignity and respect plumbs the heart of workers' relationships to their jobs. It is striking how often this twinning is expressed through the grievances and aspirations of women workers.

Throughout the last century and more, for example, women apparel workers have complained about sanitary conditions. Overflowing toilets, or insufficient numbers of them, figure prominently in their complaints. In almost all accounts of sweatshop conditions, especially those given by women workers, bathroom conditions, and the regulation of bathroom visits—usually by men—figure vividly in workers' heartfelt complaints. A woman who worked in Manhattan's garment district described her factory in a 1998 testimony:

> When it's busy, we work up to 60 to 63 hours. The conditions in the factory are not very good. There's no air circulation. The bathrooms are outside on our floor. In the factory where I work almost everyone is from Ecuador. Those people work hard. And since they are very far from their land, they come and are afraid of losing their jobs, so they enslave themselves. Almost no one goes to the bathroom, they feel embarrassed. The bathroom is outside. They have

---

[8] Jesse Lemisch, "The American Revolution Seen from the Bottom Up," in Barton J. Bernstein, ed., *Towards a New Past: Dissenting Essays in American History* (New York: Vintage, 1967); "Jack Tar in the Streets: Merchant Seamen in The Politics of Revolutionary America," *William and Mary Quarterly* 3rd ser. 25(1968), 371-407.

[9] See Gerald M. Sider, "Cleansing History: Lawrence, Massachusetts, the Strike for Four Loaves of Bread and No Roses, and the Anthropology of Working-class Consciousness," *Radical History Review*, No. 65 (1996): 48-83, and comments by Paul Buhle (84-90), Ardis Cameron (91-97), David Montgomery (98-102), and Christine Stansell (103-107), and a reply to the comments by Sider (108-117). Herbert Gutman, "The Workers Search for Power," in H. Wayne Morgan, ed., *The Gilded Age: A Reappraisal* (Syracuse: Syracuse University Press, 1963. And *Work, Culture and Society in Industrializing America: Essays in American Working-Class and Social History*. New York: Knopf, 1976. Ira Berlin, "Herbert Gutman and the American Working Class," in Herbert G. Gutman, *Power & Culture: Essays on the American Working Class*, ed. by Ira Berlin (New York: Pantheon, 1987).

to leave the factory, go to the hallway. It's a bit dangerous because anyone can enter the bathrooms.[10]

Another garment worker, Aracely, worked in Los Angeles' garment district, a larger apparel-producing region than New York, described in the 1990s as the sweatshop capital of the United States. She was a presser who worked 12 hours each of seven days a week. She had untreated burns on her hands and complained that the bathroom was wretched. "You want to get out of there as quickly as possible."[11] Union staffer Jo Ann Mort also interviewed Leticia, a sewer in L.A. She described a shop she visited where the workers had a union contract:

> [It] is like a dream shop. Even the bathrooms are so beautiful you could eat there." By contrast, where she works, "We don't even have toilet paper, you have to bring it from home. There is no space to walk in the shop. Everything is on top of you. When it rains, you have to cover yourself because the roof has a lot of holes. Rats come out. But the pressure is the worst. They won't even let you go to the bathroom—'I need this work and I need it now,' they say.[12]

Back in 1909, the firebrand Clara Lemlich wrote: "The shops are unsanitary—that's the word that is generally used, but there ought to be a worse one used."[13]

This dimension of abuse, oppressiveness as emotional degradation, including rigorous regulation of toilet access and miserable sanitary conditions, is related to extraction of profit from the workers who are kept strictly at their jobs and are driven to produce more (a form of "speed-up"). This is simply and obviously a *quantitative* aspect of exploitation: less time in bathroom breaks, more production; less desirable facilities, less use of them, more time sewing. Let us call this the "economistic" explanation of this abuse. The alternative explanation includes the economistic one, but goes further, adding as motivating cause the *qualitative* dimension of the relation between employer and worker—that of control.

Successful employers are able to hire workers at a wage and set them to work at machines where the total cost of them is less than the revenue earned from selling the good or service the wage-earners produce. The contractor prices the piece rate he pays the workers after he has taken the contract for a certain amount per thousand dozen. More work, more profit. Undergirding the contractor's ability to keep the pace up, to keep the "girls" at their tasks, to accept the piece rate and

---

[10] Linda Rodriguez Meza. 1997. "Testimony." 5. In Andrew Ross, editor, *No Sweat: Fashion, Free Trade and the Rights of Garment Workers*. (New York, 1995), 4-8.

[11] Joanne Mort, 1997. "They Want to Kill Us for A Little Money." 193. In Andrew Ross, editor, *No Sweat: Fashion, Free Trade and the Rights of Garment Workers*. (New York, 1997). 193-198.

[12] Ibid., 196.

[13] Leon Stein, ed. 1977. *Out of the sweatshop: The struggle for industrial democracy.* New York: Quadrangle/New Times Book Company, 12-13.

thus the intensity of their work and the total wage possible to them, underneath the *leverage* the employer has, is—of course, once we examine it—not *free choice* but the constrained choice really available. Sweatshop workers are not free to be Chief Executive Officers for Disney, nor high school art teachers, nor translators at the United Nations. To keep his workers at their stations requires that the sweatshop operator maintain his laborers as people—as women, as "girls"—*who will return the next day*. They must remain as they are. In turn, they must be people whose understanding of their choices is so limited that the boss's offer of employment remains acceptable *the next day*. A person whose sense of herself is as weak, vulnerable, constrained, abused but defenseless—such a woman is more apt to come back to X's Sewing Shop or Woodward's textile mill even after being told she is a child for needing to pee.

The strategic target of such humiliation is, however, not merely an individual, but rather is directed at all of her co-workers, actual and potential. The objects of the humiliation are a group of workers of a given type who the employer has targeted as his/her "special" source of labor.

In social science terms, my hypothesis is that the regulation of bathroom behavior, the use of foul and demeaning language, even the neglect of bathroom facilities all dehumanize and intimidate workers, especially women, and keep them feeling weak and thus without recourse. Control and degradation of the woman worker's body is part of a regime of . . . *control*. To have control over a person is to exert power. Here is how a famous French philosopher put it:

> In fact nothing is more material, physical, corporal than the exercise of power. What mode of investment of the body is necessary and adequate for the functioning of a capitalist society like ours? From the eighteenth to the early twentieth century I think it was believed that the investment of the body by power had to be heavy, ponderous, meticulous and constant. Hence the formidable disciplinary regimes in the schools, hospitals, barracks, factories, cities, lodgings, families.[14]

The struggle for full inclusion, for the recognition of our own full humanity, is of course material. Anatole France sardonically reminded us of the fictional nature of equal rights without a material basis: "The law, in its majestic equality," he wrote, "forbids the rich as well as the poor to sleep under bridges, to beg in the streets, and to steal bread. That is one of the good effects of the Revolution."[15]

The legend of Bread and Roses, however, adds something beyond release from degradation; it pushes us to connect the mundane ability to buy bread with

---

[14] Michel Foucault, 1975. "BODY/POWER" Interview with Michel Foucault. Interviewers: editorial collective of *Quel Corps?* http://www.generation-online.org/p/fpfoucault6.htm. Accessed January 13, 2013.

[15] Anatole France, *Le Lys rouge* ch. vii (1894) (S. H. transl.) from Harper's: http://harpers.org/archive/2007/06/hbc-90000312.

the exalted opportunity to appreciate art and beauty. Dignity, the slogan instructs us, is a complex bundle. That the aspiration the slogan expresses is culturally attached to women and/or immigrant workers is the mirror of the special degradation such workers encounter. But on the positive side of that proposition is a more universal one: we all want the Roses—even the tough and silent men— but it is the women who are allowed to say so. The legend reaches deeply into the cravings of those the *Internationale* claims who "have been naught" but wish to be all: "Nous ne sommes rien, soyons tout."

HOW THE LEGEND WAS MADE

The main origin of the Bread and Roses tale is the publication of James Oppenheim's poem. It was, apparently, first published in a 1915 labor anthology, *The Cry for Justice: An Anthology of the Literature of Social Protest*, edited by Upton Sinclair. The editor's heading said it was based on the Lawrence strike. American Studies and History scholar Jim Zwick showed, however, by 2002, that the poem was published in 1911—before the Lawrence strike, and was probably inspired by Chicago events.[16] The original dedication suggested it was about the "women of the west"—which would include Chicago in 1911, but never Lawrence.

One may speculate as to why the poem, beautiful as it is, has been affixed to the Lawrence memory rather than Chicago. From September 1910 through February 1911, there was in Chicago a very large strike of apparel workers, mostly women—larger than the Lawrence strike. But there, the men of the garment workers AFL affiliate settled the strike at one large suit maker (Hart Schaffner and Marx) and deserted some 30,000 sweatshop workers not employed there. Not such a great moment of solidarity.

Even before Zwick had definitively shown that the poem predated the strike, in 1996 Gerald Sider found that no photo of strikers, their marches, or pickets showed the "bread and roses" phrase on a picket sign.[17] No pamphlet in the Lawrence public library files has the phrase. No real-time news article reports the phrase being used.

Some of the labor historians confronted with Sider's work argued that perhaps the phrase was from the Italian radical poet Giovannitti, a strike leader, and that it appeared in Italian. But a young history student showed years ago that Giovannitti never used the phrase "pane e rose" in his published work during or

---

[16] Jim Zwick, "Bread and Roses: The Lost Histories of a Slogan and a Poem." 2002. Originally published online at http://www.boondocksnet.com/labor/history/index.html but the site, created by Zwick, ended after his death (2008). I have a cached copy and will send it to scholars upon request. Similar material is available in Jim Zwick, "Behind the Song: Bread and Roses." *Sing Out!* 46 (Winter, 2003): 92-93.

[17] Sider, "Cleansing history."

after the strike.[18] Giovannitti's book of poems written in English, which was published after the strike and after his jailing during the strike, has no phrase even close to "bread and roses."[19] Giovannitti did eventually go to work as the educational director of Local 89 of the International Ladies Garment Workers Union (ILGWU), the Italian seamstress's local. That local reportedly used an Italian song with Giovannitti's poem and that phrase. Local 89 was formed in 1919 (after the strike). Although the phrase does not appear in Giovannitti's collected work in English, someone did obtain copyright for a song *"Pane e Rose"*—written with Giovannitti—in 1934.[20]

A reasonable conclusion, bearing in mind the difficulty in proving something did not happen, is that the slogan does not stem from the Lawrence strike, but rather is a constructed memory. From the troubadour Utah Phillips through to the Massachusetts Foundation for the Humanities to many trade union publications, and on tens of thousands of web sites, the Roses of the Bread and Roses Strike stand for those dimensions of labor and working class aspirations that embrace needs that are aided but not summarized by the ascent toward material decency.

WERE THE BREAD AND ROSES IN CHICAGO?

Confronted with these facts, one friend whose biography bridges the Old Left of the communist movement and the New Left of the 1960s, as well as recent identity politics, asked, still grasping for the truth in the legend, "Well, what about the Chicago strike?"

One early use of the phrase is the title of lectures that the labor organizer Rose Schneiderman gave on behalf of women's suffrage.[21] But Schneiderman's lectures with that title (1912) came after Oppenheim had written it. Zwick notes though, that Schneiderman worked for many years as a functionary for the Women's Trade Union League (WTUL), an organization of reform-minded affluent women who encouraged women workers to form unions. The WTUL was

---

[18] Kerri Harney. 1999. "Bread and Roses in United States History: The Power of Constructed Memory." Honors Thesis. State University of New York at Binghamton. Abridged version available online at http://www.greenstone.org/greenstone3/nzdl?a=d&c=whist&d=HASH 013432f9fd02cb7f734dd466&dt=simple&p.a=b&p.s=ClassifierBrowse. Last accessed December 26, 2012.

[19] Arturo Giovannitti. 1914. *Arrows in the Gale*. Riverside, CT: Hillacre Bookhouse. Available online at http://archive.org/stream/arrowsingale00glovrich#page/n0/mode/2up. Last accessed April 2, 2012.

[20] *The Collected Poems of Arturo Giovannitti* (New York: 1962). See also: Entry Catalog of copyright entries: Musical compositions, Part 3 by Library of Congress. Copyright Office. Pane e rose theme song w Arturo Giovannitti 1 c Oct 20 1934 E unp 94588 Giuseppe Adami New York 22&54. 1935. Discovered through Google books at: http://books.google.com/books?id=WztjAAAAIAAJ&dq=Pane+e+Rose.&source=gbs_navlinks_s.

[21] See Harney "Bread and Roses in United States History" and Zwick "Bread and Roses."

extremely active in support of the women and families of the Chicago strike in 1910–11. In 1907, he notes, a British founder of the earlier WTUL had visited Chicago and given talks there.

> She argued, wrote Zwick, that women must work for more than just increased wages. Her message was summed up in a quote she attributed to the Qur'an: "If thou hast two loaves of bread, sell one and buy flowers, for bread is food for the body, but flowers are food for the mind." The Women's Trade Union League probably turned that thought into the slogan that inspired James Oppenheim's poem.[22]

My leftist veteran friend said, upon hearing the gist of these comments, "So he (Oppenheim) could have seen the slogan carried in the Chicago strike." Her point being that as long as actual workers used the slogan, the legend was still intact. Alas, there is no evidence for that at all. The WTUL's own post-strike report makes absolutely no mention of the slogan.[23] We are left with a poet who heard a phrase used by functionaries and orators.

Is this constructed memory also a constructed sentiment—a wish by the comfortable that the afflicted would share their values? Is the story—whether from Lawrence or Chicago—a romanticized telling of a struggle for three loaves of bread?

Here is an excerpt from the post-strike WTUL report from Chicago, showing quite clearly that the sentiment is not merely the projection of more privileged sympathizers:

> When a League visitor went into one of these homes she found neither food nor coal on a bitter winter's day. The mother and their little one were surrounded by the elder children, little tots three, four, and five years old. The husband had received three letters from his employer on three successive days offering to increase the wages from fifteen to thirty dollars a week, but the striker refused and the mother rejoiced in the refusal. The visitor, awed by the mystery of life and the greatness of what she witnessed, turned and said, "Friend, how do you do it? How do you meet this suffering not for yourself, but for your children?" And the mother, looking steadily out of her quiet, patient eyes, answered, "It is not only bread we give the children,—we live not only by bread!—we live by freedom, and I will fight for it till I die to give it to my children."

Faced with some of these facts, one of the Lawrence strike historians, Ardis Cameron, suggests that the idea of the Lawrence strike as a fight for bread and

---

[22] Zwick "Bread and Roses."
[23] Women's Trade Union League of Chicago. 1911. *Official report of the Strike Committee: Chicago Garment Workers' Strike,* October 29, 1910-February 18, 1911. Chicago. Online at: http://pds.lib.harvard.edu/pds/view/3370018?n=1&jp2Res=0.25&imagesize=600&rotation=0.

roses is, as Harney put it, "an example of a "wrong" story which communicates a "right" message."[24] Women workers complain of abusive language, sexual harassment, and of miserable sanitary facilities. They complain of being called dogs and being treated like dogs. When workers—women and men—resist this treatment, they almost always articulate the twinning of material demands with claims to dignity and respect. The picket signs carried by the Black male striking sanitation workers in Memphis, in 1968, just before Martin Luther King was killed, said simply, "I AM a man."[25]

WHY IS THE LEGEND SO OBDURATE IN THE FACE OF FACTS?

The memory of the 1912 strike is constructed of our broader culture's hopes and aspirations. One definition of a myth "is a traditional tale with . . . partial reference to something of collective importance."[26] Alternatively, a view of legend includes "a symbolic representation of folk belief and collective experiences and serving as a reaffirmation of commonly held values of the group to whose tradition it belongs."[27]

We may justly continue to inquire as to why women workers or otherwise oppressed workers (like the Black sanitation workers in Memphis) should specially carry these messages. Well, one part of the answer is that only recently have we recaptured an understanding of labor struggles in this way. The *Internationale* after all was written in 1871 (words) and 1888 (music): "We have been naught, we shall be all." The culture of the literati has not recently understood workers as a class among the excluded; it has focused on the ascribed identities of gender and race as the locations of indignity. Nelson Lichtenstein noted it in his *State of the Union.*[28]

Another part of the answer is that our culture perceives brutality to which women are subjected in more emotionally laden frames that it does for men. John McClymer pointed out that only a month before the Triangle Shirtwaist Fire of 1911 a terrible Pennsylvania coal mine fire killed more people than those who perished at the Triangle. The miners are remembered now only because the historian McClymer's grandfather was killed there.[29] That women and child workers were victims in New York brings special sympathy to an

---

[24] Harney "Bread and Roses in United States History."

[25] The striking image of marchers carrying that sign may be viewed at the Reuther Library of Wayne State University website: https://www.reuther.wayne.edu/node/3642.

[26] Walter Burkert. *Structure and History in Greek Mythology and Ritual.* (Berkeley, 1982) 23.

[27] Timothy Tangherlini. p. 385. 'It Happened Not Too Far from Here. . .': A Survey of Legend Theory and Characterization." *Western Folklore,* 49.4: 371-390.

[28] Nelson Lichtenstein. *State of the Union: A Century of American Labor.* (Princeton: 2002).

[29] John F. McClymer. 1998. *The Triangle Strike and Fire.* (New York: 1998). vii.

industrial or any other accident, such is the bent of our culture. They—the women and children—are "innocent;" the male coal miners knowingly take risks and are somehow accountable, that is, co-responsible for their slaughter.[30]

Yet another part of the answer as to why the Bread and Roses symbolism continues to adhere to the story of women workers is that women workers continue to bear a particular burden of exploitation in the regime of global capitalism. Consider Bangladesh. On February 25, 2010, fire broke out on the first floor of the Garib and Garib sweater factory in Bangladesh. The thick acrylic smoke rose up to the eighth floor, impenetrably dark and toxic. The door was shut and the windows were locked. Twenty-one workers died. Almost all were women sewing machine operators.[31]

In a weird historical parallel, in December 2010 a fire broke out on the ninth floor of a factory building of the Hamim group in Dhaka. Exits were again blocked—just as they were on the ninth floor of the Triangle Factory building on March 25, 1911. Women jumped to their deaths to escape the flames. This was the exact pattern of March 25, 1911. In Dhaka that day, more than 28 died and 100 were injured. The system consumes women; its brutality mobilizes our sympathy.[32] Or perhaps and in addition our culture has deeply embedded a general underdog sympathy: Christians aver . . . *the last shall be first, and the first last* (Matthew 20:16).

The Bread and Roses legend is, as Ardis Cameron says, a wrong story in a right cause. We need the Roses because we know the bread is not enough. Dignity and respect are important in labor movements and working class struggles, so important that we construct legendary histories to instruct ourselves and those who come after us.

---

[30] McClymer has an additional explanation—the Triangle victims were familiar and thus sympathetic to New Yorkers as the heroines of the 1909 strike. I offer yet another: New York was then and is now a world class media amplifier.

[31] National Labor Committee. 2010 [March 25]. [now known as Institute for Global Labour and Human Rights]. "Twenty-one Workers Die and 31 are Injured Sewing Sweaters in Bangladesh For H&M, Mark's Work Wearhouse and Other Labels." http://www.nlcnet.org/reports?id=0002.

[32] Saad Hammadi and Matthew Taylor. 2010 [December 14]. "Workers jump to their deaths as fire engulfs factory making clothes for Gap: At least 27 die and more than 100 are injured in blaze at Bangladesh manufacturing plant." *The Guardian*. Online at http://www.guardian.co.uk/world/2010/dec/14/bangladesh-clothes-factory-workers-jump-to-death.

Editors' Biographies

Robert Forrant is a University of Massachusetts Lowell Professor of History and chaired the Lawrence-based Bread and Roses Centennial Committee. He received his PhD from the University of Massachusetts Amherst in 1994. Before that he worked as a machinist. He co-curated "The Bread and Roses Strike of 1912: Two Months in Lawrence, Massachusetts, that Changed Labor History," for the Digital Public Library of America. Recent publications include: *The Big Move: Immigrant Voices From a Mill City*, with Christoph Strobel, Loom Press (2011); and *Metal Fatigue: American Bosch and the Demise of Metalworking in the Connecticut River Valley* (2009). He serves as historian to numerous Teaching American History grants, is on the Board of the Lawrence History Center, and works with the Tsongas Industrial History Center in Lowell, Massachusetts on its National Endowment for the Humanities summer teachers' residency program.

Jurg Siegenthaler is emeritus professor of social policy at American University in Washington, DC. He received his PhD at the University of Bern and was a post-doctoral fellow at Cornell University-New York State School of Industrial and Labor Relations. He also was visiting researcher at the International Social Security Association, and the U.S. Social Security Administration. Teaching and research has mainly encompassed the social and economic history of industrialization. He has written on producers' cooperatives, long-term changes in workers' standard of living, work and technology, and published a book comparing the environmental and social costs of industrialization in a Swiss textile valley and the coal economy of Scranton, Pennsylvania. He has been a member of the Bread and Roses Heritage Committee in Lawrence, Massachusetts, and a co-coordinator of the Lawrence History Live speakers' tent at the Bread and Roses Heritage Festival on Labor Day.

Author Biographies

Robert Biggert teaches in the Department of Sociology and Anthropology at Assumption College in Worcester, Massachusetts. His interests include political sociology, comparative/historical sociology, labor history, and sociological methodology. He is researching the Bread and Roses strike by examining the *Lawrence Tribune* newspaper over the course of the strike using quantitative narrative analysis.

Janelle Bourgeois is a 2013 graduate of the University of Massachusetts Lowell with a degree in History. She is interested in the relationships between immigration, labor, and radicalism. Her research is focused on French and Belgian radicals in the U.S. labor movement.

Lawrence Cappello is a doctoral candidate in History at the Graduate Center of the City University of New York. His work centers on 19th and 20th century social and political history, particularly the history of American privacy.

Domenique Ciavattone, a student at Stonehill College, is pursuing a major she designed built on the United Nations Millennial Development Goals. A native of Bellingham, Massachusetts, she interned in Kenya during the fall semester of 2012.

Ken Estey is Assistant Professor, Brooklyn College, City University New York, Department of Political Science, and Coordinator of its Studies in Religion Program.

Frank Fletcher, a member of the business faculty at the University of Phoenix, professor in the Business Division at Midway College, Midway, is a Lawrence, Massachusetts native and graduate of the University of Massachusetts. His family has roots in the textile industry: his dad was president of Local 765 of the Textile Workers Union of America. He is co-editor of *Solutions: Business Problem Solving*, a guide to business problem solvers by Gower Publishing.

Vicki Gabriner grew up in Brooklyn, New York, the granddaughter of Yiddish-speaking Eastern European Jewish immigrants. She received a doctoral degree in Women's History from Union Institute & University (2009). Gabriner sings soprano in *A Besere Velt*, Yiddish Community Chorus, and in 2010, she helped initiate the creative process that culminated in the Chorus's musical multi-media show commemorating the centennial of the Triangle Shirtwaist Fire.

Anne Mattina is an Associate Professor of Communication at Stonehill College in Easton, Massachusetts. Her research centers on American women's public activism prior to suffrage. Publications include work on the Lowell Female Labor Reform Association, the Great Strikes 1909-1913, and the forthcoming "Yours for Industrial Freedom: Women of the IWW 1905-1930" to be published in *Women's Studies* in 2013.

Virginia M. Noon, a technical designer and quality assurance specialist, has been employed in the textile and apparel industry for more than 25 years, and has lived and worked extensively in South East Asia and China. She is an Assistant Professor in Fashion Design and Retailing at Framingham State University and a doctoral student at the University of Massachusetts Lowell in Work Environment Policy.

Clarisse A. Poirier, Associate Professor of History at Merrimack College, received her PhD in 1978 from the American and New England Studies Program of Boston University. Before joining the faculty at Merrimack, she served as the first Program Director of the Immigrant City Archives (now Lawrence History Center) and worked as a Preservation Planner for the Lawrence Community Development Department from 1980 to 1985.

Robert J. S. Ross is Professor of Sociology at Clark University. He is the co-author of *Global Capitalism: the New Leviathan* and author of *Slaves to Fashion: Poverty and Abuse in the New Sweatshops*. He is a member of the Board of Directors of the Sweatfree Purchasing Consortium and past Chair of the Section on the Political Economy of World Systems of the American Sociological Association.

Ethan Snow is the Political and Communications Director for the UNITE HERE New England Joint Board, a union representing textile, garment, manufacturing, warehousing, laundry, and food service workers in the six New England States. He earned his master's degree in Regional Economic and Social Development from the University of Massachusetts Lowell in May 2012.

Adrienne Andi Sosin chairs the education committee of the Remember the Triangle Fire Coalition. She co-authored *The New York City Triangle Factory*

Fire, a 2011 Arcadia Images of America book, and co-edited *Organizing the Curriculum: Perspectives on Teaching the American Labor Movement*. Andi taught in New York City's middle and high schools, and at Pace University, the City College of New York, and Adelphi University. She earned her doctorate in Higher & Adult Education at Teachers College, Columbia University.

Joel Sosinsky is a member of the Board of Directors for the Remember the Triangle Fire Coalition. Now retired from staff positions for the International Brotherhood of Teamsters and New York City government, he co-authored *The New York City Triangle Factory Fire* and contributed to *Organizing the Curriculum: Perspectives on Teaching the American Labor Movement*. He earned his J.D. from St. John's University School of Law and an M.P.A. from New York University.

Linda Stern has a Master's in Library Science. She worked for several years in the Massachusetts community college system, using primary sources to explore 19th-century social movements. She is currently on the board of the Boston Women's Heritage Trail, focusing her research, talks, and tours primarily on Jewish women. She is a soprano in the *A Besere Velt* Yiddish Community Chorus.

Index

Abbott, Andrew, 83
A Besere Velt (ABV), Yiddish Community Chorus, Boston Workmen's Circle (BWC), 187–204
   Ale Mentschen, 201
   Bella Ciao, 200
   concerts, 199–202
   Lawrence Textile Strike, show on, 203
   S'falt a shney, 200
   Triangle shirtwaist factory fire, show on, 196–202
   Workmen's Circle, 191–194
Activist New York, 181
Adamson, Archie, 38, 40–41, 46–47, 49–50, 53–54, 56–58
Agitprop theater, 191–192
Akhter, Babul, 183
Akter, Kalpona, 183
Alger, Horatio, 127–128
All-China Federation of Trade Unions, 215
Alliance of Textile Workers' Unions, 28
Amalgamated Bank, 178
Amalgamated Clothing Workers Union, 178
   archives of, 180
Amalgamated Life Insurance Company, 178
Amalgamated Textile Workers, 56
American Dream, concepts of, 10, 121–133
   Gilded Age and gospel of wealth, 122, 126–130
   immigrants' experiences of, 122, 128–133
   Puritan/merchant, 122–125

American Federation of Labor (AFL), 20, 38, 44, 63, 129, 221, 225
   business unionism of, 81
   exclusion of African-Americans and women, 23
   exclusion of immigrants, 150
   workers' dissatisfaction with, 149
   See also United Textile Workers (UTW)
American Society of Safety Engineers (ASSE), 179, 182
American Textile Workers Union, 138
American Wool and Cotton Reporter, 19
American Woolen Company
   consolidation in woolen industry, 81, 126–128
   employment rates in Lawrence, 40
   negotiations with Committee of Ten, 40–47, 50–51, 54–55
   president of, 6
   two-loom system, 19
   Washington Mill walkout, 219
Amoskeag mill complex, 208
Anarchists, 25, 73, 94, 96, 108, 110, 132
Apparel manufacturers. *See* Garment industry
Appleton, Nathan, 122–123, 125, 129, 133, 207
Arkwright Club (Boston), 126
Arlington Mills, 42, 50, 127–128, 145, 157
Armenian immigrant workers, 164
Arnold, Dexter, 9, 126
Artef (theater group), 190
Asch Building (Triangle Waist Company), 171, 173, 184, 201

Atlantic Mills, strikes at, 29–30, 92
Atteaux, Frederick E., 41, 43
Atwill (District Attorney), 54–55
Ayer, Frederick, 44, 127
Ayer Mill walk-outs, 22

Bacchiocchi, Emidio, 166–167
Bacon, Emory A., 160
Baer, George F., 129
Bagley, Sarah, 210
Baker, Ray, 128, 133
Bangladesh
  Center for Worker Solidarity, 178, 181, 183
  factory fires, 184, 197, 214–215, 217, 229
Barkan, Steven, 87
Barre, Vermont, 53, 72, 82, 158, 201–202
Barre Socialist Labor Hall, 72, 202
Barre Wool Combing Company strike (Massachusetts), 159–160
Bass, Suzanne Pred, 178
Bayonets, 6, 81, 94, 116*f*, 132, 156
Beck, Julian, 190
Bedard, Joseph
  labor organizing, 29–30
  on Committee of Ten, 38, 46–47, 52–55
  radicalism, 27
Benoit, Oscar, 6
Berger, Victor L., 43, 74–76, 132
Berkman, Edith, 138, 148–150
Berle, A. A., 68
Bernadino, Consiglia, 168
Bienkowski, John, 38, 46–48, 51, 53–54, 58
Biggert, Robert, 9, 79–90, 131–132
Biggs, Michael, 82, 86
Birds on Fire (Kahn), 182
Black-listed workers, 18–19, 26, 34, 56, 208, 210
Blanck, Max, 173, 176–177, 195–196
Blitzstein, Marc, 190
Bloomberg, Michael, 178
Blumenthal, Rosa, 200
Boal, Augusto, 187, 190
Bodnar, John, 12

Bolshevism, 104, 107, 136, 138
Borah, William, 74
Born, William, 38, 46–48, 53–54, 56
Boston, Massachusetts
  Columbus Day Parade, 97
  Jewish Music Festival, 201
  mill owners in, 126
  Society for the Prevention of Cruelty to Children, 68
  Teachers Union Hall, 203
  Workmen's Circle, 193–194
Boston American, 68–75, 77–78
Boston Associates, 123–126, 207–208, 210, 212
Boston Daily Globe, 48, 50–51, 55, 60, 166
Boston Herald, 68, 78
Boston Manufacturing Company, 207
Boston Workmen's Circle (BWC), Yiddish Community Chorus, 187–204
Bourgeois, Janelle, 7, 15–35
Bradbury, Alfred, 101–102
Bradley, Charles E., 97
Bread and Puppet Theater, 190–191
Bread and Roses Strike of 1912
  as name for Lawrence Textile Workers' Strike, 11, 60, 139–140, 142, 144–145, 220, 224–229
  Centennial, 12, 201
  Centennial Academic Symposium, 7, 171, 185
  Centennial Steering Committee, 191
  Labor Day Festival (2012), 13, 203
  legend of, 219–229
  new understandings of, 7–14
  See also Lawrence Textile Strike of 1912
Bread & Roses (Watson), 61, 88, 130, 203
Brecht, Bertolt, 190
Breen, John, 6, 43, 141n10
Brooklyn Historical Society, 183
Brown Building of Science (NYU), 171, 184
"Brown lung" disease (byssinosis), 210, 217

Buckley, John J., 105–107, 109–110
Burke, Jeremiah E., 104
Buscada (creative technology company), 182–183

Call, The (socialist paper), 175
Callahan, Dennis, 161
Cameron, Ardis, 8, 13, 88, 129, 131, 227–229
Campbell, Douglas, 158
Capital, 3–4, 124–126
Capitalism
   dividends, 124–125, 133
   inequities of, 11
   power asymmetry between labor and business, 83
   unregulated, 81, 127, 129
Cappello, Lawrence, 8–9, 59–78
Carnegie, Andrew, 127
Carney, Edward, 106
Cartwright, Edmund, 207
Caruso, Joseph, arrest of, 6, 8, 10–11, 53–55, 94, 159, 162
Central Labor Union (CLU), 38, 44, 71, 136
Century of Safety, A (ASSE), 182
Chang, Leslie T., 213
Chenoweth, Erica, 86
Chicago strike of 1910-11, 226–227
Child labor, 78, 119f, 204
Child Labor Acts of 1916 and 1918, 78
Children's exodus from Lawrence
   as tactic in 1912 strike, 61, 68–69, 73, 75–78, 87–89, 132, 158
   as turning point in strike, 6, 77, 79–80, 83, 87, 89–90
   children's hunger as motivation for, 88, 143–144
   events of, 59–63, 72, 82–83
   Franco-Belgian traditions of, 32–33
   implementation of, 67
   in 1919 strike, 146
   local government response to, 33, 59, 73–75, 81–82
   newspaper ad calling for children's aid, 66–67

[Children's exodus from Lawrence]
   nonviolence, role of, 59, 61–65, 73, 75–78, 86–89
   parade of strikers' children in New York City, 72, 118f
   parental consent, 70–72
   police brutality, 33, 74–75, 82, 88–89, 132, 158
   press coverage, 60–62, 66–75, 77–78
   public opinion, 8–9, 68–78, 86–87, 89
   Strikers' Children's Vacation Committee, 67
   timing of, 88
"Child Welfare Day" (National Congress of Mothers), 78
China
   garment industry, 211–217
   industrialization in, 205
   living and working conditions, 212–217
   migrant workers, 212–213, 216
   Special Economic Zones (SEZs), 206, 211–212, 217
   unions, 215
   worker protests, 216
China Labor Bulletin (CLB), 216
Chong, Dennis, 86, 89
Ciavattone, Domenique, 153–169
Citizens Association, 97
Citizens' Committee, 39–40, 45
City Council Resolution, 1912, 91
City Lore, 179–180
Civic religion, 106
Civil rights movement, 63, 188–189, 191–192
Civil War, 125–126
Clinton, Massachusetts, strike in, 161–162
Clinton Wire Cloth, 161
Cloth From Which We are Cut, The (A Besere Velt), 187–204
Cloward, Richard, 85
Cold War, 9, 93, 107–108
Coldwell, Joseph, 164–166
Cole, Arthur H., 127
Cole, David B., 128
Cole, Donald, 58

Columbus Day Parades (Lawrence), 97–99
  See also God-and-Country Parade (1912)
Committee of Ten, 37–58, 89
  arbitration, 39
  direct negotiations with textile corporations, 38–46
  mediation, 38–39
  members, activities of, 46–58
  private negotiations with American Woolen Company, 40–47, 50–51, 54–55
  strike settlement, 46
  wages, negotiations over, 45–46
"Committee of Ten Which Met the Mill Bosses—and Won, The" (photograph), 37, 117*f*
Committee on Safety, 175
Communist Party, 138, 147–148, 150
Congressional hearings. *See* United States House of Representatives
Contentious politics theory, 85
Cooperative Franco Belgian grocery store, 32
Cooperatives, 7–8, 18, 20–22, 25–27, 29, 31–32, 34, 114*f*, 137, 202n25
Cooper Union, 180–181, 194
Copland, Melvin T., 129
Cornell University, Kheel Center, 180, 198
Corporations
  consolidation of, 126–128
  direct negotiations, 38–46
  textile industry, 122–126
  See also specific corporations
Cotton Claims Bureau, 126
Cowan, Paul, 13
Cradle Will Rock, The (Blitzstein), 190
Credit Suisse, 215
Cry for Justice, The (Sinclair), 225
Cuban missile crisis, 107
Curley, James M., 103
Cushing, Grafton D., 48
Cushing, John, 206

Danker, Anita, 164
Deaths of workers, 135, 167, 206, 210, 228–229

[Deaths of workers]
  See also LoPizzo, Annie; Ramey, John; Triangle shirtwaist factory fire (1911)
Debs, Eugene, 136, 202
DeCourcy, Charles A., 104
Defense Committee for Ettor and Giovannitti, 34, 47
Democrats, 150
Dengler, Eartha, 13
Deng Xiaoping, 205, 211
Dennison, Beulah, 109
Derby, Doris, 189
Detollenaere, August, 17–31, 34–35
Dhaka, Bangladesh, 229
Di Fayer Korbunes, 181
DiFranco, Ani, 220
Dignity and respect, struggle for, 11, 122, 183, 203, 219, 222, 225, 228–229
Dilavore, Jack, 145–147
Dingley tariff, 17
Disease. *See* Occupational diseases
Dividends, 124–125, 133
Dix, John Alden, 176
Dongguan City, 212–214
Draper, Eben, 162, 164, 167–168
Draper strike, 162–169
Dreier, Mary, 176
Dubofsky, Melvyn, 131
Duck Mills, 42

Eaton, Fred H., 100
Eaton, William, 101
Ebert, Justus, 57
Education and Labor Collaborative (ELC), 179–180
Eight-hour day movement, 29, 136
Ellis, George H., 45
El Teatro Campesino, 188
Ely, John, 138
Employers Mutual Protection Association, 195
Erdener, Yilderay, 140–145
Essex Company, 2–3, 208
Estey, Kenneth, 9, 91–111

Ettor, Joseph
  acquittal of, 55
  arrest of, 6, 8, 10–11, 38, 43, 49, 52, 65, 81, 94, 132, 156, 221
  defense committee for, 162
  Draper strike, 164, 167
  imprisonment of, 159, 169
  in Committee of Ten, 37–43, 46–47, 49–51, 117*f*
  indictment of, 53
  labor organizing, 28, 31, 140–141
  leadership of strike committee, 63–64, 66, 88, 130
  on scabs, 72
  on violence, 71
  trial of, 54–55
Evans, Scott Alan, 182
Everett Mills, 4–5, 15, 130, 219

Fabric, Flames, and Fervor (Looking for Lilith), 182
Factories
  inspections, 215
  sanitary conditions, 222–224, 228
  See also Fires; Triangle shirtwaist factory fire (1911); Working conditions
Factory Investigating Commission (FIC), 176, 196
Fair Labor Standards Act (1938), 176
Fall River, Massachusetts, 211
"Fangs of the Monster at Lawrence, The" (Sanger), 11, 69
Fasanella, Ralph, 13
Fassel, Samuel, 159–160
Federal Theatre Project, 190
Federated Jewish Charities, 40
Feigenbaum, Benjamin, 194
Ferrante, Theresa, 168
Fires, 173–174, 184, 197, 229
  See also Triangle shirtwaist factory fire (1911)
Flag Day, 98–99
Flags, American, 91, 95–99, 107–108
Flesh & Blood So Cheap (Marrin), 182
Fletcher, Frank, 121–133

Flynn, Elizabeth Gurley "Rebel Girl"
  at Clinton strike, 161
  children's exodus, 67, 70, 72, 75, 78
  defense committee for Ettor and Giovannitti, 162
  Draper strike, 164, 169
  labor organizing, 64–65
  on "No God, No Master" banner in IWW parade, 94–95
  strike leadership, 37, 65–66, 132, 151, 155
Flynn, Kathy, 142–143
Foner, Moe, 13
Foner, Phillip, 60–61, 82
Foreign trade, strike outcomes and, 80–81
Forrant, Robert, 1–14, 191
40 Years Workmen's Circle, 187
Fosdick, Harry, 57
Foss, Eugene, 39, 47–48, 60, 89
France, Anatole, 224
France, textile industry in, 17–18
Franco-Belgian Co-operative, 7–8, 18, 34, 114*f*
  labor organizing, 20–22, 25–35
  support for Atlantic Mill strike, 29–30
Franco-Belgian Hall, 16, 114*f*
  labor organizing meetings at, 22, 30, 32–34
Franco-Belgian immigrants
  attitudes toward women, 33
  radicalism of, 16, 25–27, 33–35
Franzosi, Roberto, 82
Free Southern Theater (FST), 189
Freiheit, 190
Freire, Paulo, 192
French-Canadians, 27, 32, 34–35, 151, 211
French Confederation of Labor, 24
French Textile Federation (IWW), 18, 23–26, 29
From the Fire (Swados), 181–182
Fulden, Anna, 158

Gabriner, Vicki, 12, 187–204
  civil rights organizing, 192
  point person for Triangle show, 196

Gallatin, Lisa, 193, 196, 198
Game theory, 85–87, 89
Gamson, William, 85
Gap, Inc., 197, 214, 229n32
Garbelnick, Julia Dublin, 139–145
Garment industry, 205, 217, 222–223
   China, 211–217
   New York City, 171–173, 183, 194, 216
   "ready-to-wear" clothing, 172, 216
   See also Triangle shirtwaist factory fire
General Strike Committee, 137
Geraghty, Thomas M., 80–81
German immigrants, 47
   strikes led by, 19
Giannini, Ettore, 37–38, 46–48, 52–53, 55–56, 58
Gibson, Charles Dana, "Gibson Girls," 172
Gilbert, Moses, 189
Giovannitti, Arturo, 63, 225–226
   acquittal of, 55
   arrest of, 6, 8, 10–11, 52, 65, 81, 88, 94, 132, 156, 221
   defense committee for, 162
   Draper strike, 164, 166
   imprisonment of, 159, 169
   indictment of, 53
   trial of, 54–55
Global economy, 197, 206
   strike outcomes and, 80
   See also China
Goaziou, Louis, 25–26
God-and-Country Parade (1912), 9, 109–111, 115*f*
   doctrine of, 95–96
   Lawrence City Council Resolution, 91, 96
   opposition to IWW, 92–93
   sculpture as memorial of, 101–103
God-and-Country Parade (1962), 104–111, 115*f*
   as secular, 106
   opposition to communist Soviet Union, 93, 107–108
   time capsule (from 1912), 92, 104–105
Golden, John, 50, 70, 76, 160

Goldman, Emma, 202
Gompers, Samuel, 129
Gospel of Wealth, The (Carnegie), 122, 127
Graham, Tolle, 191–192
Grand Army of the Republic, 97, 99
Grassroots history, 16
Great Britain, industrialization in, 122, 207, 209
Greater Lawrence Chamber of Commerce, 110
Great Lawrence Textile Strike. See Lawrence Textile Strike of 1912
Great Stone Dam (Merrimack River), 2
Greek immigrants, 161, 211
Green, James, 13
Greenbie, Sydney, 70
Greene Brothers, 165, 168
Gregory, Frances, 125
Grey Art Gallery, 182
Guangdong Province, 212–215
Guerrilla theater, 191

Halbwachs, Maurice, 12
Halluin, France, strike in, 22
Hamim group, 229
Hannagan, Paul, 96
Hanson, Harriet, 40
Hardwick, Thomas, 76–77
Harney, Kerri, 228
Harper's Weekly, 5
Harris, Isaac, 173, 176–177, 195–196
Harvard University, 126–127, 153, 156, 221
Havel, Vaclav, 190
Haverhill, 97, 143
Hayes, Martin, 73
Haywood, William "Big Bill"
   announcement of end of strike, 16, 33
   children's exodus, 60, 74–75, 78, 88
   Draper strike, 167
   on morality of tactics, 63
   on strikers' victory, 79
   on worker unity, 155
   strike leadership, 37, 45, 49–50, 64–66, 88, 131–132, 159

Hearst, William Randolph, 68–69, 71, 73, 76
Heinold, Rose, 161
Hennessey, James F., 115*f*
Herald, 73
Hewett, Peter, 105–106, 109
Hill, Jim, 30
Hine, Lewis, 119*f*
Hirsch, Michael, 180, 182
Holliday, Thomas, 38, 41, 46–48, 50–51, 53–56, 58
Holman, Dudley M., 39
Hong Kong, 212
Hooper, Ken and Will, 122
Hoover, J. Edgar, 110
Hopedale, Massachusetts strike, 162–169
Horne, James D., 100
Howard, Caleb, 166
Howe, Elias, 216
Hugo, Victor, 35

ILGWU. *See* International Ladies Garment Workers Union
Il Progresso, 175
Il Proletario, 160
Immigrant City (Cole), 58
Immigrants
   American Dream, concepts of, 122, 128–133
   Armenian, 164
   French and Belgian, 15–35
   German, 19, 47
   Greek, 161, 211
   in Lawrence, Massachusetts, 3.128–129, 17–19, 155
   Irish, 208, 211
   Italian, 27, 29–30, 151, 164–166, 174
   Jewish, 106, 139, 174, 192–194
   Lithuanian, 139
   Polish, 15, 29–30, 47, 130, 154–155, 158, 164, 211
   strike outcomes and, 80
   strikes, 163–164
   textile industry, 128–129
   Ukranian, 147

[Immigrants]
   union organizing and, 128–129, 150–151
   women, 154–159
Industrialization, 205–213
   consolidation of corporations, 126–128
   moral and social effects of, 123–124
   See also Capitalism; Garment industry; Textile industry; Working conditions
Industrial organization and competition, role in strike outcomes, 80–81
Industrial Relations Committee, 64
Industrial safety. *See* Workplace safety
Industrial Workers of the World (IWW), 221
   arrest of members, 56
   Communism and, 93
   Draper strike and, 163–164
   Eastern United States, organizing in, 29, 81
   free speech fights, 62, 65, 75
   French Textile Federation, 18, 23–26, 29
   General Executive Board, 92
   Haywood, William, 79
   ideology of, 53–54, 64, 77, 91–92, 130–131, 133
   labor organizing, 92
   Lawrence, labor organizing in, 22–25, 30
   Lawrence Textile Strike of 1912, role in, 31–34, 60–61, 66–67, 70–73, 88, 153–159
   Local 20, 25, 27–28, 39, 47, 53, 63, 92
   mobility of leaders, 8
   "No God, No Master" slogan, 94–95, 107–108
   nonviolence, use of, 76, 155
   opposition to, 6, 9, 92, 99, 103, 107–108, 115*f*
   parade on September 29, 1912, 53–54
   Paterson silk workers' strike, 81, 162, 164
   press coverage, 28
   strike committee (Lawrence Textile Strike of 1912), 16, 38–39, 43–45, 61

[Industrial Workers of the World (IWW)]
  syndicalism, 130–131, 133
  violence, use of, 64
  women in, 160, 169
  workers' support for, 50–51, 133, 163
  writings on the Lawrence Textile Strike, 57
  See also National Industrial Union of Textile Workers (NIUTW)
Insurance companies, fire, 173
Internationale, 203, 221, 225, 228
International Labor Rights Forum (ILRF), 183
International Ladies Garment Workers Union (ILGWU), 171, 173, 175, 177, 197, 216
  archives of, 180
  Heritage Fund, 179
  Local 25, 179, 194
  Local 89, 226
  Pins and Needles, 190
Irish immigrants, 208, 211
Isler, Fred, 24
Italian immigrants, 27, 29–30, 151, 164–166, 174
Italian Socialist Federation (ISF), 66–67, 153–155, 157, 160
IWW. *See* Industrial Workers of the World

Jackson, Patrick, 207
James, C.T., 124
Jewish Daily Forward, The, 174–175
Jewish immigrants, 106, 139, 174, 192–194
Jones, Jack, 65

Kahn, Barbara, 182
Keller, Helen, 10–11, 202
Kemp, Brad, 182
Kennedy, Edward, 109
Kennedy, John F., 110
Kerrigan, Charles, 214
Kheel Center, Cornell University, 180, 198

Kimball, William T., 101
Knebel, Simon, 76–77
Knights of Columbus, 95
Knights of Labor, 20, 25
Krushchev, Nikita, 107
Kunhardt Mills, 42

Labor law, 198, 215, 217–218
  Child Labor Acts of 1916 and 1918, 78
Labor organizing
  arrest as tactic, 65
  international, 183
  in woolen industry, 129
  lumber and mine workers, 65
  management opposition to, 173–174
  militancy, 135–151
  radical, 16, 22–23, 136, 138, 147n16, 153, 202
  strength, impact on strike outcomes, 80
  See also Industrial Workers of the World
Lafskoski, Domacilla, 157
Lancaster Gingham Mills, 161
La Paix (cooperative), 20
Lapworth Manufacturing, 165
Lawrence, Abbott, 2, 125, 135, 208
Lawrence, Massachusetts
  1919 strike, 135–137, 145–147
  1922 strike, 104, 147
  1931 strike, 135, 138, 147–151
  City Council, 39, 81, 91, 96, 98, 105
  immigrant populations, 3.128–129, 17–19, 155
  industrial development in, 2–4, 9, 93, 208, 217
  Lawrence Common, 12, 16, 46, 93, 99–100, 102–103, 111, 120*f*
  living conditions, 4, 63, 77, 88, 116*f*, 121, 129–130, 135, 142–145
  North Canal, 2–3
  panoramic view of, 113*f*
  patriotism, 95–100
  population, 2–3, 128–129
  religion and municipal interests, 93, 98, 106

[Lawrence, Massachusetts]
  Shattuck Flagstaff, 92–93, 100–104, 109
  tenements, 116*f*, 140
  trade unions, 28, 44, 128–129, 138, 148
  unemployment, 138
  working conditions in textile industry, 121, 135, 148, 158–159, 210
  See also God-and-Country Parades; Lawrence Textile Strike of 1912
Lawrence Daily American, 99
Lawrence Daily Eagle, 100
Lawrence-Eagle Tribune, 107–108
Lawrence Eagle-Tribune, 110
Lawrence Evening Tribune, 52, 55, 73
Lawrence History Center, 13, 113*f*–118*f*, 120*f*, 139, 203
Lawrence Machine Shop, 3
Lawrence Survey, The, 3
Lawrence Telegram, 96, 98–100
Lawrence Textile Strike of 1912
  beginning of, 15–16, 130
  causes of, 1, 4, 10, 63, 121, 154, 219–221
  communication, 8, 156–157
  cooperatives, 7–8
  demands and goals of, 13–14, 31, 51, 79
  dynamite planted to frame strikers, 6, 43, 55, 81, 132
  events of, 4–7, 15–16, 31–34, 37, 130–133, 135–136, 154–159
  French and Belgians in, 31–34
  government responses to, 39, 59, 65, 73, 131
  influence on subsequent strikes, 9, 154–169
  militia presence, 6, 65, 116*f*, 221
  New York Lawrence Strike Committee, 70
  oral histories, 135, 139–145
  organization and organizing, 7–8
  parades, 50
  picketing, 50, 131, 157
  police violence, 51, 88
  press coverage, 6, 8, 43, 45, 48, 50–51
  public opinion on, 60

[Lawrence Textile Strike of 1912]
  relief for strikers, 61, 66
  remembrance and legend of, 10–13
  reports of end of strike, 50–51
  settlement, 33, 46
  significance of, 139, 153
  solidarity among workers, 48, 50, 71, 154, 156
  soup kitchens, 32, 131, 157
  strike committee, 47–48, 63, 131, 155
  tactics, 85
  timing of, 8–9, 88
  women, importance of, 49–50, 131, 154–159
  workers' victory in, 16, 38, 58, 61, 79, 89, 136, 139, 153, 155, 159, 169, 203
  See also Bread and Roses Strike; Children's exodus from Lawrence; Committee of Ten; God-and-Country Parade (1912)
Lefebre, Lawrence, 13
L'Emancipation, 18, 25–27, 30, 32–33
Lemlich, Clara, 176, 194, 196, 199, 201, 223
Leveroni, Frank, 53
Lichtenstein, Nelson, 228
L'Internationale, 28
Lippman, Walter, 77–78
Lipson, Samuel, 41, 46–47
Lis, Josephine, 158–159, 162
Lithuanian immigrants, 139
Living Newspaper, 190, 198
LoLo, LuLu, 181
LoPizzo, Annie
  parade in honor of, 94
  shooting death of, 6, 10–11, 38, 43, 54, 65, 81, 88–89, 132, 156
Lovejoy, George E., 97–98, 100
Lowell, Francis Cabot, 122–123, 207–209, 216
Lowell, Massachusetts
  as model factory town, 2, 123–124, 207, 216–217
  Columbus Day Parade, 97
  cooperation with workers in Lawrence, 24

[Lowell, Massachusetts]
"Mill Girls," 123, 208–209
working conditions, 206–211
Lowell Female Labor Reform Association (LFLRA), 210–211
L'Union des Travailleurs, 25–26

Macroeconomic conditions, strike outcomes and, 80
Mahoney, Jeremiah J., 48, 52
Malina, Judith, 190
Maltese, Serphin, 180
Margot Gayle Fund, 179
Margules, Adela, 201–202
Margules, Jane, 201
Margules, Rita, 201
Maroni, Lorenzo, 46–48
Marrin, Albert, 182
Marston Mills, 92
Marxism, atheistic, 108
Massachusetts
 Foundation for the Humanities, 226
 Labor Commission, 4
 legislation reducing hours in work week, 4, 15, 30, 154
 Legislative Committee on Conciliation, 44–45
 State Board of Conciliation and Arbitration, 39, 41–42
 See also Boston; Lawrence; Lowell
MassCOSH (Massachusetts Coalition for Occupational Safety and Health), 191–192
Mattina, Anne F., 153–169
McCarthy, Joseph, 100
McClymer, John, 228
McFadden, Elizabeth, 78
McGill, Pearl, 157, 159, 161–162
McIntire, Carl, 109
McKinley tariff, 17
McPherson, John, 130
Meany, John F., 48
Mechanics Block, 2
Mediation
 Committee of Ten, 38–39
 strike outcomes and, 80

Memorials
 1912 Strikers' Monument, 12, 111
 God-and-Country Parade (1912), 101–103
 Shattuck Flagstaff, 92–93, 100–104, 109
 Triangle factory fire, 10, 12, 171–185, 187–204
 Triangle Fire Memorial, 184–185
Memory, 12–13
Menders and mending, 49–50
Menzie, James R., 101
Merolini, Palmira, 163, 165–166, 168
Merrimack Manufacturing Company, 208
Merrimack River, 2–3, 113*f*, 123, 207–208, 216
Metropolitan Klemzer, 181
Mikol, David, 23
Milford, Massachusetts strike, 162–169
"Mill Girls" (in Lowell), 123, 208–209
Missoula, Montana, 62, 65
Mitchell, Max, 40–42, 44
Mix, Tom, 202
Monopolies, 81, 127
Monti, Ersal, 168
Moody, Paul, 207
Morality, 30, 61–62, 64, 75, 122–124
Moral support, 20–21, 157
Mort, Jo Ann, 223
Murphy, "Silent Charlie," 176
Museum of the City of New York, 181
My Country 'Tis of Thee, 98

National Association of Wool Manufacturers, 126
National Congress of Mothers, 78
National Consumers League, 175
National Industrial Union of Textile Workers (NIUTW), 24, 28, 92
National Labor Committee, 214
National Labor Relations Act (1935), 176–177
National Labor Relations Board, 177
National Textile Workers Union (NTW), 137–138, 148
Negotiations. *See* Committee of Ten

Neill, Charles P., 1, 4, 50
Newman, Holly, 198–199
Newspapers
    ad for children's aid, 66–67
    in Lawrence, 31
    radical, 25–26
    socialist, 66–67
    See also Press coverage
New York Call, 11, 66–70, 74, 175
New York City, 53, 72, 216
    Central Labor Council, 177–179
    Fire Department (FDNY), 171, 174, 177
    garment industry, 171–173, 183, 194, 216
    Landmarks Preservation Commission (NYCLPC), 184
    Workmen's Circle Cemetery, 194
    See also Triangle shirtwaist factory fire
New York City Tenement Museum, 182
New York City Triangle Factory Fire (Images of America), 182
New York Herald, 68
New York State
    Department of Labor, 176
    Fashion Institute of Technology, 182
    Legislature, 176, 196
New York Times, 60, 174
New York University, 177, 184, 195
"No God, No Master," 53, 94–95, 99
Nonviolence, use as strike tactic, 59, 61–65, 73, 75–78, 86–89
Noon, Virginia M., 205–218
Norway Worsted Mill, 159

O'Brien, Michael S., 44, 100–101
Occupational diseases, 176, 210, 217, 220
Occupational Safety and Health Act (1970), 176
Occupational Safety and Health Administration (OSHA), 198
Occupy Wall Street (OWS), 183–184
Olneyville, Rhode Island, 19
O'Neal, John, 189
"One big unionism," 139, 153
On the Line (singing group), 193

Oppenheim, James, 220–221, 225–227
O'Reilly, James T., 95–97, 101, 104, 106, 115*f*
    Golden Jubilee (1924), 103–104
O'Sullivan, Mary K., 121, 131
Outlook, The, 5–6, 31, 57
Out of the Sweatshop (Stein), 198

Pacific Mill, 52
Paglia, Jennie Calitri, 165–166
Pakistan, 214
Parades, 50, 160, 165–166
    for victims of Triangle factory fire, 175
    strikers' children in New York City (1912), 118*f*
    See also God-and-Country Parades
Paternalistic management, 123–124, 133, 162
Paterson, New Jersey, 24, 92, 162, 164, 167
Patriots Day, 102
Pearl River Delta, 215–217
Pemberton Mills, 42
Peradelia, Serafina, 156
Perkins, Frances, 10, 176–177, 195, 198
Philadelphia Inquirer, 60, 68, 78
Phillips, Utah, 220, 226
Picavet, Louis, 27–28
Picket lines, 5, 50, 160
    moving, innovation of, 157
Piehler, Christopher, 182
Piesco, Ralph, 163
Piety, 122
Pinkerton detectives, 52, 156
Pins and Needles (ILGWU), 190
Piscitello, Ignatius, 13
Piven, Frances Fox, 10, 85
Poirier, Clarisse A., 8, 37–58
Police brutality, 6, 33, 51, 74–75, 82, 85–86, 88–89, 132, 137–138, 147, 158, 160–161, 165–168
Polish immigrants, 29–30, 47, 158, 164, 211
    women's walkout of Everett Mill, 15, 130, 154–155
Pottier, Eugene, 28

Press coverage
  children's exodus from Lawrence,
    60–62, 66–75, 77–78
  Industrial Workers of the World
    (IWW), 28
  Lawrence Textile Strike of 1912, 6, 8,
    43, 45, 48, 50–51
Price, George, 176
Product of the Mill, The (McFadden), 78
Progressive Movement, 130
Progressive Women's Club of Lawrence,
  157

Qiaotou, China, 205

Radical labor organizing, 16, 22–23, 136,
  138, 147n16, 153, 202
  See also Industrial Workers of the
    World (IWW)
Ramey, John, bayonet death of, 6, 81, 94,
  132, 156
"Ready-to-wear" clothing, 172, 216
"Rebel Girl." *See* Flynn, Elizabeth Gurley
Recchia, Maria, 167
Red Cross, 175, 182
Reilly, Father, 95
Relief for strikers, 47, 137
Remember the Triangle Fire Coalition
    (RTFC), 171, 177–185, 201
  "Bells" (interactive social media
    event), 181
  "Chalk Project, The," 178
  grant funding, 179
  "Names Map," 179
  Open Archive and Museum, 179,
    182–183
  Triangle Fire Memorial, 184–185
  web site, 178–179
Report of the Lawrence Survey, The, 116
*Report on Strike of Textile Workers in
  Lawrence, Massachusetts in 1912*
    (Bureau of Labor), 1, 4
Republicans, 150
Revolutionary syndicalism. *See*
  Syndicalism

Riley, Edward, 38, 40, 44–50, 53–54, 56,
  58
"Robber Barons," 127
Robeson, Paul, 190
Robinson, Earl, 190
Rocco, Angelo, 27–28, 31, 63
Rochefort (mayor of Lawrence), 104
Roman Catholics, patriotism of, 95–96,
  106
Roosevelt, Eleanor, 177
Roosevelt, Franklin D., 195
Rosenfeld, Morris, 174–175
Ross, Robert, 11, 219–229
Roubaix, France
  cooperatives, 20
  textile workers' strikes, 17–18
Roulston, Jane, 70
Russian Revolution, 107

Sabatucci, Elizabeth, 168
Sacco, Ferdinando (Nicola), 147, 163
Sacco and Vanzetti Defense Committee,
  147n16
Sachs, Anna, 158
Sanchioni, Adrianna, 168
Sanclemente, Angie, 168
Sandberg, Louise, 104–105
Sanger, Margaret, 10–11, 67, 69, 77, 158
Saunders, Daniel, 2
Savage, Kirk, 12
Scabs, 24, 31, 71–72, 156, 164
Scabs mugging, 157, 161–163
Scanlon, Michael A., 39, 44, 47, 65, 70,
  81, 97, 99, 102–103
Schneiderman, Rose, 175–177, 196,
  199–200, 226
Schumann, Peter, 191
Schwartz, Judith, 203
Scudder, Vida, 74, 157
Sensationalism, 68, 71
September 11, 2001 attacks, 174
Sergel, Ruth, 178–179, 181–182
Shapleigh, Elizabeth, 221
Shattuck, Dorothy, 102
Shattuck, Joseph, 100, 102
Shattuck Flagstaff, 92–93, 100–104, 109

Shaw, Kim, 200
Shenzhen, China, 211–212, 214, 217
Shinberg, Pearl, 143
Shirtwaist Kings, 173
Shirtwaists, description of, 172
Sholik, Mary, 158
Sider, Gerald, 225
Siegenthaler, Jurg, 1–14
Sketch of the Life and Labors of the Rev. James T. O'Reilly, A (Walsh), 103
Skowhegan, Maine, 92
Sloan, Dolly, 11
Smith, Alfred E., 176, 196
Smith, Anna Deveare, 190
Smith, Gilbert, 23, 38, 46–48, 53–54, 57–58
Smolskas, Jonas, 6, 99
Snow, Ethan, 9, 135–151
Social activism and movements, 10, 85, 183–184, 188–191
Social change, 16, 34–35, 188–191, 193, 209
Socialism, 21, 25, 64
Socialist Party
  Labor Temple, 67, 69
  strike relief provided by, 81
  women's committee of, 67
Socialist Trade and Labor Alliance (STLA), 19–20, 23
Social justice, 13, 184, 191, 193, 197–198
Society for the Prevention of Cruelty to Children (Boston), 68
Solidarity (IWW), 29, 33, 64, 75
Solidarity among workers, 48, 50, 71, 154, 156, 169, 183
Solis, Hilda, 178
Solomon, Alisa, 191
Songxia, China, 205
Sonia, Margaret, 156
Sosin, Adrienne, 12, 171–185
Sosinsky, Joel, 12, 171–185
Sousa, John Philip, 202
South Congregational Church, 97–98
Soviet Union, 93, 107–108
Special Economic Zones (SEZs), 206, 211–212, 217
Spokane, Washington, 62, 65

Star Spangled Banner, 78, 98–99, 102
State of the Union (Lichtenstein), 228
Stein, Leon, 172, 173n8, 174–175, 177, 182, 198
Steindl, Emma and Lillian, 52, 157
Stephan, Mana J., 86
Stern, Linda, 12, 187–204
Steuer, Max, 176–177
STLA (Socialist Trade and Labor Alliance), 19–20, 23
St. Mary's (Lawrence), 95, 106
Stockholders, 124–125, 133
Stone, Orra, 3
Storrow, Charles, 208
Stowe, Harriet Beecher, 190
Street theater, 191
Strike breakers, 156–157, 161, 165–168
Strikers' Children's Vacation Committee, 67
Strikers' Monument, 1912, 12, 111
Strikes
  as social process, 83
  collective bargaining, 83
  definition of, 82
  government and police, role in, 82
  in France, 18
  macro-explanations of, 80
  meeting of workers, 120*f*
  micro-explanations of, 80–81
  outcomes, 80–81, 83, 137
  protests, 83
  repression of, 83, 85–87, 87*f*, 137–138
  tactics, 59–63, 83, 87*f*, 164
  trajectories, 83, 84*f*
  turning points, 83
  violence by strikers, 71–72
  See also Bread and Roses strike; Lawrence Textile Strike of 1912
Student Nonviolent Coordinating Committee (SNCC), 188
Sturgis, Richard Clipston, 101
Sullivan, John, 59, 73, 77
Swados, Liz, 181–182
Sweatshop labor, 198, 204, 214, 222–224
Sweetser, E. LeRoy, 65, 73–74, 82
Syndicalism, 22–23, 64, 77, 130–131, 133, 153

Taft, Helen "Nellie," 43, 74, 158
Taft, William Howard, 60
Taiping Handbag Factory, 212
Taiwanese businesses, 212–213
Tanguay, Eva, 119*f*
Tariffs, protectionist, 17
Tarzeen factory (Bangladesh), 184
Telegram, 97
Temple Emmanuel, 106
Teoli, Carmella, 158–159
Textile industry
  closing of mills, 138
  corporations, 122–126
  French manufacturing methods, 17
  immigrant workers, 128–129
  in Northern and Southern United States, 149
  power looms, 162, 207
  turbulence following World War I, 136
  two loom system, 19
  wages and wage cuts, 4, 15, 45–46, 124, 138, 146, 147n17, 149, 210
  working conditions, 121, 135, 148, 158–159, 206–211
  See also Garment industry; Lawrence Textile Strike of 1912
Textile Workers Organizing Committee, 211
Textile Workers Protective Association, 22
Theater of Social Change, 188–191
Theatre of the Oppressed (Boal), 187, 190
Thompson, James P., 15–16, 23–24, 29
Thompson, R.G., 159
Timpson, Anne Burlak, 147–151
Transcendentalism, 162
Trautman, William, 61
Tremblay, Joseph T., 110
Tresca, Carlo, 94, 147n16
Trial of a New Society, The (Ebert), 57
Triangle, A Puppet Play with Live Music (Kemp), 182
Triangle Factory Fire Project (Piehler and Evans), 182
Triangle Fire, The (*American Experience* documentary), 182

Triangle Fire, The (Stein), 172, 182
Triangle Fire Memorial Association (Facebook group), 180
Triangle: Remembering the Fire (HBO documentary), 180, 182
Triangle shirtwaist factory fire (1911), 10–11, 187–204, 216, 228
  50th anniversary memorial, 171, 177
  centennial commemoration, 10, 12, 171–185, 194
  factory safety laws resulting from, 175–177
  history of, 172–178, 195–196
  parade for victims, 175
  publications, art works, and conferences commemorating, 180–183, 187–204
  "Remembering the Triangle Factory Fire" (website), 180, 198
  See also Remember the Triangle Fire Coalition (RTFC)
Triangle: The Fire That Changed America (Von Drehle), 198
Triangle Waist Company, 173, 195
  See also Triangle shirtwaist factory fire (1911)
Tripp, Anne Huber, 81
Tuberculosis (TB), 210
Turning points, definition of, 83

Ukranian immigrants, 147
Uncle Tom's Cabin (Stowe), 190
Unions, 197–198
  conservative, 23, 27–28, 147n15
  demands for safer working conditions, 174
  See also specific unions
Unitarian Church, 100
United Mine Workers of America, 25
United States Bureau of Labor, 4, 60
United States House of Representatives
  Committee on Rules, 43, 46–47, 74, 132
  hearings and investigation of Lawrence Textile Strike, 1, 6, 43, 45, 60, 74–77, 89, 132, 158–159

United Students Against Sweatshops (USAS), 183
United Textile Workers (UTW), 24, 50, 70, 136, 138, 160, 221
United Textile Workers of America (UTWA), 129
"Uprising of the Twenty Thousand" (strike), 194–196

Vanzetti, Bartolomeo, 147
Vendor Compliance Auditors (VCOs), 214
Victorian Society in America, 179
Violence
　use by police, 6, 33, 51, 74–75, 82, 85–86, 88–89, 132, 137–138, 147, 158, 160–161, 165–168
　use by strikers and protesters, 85–86, 160–161, 165
　See also Nonviolence, use as strike tactic
Von Drehle, David, 198
Voorhees, R. G., 123
Vorse, Mary Heaton, 5

Wages and wage cuts, 4, 15, 45–46, 124, 138, 146, 147n17, 149, 210
Wagner, Robert F., Sr., 176, 196
Waistmaker's Opera (student performance), 182
Walker, Scott, 197
Wal-Mart
　demonstrations against, 184
　unions and, 215–216
Walsh, Alice L., 103
Waltham, Massachusetts, factory in, 122–123, 207
Waltham/Lowell manufacturing model, 122–125
Washington Mills, 52, 127, 219
Watson, Bruce, 61, 88, 130, 203
Weavers
　Franco-Belgian, 17–19
　strikes, 24, 29–32, 161
　union, 22
　working conditions, 148, 210

Welsh, Mary, 161
Welzenback, Annie, 38, 41, 43, 46, 49–50, 52–55, 57–58, 155, 157
White, William, 74
Whitman, William, 127–128
Wiggin, Parry C., 41
Wilson, William, 75
Wilson, Woodrow, 99
Wilson-Gorman Tariff, 126–127
Wisconsin, 197
Wiseman, Thomas, 80–81
Wobblies, 62–64, 154–155, 157–159, 161
　See also Industrial Workers of the World (IWW)
Women
　as strikers and activists, 15, 33, 49–50, 131, 153–169
　ideas of feminine propriety, 154, 169
　industrial violence and, 10–11
　police brutality against, 59–60, 160–161, 165–168
　police perceptions of, 5, 118*f*, 158
　See also Triangle shirtwaist factory fire
Women's Trade Union League (WTUL), 10–11, 157, 175–176, 195–196, 226–227
Wood, William M., 6
　as head of American Woolen Company, 19, 127–129
　concessions to strikers, 79, 89, 132
　strike negotiations with Committee of Ten, 40–44, 49–50, 54–55, 117*f*
Wood Mill, 50, 127
　walk-outs, 138
Woolen and worsted industry
　consolidation in, 81, 126–128
　French operatives in, 17–18
　worsted wool cloth, production of, 3–4
Woonsocket, Rhode Island, 24–25
Workers
　alternative social institutions, 16
　degradation and exploitation of, 223–225
　skilled, 49
　unskilled, 49, 63, 130, 132
Worker's Compensation Insurance, 176
Workers' rights, 177, 214, 217

Workers United, 177–179
Working conditions, 10, 121, 123–124, 135, 148, 158–159, 173–175, 194, 204, 206–217, 222–224
Workmen's Circle, 191–194, 196–199
  Center for Jewish Culture and Social Justice, 193
  See also Boston Workmen's Circle (BWC), Yiddish Community Chorus
Workplace safety, 197–198, 204, 210, 215–217
  activism for, 183–184
  regulations, 173
Work Projects Administration (WPA), 190
Work week, reduction in hours of, 4, 15, 30, 154
World Federation of Mothers, 78

WTUL. *See* Women's Trade Union League
Wuyi, China, 205

Xintang, China, 216

Yiddish Community Chorus, Boston Workmen's Circle (BWC), 187–204
Yiddish theater, 190
Yiwu, China, 205
Youngsjohn, J., 24
Yue Yuen, China, 213–214

Zhejiang, China, 205
Zinn, Howard, 1
Zwick, Jim, 225–227